HOW DID THIS HAPPEN?

HOW
DID THIS
HAPPEN?
TERRORISM
AND THE NEW WAR

EDITED BY

363, 3209

JAMES F. HOGE, JR., AND GIDEON ROSE

EDITOR AND MANAGING EDITOR OF *FOREIGN AFFAIRS*

PublicAffairs
NEW YORK

CONTENTS

INTRODUCTION

■

JAMES F. HOGE, JR., AND GIDEON ROSE

With the Cold War over and the economy booming, the United States relaxed during the 1990s, letting go the tension it had sustained for decades. All that changed on September 11, 2001. Suddenly the world rushed in, striking brutally at symbols of the very wealth and power that had underwritten the public's geopolitical nap. The nation awoke that morning to find itself at war. But it was a strange kind of war, one without front lines or massed troops, fought in the shadows against an elusive enemy, without a clear sense of where it would lead or how it would end. When the attacks against the World Trade Center and the Pentagon were followed by a spate of letters bearing anthrax bacteria, shock and anger turned to panic. Citizens debated the merits of different gas masks, and politicians considered overriding pharmaceutical patents in order to produce massive quantities of antibiotic drugs that experts agreed were inappropriate for all but a few potential victims and would be necessary only for a vastly larger and more systematic attack.

Neither complacency nor hysteria, obviously, are good ways of approaching American national security. Measured determination is more appropriate, grounded in facts and sound judgments about the nature of the challenges facing the country and the alternative responses available. This book is designed to offer such facts and such judgments, to provide the basis for informed discussion of what has happened and where to go from here. The authors of the chapters are leading experts in their respective fields, and many of them issued warnings about lurking dangers or glaring vulnerabilities long before the current crisis. Now, belatedly, we know to listen.

The first question the book addresses is posed by its title: How did this happen? The short answer is because some very determined people wanted to make it happen and were able to outwit the defenses erected against them. Causation is a complex issue, however. Airplanes crashed into the World Trade Center and the Pentagon because hijackers had boarded them intent on committing an act of radical evil. Yet, much earlier, the terrorists themselves had become guided missiles, driven by the training and support they had received, by a perverse interpretation of one of the world's great religions, and by a hatred for the United States and all that it stood for. They were able to carry out their mission, furthermore, only because they managed to evade the searching eyes of American intelligence agencies and slip through a porous domestic security system.

During the final years of the twentieth century, the number of terrorist attacks worldwide declined, but the number of casualties per attack rose. Experts felt the latter trend was ominous. They generally agreed that the risk of a catastrophic strike was still low, but worried that a new kind of terrorist driven by fanaticism and hatred rather than limited political objectives might try to cause true mass destruction. They were right to worry.

One man in particular epitomized the changing face of the threat. Osama bin Laden, son of a Saudi construction magnate and supporter of the Afghan *mujahideen* in their struggle against Soviet occupation, developed a vast terrorist network and organized a series of deadly attacks on U.S. installations around the world. He sought to oust Americans from the Middle East, overthrow so-called moderate Arab governments, and create a unified Muslim nation based on a puritanically oppressive theology.

Bin Laden saw the stationing of U.S. troops in Saudi Arabia, the 1991 war against Iraq, and American support of Israel as just the latest episodes in a long history of Western humiliations of the Muslim world. Media coverage of Palestinians hurt or killed during clashes with Israelis, meanwhile, fanned the rage of his followers and of Arabs and Muslims more generally—many of whom found bin Laden's radicalism appealing as a response to the poverty, frustration, and repression of their daily lives.

Bin Laden's attacks have been planned carefully and financed through an extensive network of funding sources and secure economic pathways. The success of the most recent strikes, however, also depended on the vulnerabilities of an open and ill-prepared society. Intelligence services cannot foil all terrorist plots, and developing appropriate benchmarks against which to judge those services' performance is difficult. Still, the September 11 attacks required extensive preparations in the United States and elsewhere, and fragments of information scattered here and abroad might have rung alarm bells had the dots been connected. Diminished human intelligence resources, a scarcity of regional experts, and poor coordination among information-gathering agencies helped keep the picture from being pieced together. In the execution of the operation itself, meanwhile, the terrorists boldly exploited the loopholes in the U.S. immigration and commercial aviation security systems, which were designed less to guarantee protection than to speed people and planes through as fast as possible.

Although they succeeded in bringing down the twin towers, the terrorists will not manage to provoke the "clash of civilizations" that their leader desires, nor will they spur drastic changes in the U.S. presence in the Middle East. But they have changed the world in other ways, etching the divide between the twentieth and twenty-first centuries far more sharply than the millennium celebrations ever did. Three challenges in particular now loom large: how to fight back against the people responsible, how to reduce our vulnerability to future attacks, and how to engage the world so as to lower the number of future attackers and those who might support them.

America is now at war. It accepts that the struggle will be lengthy, will involve casualties, and may have no neat or clear end. The initial targets are in Afghanistan, but Washington has vowed to pursue terrorists elsewhere as well. Disparate and uneasy states have been corralled into playing supporting roles in the coalition, but how many will stay on stage as the action proceeds remains to be seen. Some of the more tentative backers are states that have themselves been accused of supporting terrorists.

As the conflict has reshaped diplomatic relations, so has it disrupted the debate about the transformation of the U.S. armed forces to meet the challenges of the post–Cold War world. That debate had pitted believers in new threats and new responses against the entrenched supporters of the status quo, and had taken place within what seemed to be a relatively narrow budgetary constraint. After September 11 the funds will be there, but the question of what to spend them on remains open. The Bush administration's arguments about new and unconventional threats have been validated, but its early responses to those threats—notably an overemphasis on missile defense and an aversion to messy foreign interventions—have not.

Larger budgets remove some of the pressure to make choices between new force structures and expensive Cold War weapons systems. For the immediate future, there is money for both. Still, there will be debate about the kinds of adaptations that will be necessary if the war on terrorism becomes a central task of American foreign policy in the years ahead and if the armed forces are expected to help wage it. However the military is reconfigured, trying to prevent and respond to the proliferation of weapons of mass destruction will be among its top priorities.

At home, the open, secure life Americans took for granted is under stress. Fear is palpable—of bombings, hijackings, and biological or chemical attacks. Some curtailment of civil liberties is to be expected, along with the inconvenience of tightened security and the cost of making America safe in a shrunken world. The faltering economy now worries a public that had gotten used to lasting prosperity. Washington is offering confidence-building talk and fiscal-stimulus muscle, including a $15 billion bailout of the airlines. But the pressures of economic slowdown and enlarged public expenditures are canceling out yesterday's budget surpluses. If no quick upturn emerges, deficits loom.

In the realm of homeland security, the hijackings have provoked a scramble to improve protection of airplanes, airports, nuclear power plants, and other vulnerable facilities. For their part, the anthrax incidents have prompted an urgent re-evaluation of the public health system's readiness to counter future biological attacks. Other sectors cry out for similar attention. The exponential growth in transnational commerce has left American borders and ports underguarded and ill equipped to police increased flows of goods and people. Private aviation remains far less regulated than its commercial counterpart. Critical infrastructure in telecommunications and other areas remains vulnerable to mass disruption. None of these challenges is yet receiving the attention it deserves. Nor is it clear that the new director of the Office of Homeland Security, Tom Ridge, will have the authority to effectively coordinate the efforts of disparate government bureaucracies and congressional committees.

The attacks of September 11, finally, have driven home the need for the cooperation and support of partners abroad in achieving crucial American goals. Recent opinion polls show a sharp increase in public support for engagement. At the government level, the Bush administration has moved swiftly to reduce frictions between the West and its former Cold War adversaries, Russia and China, in order to address new common threats. Globalized scourges such as terrorism, drugs, and organized crime cannot be effectively countered by one nation, no matter how powerful. The same can be said of transnational problems such as infectious diseases and global warming. Even nation-building is being dusted off as a requirement in some instances. President George W. Bush's call for the United Nations to lead such an effort in Afghanistan once the military campaign is over stands in stark contrast to the abandonment of that country after the Soviet occupation was repulsed in the 1990s.

The time may have come, as well, for the United States to reconsider whether the close relations it maintains with repressive authoritarian regimes to assure regional stability in the short term truly serve its interests in the long term. In the Arab world in particular, populations that are experiencing explosive growth and high levels of unemployment are effectively being abandoned by inefficient, corrupt, and repressive regimes. Seeing little alternative, many answer the call of radical Islamist movements. For its own safety and stability, accordingly, the United States should consider pressing for the gradual opening of political and economic spaces to allow the people of this region to partake of the fruits of modernity and not just its toxins.

As we mourn the dead, we must also absorb the lessons, some of which are grim. Additional terrorist attacks on America are likely. Chemical and biological weapons may be used. September 11, an outrage and a tragedy for us, is an inspiration for terrorists. Only preparedness, determination, and, ultimately, self-confidence can offset the forebodings. The moral that Winston Churchill chose for his towering history of a previous global conflict is as apt now as it was then:

In War: Resolution.
In Defeat: Defiance.
In Victory: Magnanimity.
In Peace: Goodwill.

HOW DID THIS HAPPEN?

THE ORGANIZATION MEN
ANATOMY OF A TERRORIST ATTACK

■

BRIAN M. JENKINS

The September 11 attacks underscore some long-range trends in terrorism and tell us a great deal about the perpetrators' mindset, organization, capabilities, and intentions. The attacks also demolish some things we thought we knew while raising fresh questions for analysts to ponder.

It will take many months of investigation before we can assemble all of the details of what happened, and we will probably never know the entire story. Even without access to classified intelligence, however, it is possible to offer a preliminary sketch based on news reports and past testimony. There has been an avalanche of reporting by the news media, often based on their own massive investigations. One must handle this information with care, for it carries the potential for hidden and not-so-hidden agendas. It is collected and reported under time pressure, unfiltered and often unchecked. It varies greatly in quality. It is space-constrained. Uncertainty is banished, and a shorthand phrase, an elegant quote, or a colorful metaphor can trump analysis. Nonetheless, it is rich ore to be mined. It can be supplemented, moreover, with material that has emerged from investigations, indictments, and trials of other terrorists.

This last point presumes that the people behind the September 11 attacks were associated with those behind other recent strikes, but such a link seems clear. The hijackers seem connected to those who sponsored and executed the 1995 bombing of the Military Cooperation Program building in Riyadh, Saudi Arabia; the 1998 bombings of the American embassies in Kenya and Tanzania; the foiled terrorist plot to carry out bombings in the United States and elsewhere at the turn of the millennium; and the October 2000 attack on the U.S.S. *Cole* in Yemen—in other words, Osama bin Laden and his lieutenants.

For this not to be the case, the United States, the nations of the North Atlantic Treaty Organization and other allies, and the world's skeptical and aggressive news media would all have to have signed on to a massive disinformation campaign. Ingenious and elaborate conspiracy theories will always be on offer, but a propaganda conspiracy of that magnitude stretches credulity. At the same time, it is probable that bin Laden, despite his un-doubted role and newfound celebrity status, is not the Ian Fleming supervillain he has been made out to be. Leadership among self-appointed fanatics is always more complex than that.

We are deluged with material but still know too little. And this chapter, written only a month after the event, can be only analy-sis on the fly, a blurry snapshot rather than a diagram. Neverthe-less, one can look at what happened and how it happened and learn something about the terrorists' capabilities. One can then proceed to the "why"—the mind-set, motives, and strategy be-hind the attack, examining things from the terrorists' point of view. Discerning the logic behind their terrible violence, of course, in no way lessens condemnation of their acts. Cold-blooded mass murder requires cold-blooded analysis, the careful selection of words to convey precise meaning uncluttered by emotional rhetoric.

A LOW-TECH AFFAIR

On September 11, four separate teams of terrorists, 19 men in all, hijacked four airliners. They crashed two of them into the towers of the World Trade Center in New York and one into the Pentagon just outside of Washington, D.C. In the fourth aircraft, passengers realized what the hijackers intended to do and strug-gled to regain control of the plane. It crashed in Pennsylvania, killing everyone on board.

We may never know exactly how the hijackers seized control

of the aircraft. The little evidence we have suggests that they did it with small knives and box cutters along with claims that they had a bomb. The hijackers may have walked through airport screening procedures with these items (which passengers at the time were allowed to carry on board), or they may have had confederates at the airports who handed the items to them on the other side of security checkpoints or concealed them aboard the planes in advance. Some of the hijackers had trained in the martial arts; they were the muscle while the others, trained as pilots, flew the planes. They may or may not have worn red bandannas.

Add to their weapons, real and imagined, the element of surprise, the fact that they were a team rather than a lone hijacker, the likely swift initial act of violence to intimidate would-be challengers, the typically low passenger loads on Tuesday morning transcontinental flights, and the history of previous hijackings, which suggested that compliance rather than foolish resistance was the safest course of action.

The takeovers had to be coordinated in time. With the first crash, the authorities would realize what was up. Security would tighten. Airliners might be grounded—as in fact they were. Jets might even scramble to shoot down the hijacked planes before they reached their destination. The attacks had to be carried out in quick succession.

This simple account, if fairly accurate, suggests that the hijackers had knowledge of airport security procedures, which would have been easy to obtain through observation. How they persuaded or coerced the pilots to surrender the controls we do not know, but the hijackers expected no difficulty in entering the cockpits—they knew the doors were flimsy—and, unarmed, expected no surprises on the other side of the door. Security was fatally predictable.

Familiarity with passenger loads could have been gained through conversations with booking agents and through trial runs. Confederates among airport ground staff may or may not have been used, but their recruitment would not have presented any great obstacle. The "weapons" they used were readily available items.

The coordination of the final attack required communications between the teams. The operation itself required clear weather in both New York and Washington. Bad weather could have delayed flights, destroyed simultaneity, and obscured their targets. The hijackers had to be able to postpone the operations days, if not hours, beforehand if the weather looked bad. Cell phones would have sufficed to coordinate this aspect of the attacks.

In previous operations, we know there were separate teams: A surveillance unit reconnoitered possible targets and gathered intelligence, possibly years in advance. Its reports included careful evaluations of security. A higher echelon selected targets and reviewed plans. A logistics team provided support. And an attack team carried out the operation.

Indeed, this was fundamentally a low-tech affair. Ingenuity rather than technological sophistication enabled the terrorists to enter the domain of mass destruction, killing more than 5,000 people without resorting to chemical or biological weapons or improvised nuclear devices.

CASUALTIES OF EPIC PROPORTIONS

Those who had previously forecast that terrorist violence would escalate were right. The September 11 attacks conformed to a trend of escalating lethality even as the volume of international terrorism had declined. Large-scale indiscriminate violence had become the reality of contemporary terrorism before this most recent strike. Previously, terrorists had achieved this in one of two ways: by detonating truck bombs or by smuggling small bombs aboard commercial airliners. The worst incidents tell the story: 325 people killed in the 1985 crash of an Air India flight; more than 300 killed in 1993 by car bombs in Bombay; 270 killed in the 1988 crash of Pan Am flight 103; 241 killed in 1983 by a truck bomb in Beirut; 171 killed in the crash of a UTA flight in 1989; 168 killed by a truck bomb in Oklahoma City in 1995; 115 in the 1987 sabotage of a Korean airliner.

These were ominous but rare events. Of more than 10,000

incidents of international terrorism recorded since 1968, only 14 prior to September 11 had resulted in 100 or more fatalities. This suggests that self-imposed constraints limited terrorist violence; in the past, terrorists could have killed more but chose not to. Why? Because wanton violence could be counterproductive. It might have tarnished the group's image, threatened its cohesion, alienated perceived constituents, and provoked ferocious crackdowns. The increasing incidence of large-scale violence before September 11 suggested that these constraints were eroding. Terrorism requires shock, which was increasingly difficult to sustain in a world that had become inured to the growing volume of violence, and so escalation was necessary.

A fundamental change in terrorist motives had further eroded the constraints. Terrorism in the 1970s and 1980s was driven largely by ideology or the narrow nationalism that spawned separatist violence. Toward the end of the century, however, proclaimed religious beliefs increasingly provided its context. This shift is significant. Those convinced that they have the mandate of God to kill their foes have fewer moral qualms about mass murder and care less about constituents. They have no political agenda to promote. And in the minds of the devout, death in God's cause brings reward in the hereafter. Suicide attacks and mass murder often go hand in hand. For these reasons, analysts predicted that religiously inspired terrorists would be capable of the worst destruction, and they were correct.

Islam, a peaceful religion, has no monopoly on horrific violence. Advocates of the sword (or the bomb, or poison) can be found in every religion. But in the last quarter of the twentieth century, the continuing bloody quarrels of the Middle East were increasingly framed in religious terms, which were in turn exploited to inspire and excuse higher and higher levels of violence, directed against the West in general and the United States in particular. Analysts correctly assumed that Middle Eastern religious fanatics posed the greatest terrorist threat to America.

In February 1993, a local conspiracy of religious fanatics, assisted by a man named Ramzi Yousef, set off a huge truck bomb in the underground parking garage of the World Trade Center.

Their hope had been to topple one of the towers into the other, killing tens of thousands of people. The bomb caused extensive damage but killed only six. Yousef took flight and then later turned up in the Philippines, where he planned to sabotage 12 U.S. airliners flying in the Asia-Pacific region. This plan was breathtaking in its ambition; had it succeeded, it would have resulted in thousands of fatalities. Through sheer luck, Philippine authorities discovered the plot and special security measures prevented its execution. Yousef fled to Pakistan, where he was later apprehended. These events alerted us to the new terrorist mindset we faced. It sought casualties of epic proportions.

Even when terrorists tried, however, killing in quantity proved hard; the upper limit of several hundred fatalities seemed difficult to breach. Many, therefore, became convinced that terrorists seeking higher body counts would eventually resort to so-called weapons of mass destruction: chemical, biological, or even nuclear devices. As the recent anthrax mailings demonstrate, that possibility still cannot be dismissed, but too often overlooked was another, technologically less demanding solution: the multiple coordinated attack.

Coordinated terrorist attacks are not new. Almost 31 years before the events of September 11, on September 6, 1970, the Popular Front for the Liberation of Palestine hijacked three airliners and a fourth one the next day. Three of the hijackings succeeded; one failed. The three hijacked aircraft were flown to a desert airfield in Jordan, giving the hijackers several hundred hostages, all of whom were eventually released. Palestinian terrorists planted bombs aboard two separate Pan Am flights in August 1982. Sikh separatists tried to bring down three flights in June 1985. In 1994, Ramzi Yousef wanted to bring down 12 airliners. In 1998, followers of Osama bin Laden simultaneously attacked two American embassies in Africa.

Coordinated attacks enable terrorists to enter higher domains of violence, but they often fail. They have come to be seen as a kind of terrorist feat, an opportunity to demonstrate organizational skills. Sincerity of belief in one's God and implacable hatred for one's foe do not preclude sheer showmanship, especially when that showmanship may not only bring perverse acclaim from other terrorists but also enhance a leader's reputation among people who feel that they have suffered defeat and humiliation.

Those who approved and supported the September 11 attacks may well have anticipated an even higher level of casualties than actually occurred—something in the realm of tens or hundreds of thousands. The attacks were designed to have been a blow unprecedented in the annals of terrorism, beyond the carnage of war: the cruel punishment, the ultimate payback. In that sense, we were lucky.

THE TERRORISTS' SECRET WEAPON

The terrorists' secret weapon on September 11 was not high technology but human resolve. Coordinated attacks can succeed only if those carrying them out are willing to sacrifice their own lives. That the attackers did so wiped out several assumptions about suicide attacks. Analysts had previously viewed suicide attacks as not easily exportable. Suicide attackers themselves were thought to be a form of guided missile, but the kind requiring direct observation and targeting to be effective. The recruitment and psychological maintenance of a suicide attacker required handlers. Suicide attacks had to be launched close to the target. Without isolation and reinforcement, time and distance would erode the attacker's resolve.

The principal perpetrators of the September 11 attacks, however, had lived in the United States for months beforehand, leading apparently normal lives, interacting with society, in some cases traveling abroad. They had ample temptation and opportunity to change their minds, but they did not do so. We do not yet know if any associates dropped out of the plot before its denouement.

Group suicide attacks are extremely rare. And yet on September 11, at least 19 perpetrators went to their deaths. It is possible that as many as 13 did not know it was a suicide mission. Only six suicide notes have been discovered, and it is possible that the final letter urging the hijackers "to crave death" was not read by all. Perhaps some were told only that they would hijack an airplane, although questions about where they would go and how they would continue to hold their hostages without weapons must have crossed their minds. Their knowledge of previous terrorist operations might also have raised the suspicion that this was a one-way mission. Testimony from relatives and friends that they did not appear suicidal is meaningless. We may never know the truth, but no matter; at least six were determined to kill themselves in order to carry out their mission.

The profile of the September 11 attackers also differs from the profile of the typical suicide bombers seen in the Middle East, who for the most part appear to have been poor, not very well educated, and possibly psychologically damaged young men in their early 20s. Analysts believed that with greater maturity, status, and education, the proclivity to suicide would decline. This would normally have been a good bet, but the September 11 attackers were older—particularly those who clearly knew it was to be a suicide mission. They had better educations and appear to have been far more sophisticated than their predecessors. The profile of suicide attackers now requires revision.

Part of the explanation for the radical differences of the September 11 attacks lies in the nature of the bin Laden network, which taps into a much larger human reservoir than any previous terrorist organization. Previous terrorist groups could field perhaps several dozen, at most a few hundred active members, but the war in Afghanistan created a network that spanned the Arab world and drew in recruits from the most fanatical elements in the more distant corners of Islam. Not all were members of a single bin Laden organization, but the contacts among them enabled operations to draw on multiple resources. Analysts estimate the number of activists in the bin Laden network to be several thousand, an order of magnitude larger than the largest traditional terrorist group. This is sufficient to permit specialization: scientific, military, aviation, or, in another form, the willingness to commit suicide. With several thousand potential volunteers, 5 to 20 willing to die can be found.

The cultural context, moreover, cannot be overlooked. All cultures have produced their share of martyrs and heroes who readily sacrificed their lives for causes in which they believed. The fanatical obedience of the assassins who nine centuries ago struck terror in the minds of their foes is but one example. In recent years, suicide has become the benchmark of religious devotion and political commitment among "true believers" in the Middle East.

PAVING THE WAY OR STRATEGIC DECEPTION?

Training for the September 11 attacks began more than a year before the hijackings. It seems likely that the operation was laid out and approved some time before that. We know from testimony at the trial of those charged with the bombings of the American embassies in 1998 that bin Laden's network started moving assets into place for those attacks not later than 1994. One of bin Laden's key associates reportedly visited the United States in 1995 to check on the status and reliability of the local cells. This would mean that planning and preparations for the embassy bombings, the intended millennium attack at the Los Angeles International Airport (LAX), and the bombing of the U.S.S. *Cole* overlapped with planning and preparations for the September 11 attack. If other plots uncovered by authorities or believed to have been aborted are added, then this is an organization dealing with several major operations at the same time. It also raises the possibility that other terrorist operations were in various stages of preparation when the September 11 attacks took place; we may not learn about these plans for weeks or months or years.

Security considerations would require that the projects be kept compartmentalized. Operatives in one operation could not be allowed to know about other operations. The September 11 attacks were clearly the most audacious and had to be protected at all costs. This raises important questions. Were the actual and planned embassy bombings, the airport attack, and the attack on the *Cole* part of campaign building to the climactic attack of September 11? Were the other operations used to test responses and provide opportunities for the terrorists to learn lessons even if the operations themselves failed?

Were there two sets of terrorists involved: one or more terrorist "B teams" who carried out lower-level, albeit still spectacular actions, while a separate "A team" prepared the strategic September 11 strike? Is it conceivable that the other operations functioned as diversions to distract authorities from the September 11 attack? But then the planned attack at LAX, which was prevented only by a U.S. Customs Service official's fortunate discovery of explosives in the trunk of a terrorist's car, seems very risky. Had the LAX attack succeeded, it might have provoked heightened aviation security, thereby making the September 11 attacks more difficult. Yet the terrorist planners might have been confident that aviation security would not fundamentally change. As indeed it did not: The clear signal that bin Laden's terrorists were looking at airports produced no security changes. Lulled by luck, we slept. Could it be that the LAX bomber was supposed to be apprehended, to provide a false sense of security?

BIN LADEN'S PURPOSE

Terrorist operations must be judged not on the basis of what they do to the targets but what they do for the terrorists' leaders. What purpose did killing more than 5,000 people serve? Hatred provides a partial explanation. Bin Laden and his lieutenants speak often of punishment, which in their view is willed by God. More important, punishment is popular in the Middle East, where hatred of America is widespread and deeply felt. Bin Laden has also spoken of a more specific goal: bringing about the withdrawal of American military forces from the Middle East. His forces cannot drive them out, but the American public, if sufficiently terrified and confronted with growing anger in the Middle East, could decide that staying there is not worth the cost. That would make bin Laden the first Arab leader since Saladin to liberate sacred ground. The attacks would also demonstrate that America is not invincible, that it can be struck at the very symbols of its economic and military might. This result would enhance bin Laden's personal reputation as the only man able to strike such blows. We must keep in mind that these are people who drove the Soviet Union, then a superpower, out of Afghanistan.

U.S. leaders may have unwittingly enhanced bin Laden's reputation by labeling him the pre-eminent organizer and financier of international terrorism, thereby sending hundreds, even thousands, of recruits to his tent. The September 11 attacks and America's reaction to them could help bin Laden advance his own particular interpretation of Islam, which sanctifies violence as just and necessary, and facilitate his recruitment of young fanatics, thereby restocking his human arsenal.

The attacks of September 11 have also led to war, a war that bin Laden has characterized (and many in the Middle East see) as a U.S. assault on Islam, further elevating bin Laden's appeal and authority. The same "religious war" may well discredit the governments of Saudi Arabia (bin Laden's bitter foe), Egypt, Algeria, and others if they sign on with the U.S.-led coalition.

TERROR, INC.?

In the 1990s, analysts began to talk of a new kind of terrorist organization, one that was less structured and more fluid than the quasi-military terrorist organizations of earlier decades. To describe relationships that were not strictly hierarchical, one spoke of universes of like-minded fanatics in which there were galaxies and constellations from which ad hoc conspiracies and individual actors emerged. Such descriptions applied to the conspirators in the 1993 World Trade Center bombing, who prior to the attack had belonged to no terrorist organization. They applied to Timothy McVeigh and his co-conspirators in the Oklahoma City bombing. Ramzi Yousef's ability to plug into the World Trade Center conspiracy and then to Muslim fanatics in the Philippines seemed to confirm a loosely structured terrorist intranet.

Only with great caution should we apply this looser construct to Osama bin Laden's enterprise, however, for it comprises several things at once. The deployment of salaried operatives worldwide, the collection of intelligence, the acquisition of false documents, the provision of stipends for sleeper agents (those taking flight training in the United States), the movement of funds and terrorist recruits, the operation of training camps, and the coordination of multiple attacks require a lot of organization. There is evidence of formal membership (new members take oaths), of a hierarchy (an approval process), of specialization by function (intelligence, logistics, training), and of division of responsibilities (into religious and legal matters, public affairs, training and operations). The network appears to have the equivalent of a "board of directors" in the form of a powerful advisory group, line managers, and employees who, according to one former disgruntled insider, display all of the attributes of bureaucracy—gripes about compensation and working conditions, jealousies, corruption, and betrayal.

This enterprise does not look quite like a military headquarters, although some of its attributes are similar. It differs from a Mafia crime family, although there are some similarities. It more closely resembles a multinational corporate structure, which would fit with bin Laden's business background. At the same time, it is vitally concerned with proselytization—making it more like a political campaign headquarters. And yet it also appears very traditional, with powerful personalities and family, clan, and long-standing local connections providing the basis for loyalty and influence.

Al Qaeda (its name means "the base") has a structure designed to move money through formal financial institutions and traditional, informal means. Treasury Secretary Paul O'Neill described this financial network as "spider webs."

Al Qaeda's funds, which derive from bin Laden's own investments and from wealthy supporters, are spent supporting religious schools, business enterprises in which bin Laden may have a purely financial or future operational interest, terrorist training camps, the salaried agent network, deserving allied organizations, support for the Taliban, and terrorist operations. The last probably account for a small portion of the total budget. Terrorism is not costly. A few hundred thousand dollars would have sufficed to cover the September 11 operation.

Cutting across the more formal structure is a horizontal network of relationships with other organizations who subscribe to bin Laden's bellicose interpretation of Islam. These groups enable bin Laden to tap into local resources for operational support and provide recruits for training camps where the international connections are cemented, giving the enterprise a vast alumni base to draw on. Through these links with other groups and by carrying out operations, bin Laden gets to put his brand on the entire enterprise, which adds to his personal reputation, spreads his form of Islam, and attracts more recruits to the cause.

We do not know the operational code of bin Laden's "politburo," whether he has absolute power or is a non-executive chairman—the "commander" or the "face." Nor do we know the role played by "board" or "committee" members, or exactly how decisions are made.

The September 11 attacks, however, must have been handled differently from the others. An operation of this magnitude and consequence must have been approved at the highest level of the organization, by bin Laden himself, with the support of his advisers. It must have been closely monitored. The September 11 attacks would certainly have affected all other activities, and all those other activities must have been adjusted or suspended in accord with the main attack's trajectory.

THE END GAME

In recent videotaped messages, Osama bin Laden has increasingly referred to the Palestinian cause as the basis for his campaign. He sees it as an issue that is likely to win broad support in the Arab world. These public messages and shifts in explanation show a politician seeking a constituency. Terrorism is not his end, and religious belief, however sincere, is not his sole motive for violence. His is the politics of mass mobilization. Without constituents, terrorist violence becomes meaningless. But constituents impose constraints. The violence unleashed on September 11 inspires some, but bin Laden must weigh the risks of going too far. The deaths of innocent fellow Muslims in the attack cannot be easily dismissed. It must be explained, justified. Not every Muslim buys into bin Laden's brand of Islam or his assertion of religious leadership; in fact, most do not.

The attacks on the American embassies in Africa prompted a salvo of cruise missiles. The attack on the U.S.S. *Cole* brought no response. From the terrorists' perspective, the United States did not seem eager to engage bin Laden militarily. But bin Laden and his lieutenants knew that the September 11 attacks would bring a ferocious reply. Their strategy depended on provoking the United States into what would be seen in the Muslim world as an assault on Islam, and we may reasonably guess that they prepared for it.

They must have known that their network would come under enormous pressure from the United States, its allies, and those it could enlist in its campaign. To survive, the organization has probably protected its key operatives, arranged alternate routes of finance, and prepared hideouts, escape plans, and deception operations. All these arrangements would have been in place before September 11.

The survival of the leadership, especially bin Laden, would be paramount, not because they fear death more than those who slammed the planes into the World Trade Center, but because they believe that continuation of the struggle depends on their leader's survival. To remain the rallying point of the Islamic uprising requires that they also be able to continue communicating—hence bin Laden's videotaped messages. And it would inspire the masses and enrage their foes still more if, even while hunted by U.S.-led forces, they could carry out further terrorist attacks, doomsday operations counting down to launch without further instruction from the center. September 11 must be viewed as the beginning of Osama bin Laden's end game. It was almost certainly not planned to be his last move.

THE UNEASY IMPERIUM

PAX AMERICANA IN THE MIDDLE EAST

■

FOUAD AJAMI

From one end of the Arab world to the other, the drumbeats of anti-Americanism had been steady. But the drummers could hardly have known what was to come. The magnitude of the horror that befell the United States on Tuesday, September 11, 2001, appeared for a moment to embarrass and silence the drummers. The American imperium in the Arab-Muslim world hatched a monster. In a cruel irony, a new administration known for its relative lack of interest in that region was to be pulled into a world that has both beckoned America and bloodied it.

History never repeats itself, but when Secretary of State Colin Powell came forth to assure the nation that an international coalition against terrorism was in the offing, Americans recalled when Powell had risen to fame. "First, we're going to cut it off, then we're going to kill it," he had said of the Iraqi army in 1991. There had been another coalition then, and Pax Americana had set off to the Arab world on a triumphant campaign. But those Islamic domains have since worked their way and their will on the American victory of a decade ago. The political earth has shifted in that world. The decade was about the "blowback" of the war. Primacy begot its nemesis.

America's Arab interlocutors have said that the region's political stability would have held had the United States imposed a settlement of the Israeli-Palestinian conflict—and that the rancid anti-Americanism now evident in the Arab world has been called up by the fury of the second *intifada* that erupted in September

2000. But these claims misread the political world. Long before the second *intifada,* when Yasir Arafat was still making his way from political exile to the embrace of Pax Americana, there was a deadly trail of anti-American terror. Its perpetrators paid no heed to the Palestinian question. What they thought of Arafat and the metamorphosis that made him a pillar of President Clinton's Middle East policy is easy to construe.

The terror was steady, and its geography and targets bespoke resourcefulness and audacity. The first attack, the 1993 truck bombing of the World Trade Center, was inspired by the Egyptian cleric Sheikh Omar Abdel Rahman. For the United States, this fiery preacher was a peculiar guest: he had come to *bilad al-Kufr* (the lands of unbelief) to continue his war against the secular regime of Egyptian President Hosni Mubarak. The sheikh had already been implicated in the 1981 murder of Mubarak's predecessor, Anwar al-Sadat. The young assassins had sought religious guidance from him—a writ for tyrannicide. He had provided it but retained a measure of ambiguity, and Egypt let him leave the country. He had no knowledge of English and did not need it; there were disciples and interpreters aplenty around him. An American imperium had incorporated Egypt into its order of things, which gave the sheikh a connection to the distant power.

The preacher could not overturn the entrenched regime in his land. But there was steady traffic between the United States and Egypt, and the armed Islamist insurgency that bedeviled Cairo inspired him. He would be an Ayatollah Khomeini for his followers, destined to return from the West to establish an Islamic state. In the preacher's mind, the world was simple. The dictatorial regime at home would collapse once he snapped its lifeline to America. American culture was of little interest to him. Rather, the United States was a place from which he could hound his country's rulers. Over time, Abdel Rahman's quest was denied. Egypt rode out the Islamist insurgency after a terrible drawn-out fight that pushed the country to the brink. The sheikh ended up in an American prison. But he had lit the fuse. The 1993 attack on the World Trade Center that he launched was a mere dress rehearsal for the calamity of September 11, 2001. Abdel Rahman had shown the way—and the future.

There were new Muslim communities in America and Europe; there was also money and freedom to move about. The geography of political Islam had been redrawn. When Ayatollah Khomeini took on American power, there had been talk of a pan-Islamic brigade. But the Iranian revolutionaries were ultimately concerned with their own nation-state. And they were lambs compared with the holy warriors to come. Today's warriors have been cut loose from the traditional world. Some of the leaders— the Afghan Arabs—had become restless after the Afghan war. They were insurrectionists caught in no-man's-land, on the run from their homelands but never at home in the West. In Tunisia, Egypt, and Algeria, tenacious Islamist movements were put down. In Saudi Arabia, a milder Islamist challenge was contained. The counterinsurgencies had been effective, so the extremists turned up in the West. There, liberal norms gave them shelter, and these men would rise to fight another day.

The extremists acquired modern means: frequent flyer miles, aviation and computer skills, and ease in Western cities. They hated the United States, Germany, and France but were nonetheless drawn to them. They exalted tradition and faith, but their traditions could no longer give them a world. Islam's explosive demography had spilled into the West. The militant Islamists were on the move. The security services in their home countries were unsentimental, showing no tolerance for heroics. Men like Abdel Rahman and Osama bin Laden offered this breed of un-settled men a theology of holy terror and the means to live the plotter's life. Bin Laden was possessed of wealth and high birth, the heir of a merchant dynasty. This gave him an aura: a Che Guevara of the Islamic world, bucking the mighty and getting away with it. A seam ran between America and the Islamic world. The new men found their niche, their targets, and their sympathizers across that seam. They were sure of America's culpability for the growing misery in their lands. They were sure that the regimes in Saudi Arabia and Egypt would fall if only they could force the United States to cast its allies adrift.

NOT IN MY BACKYARD

Terror shadowed the American presence in the Middle East throughout the 1990s: two bombings in Saudi Arabia, one in Riyadh in November of 1995 and the other on the Khobar Towers near Dhahran in June of 1996; bombings of the U.S. embassies in Tanzania and Kenya in 1998; the daring attack on the U.S.S. *Cole* in Yemen in October 2000. The U.S. presence in the Persian Gulf was under assault.

In this trail of terror, symbol and opportunity were rolled together—the physical damage alongside a political and cultural message. These attacks were meant for a watchful crowd in a media age. Dhahran had been a creature of the U.S. presence in Saudi Arabia ever since American oil prospectors turned up in the 1930s and built that city in the American image. But the world had changed. It was in Dhahran, in the 1990s, that the crews monitoring the no-fly zone over Iraq were stationed. The attack against Dhahran was an obvious blow against the alliance between the United States and Saudi Arabia. The realm would not disintegrate; Beirut had not come to Arabia. But the assailants— suspected to be an Iranian operation that enlisted the participation of Saudi Shi'a—had delivered the blow and the message. The foreigner's presence in Arabia was contested. A radical Islamist opposition had emerged, putting forth a fierce, redemptive Islam at odds with the state's conservative religion.

The *ulama* (clergy) had done well under the Al Saud dynasty. They were the dynasty's partners in upholding an order where obedience to the rulers was given religious sanction. No ambitious modernist utopia had been unleashed on them as it had in Gamal Abdel al-Nasser's Egypt and Iran under the Pahlavis. Still, the state could not appease the new breed of activists who had stepped forth after the Gulf War to hound the rulers over internal governance and their ties to American power. In place of their rulers' conservative edifice, these new salvationists proposed a radical order free from foreign entanglements. These activists were careful to refrain from calling for the outright destruction of the House of Saud. But sedition was in the air in the mid-1990s, and the elements of the new utopia were easy to discern. The Shi'a minority in the eastern province would be decimated and the Saudi liberals molded on the campuses of California and Texas would be swept aside in a zealous, frenzied campaign. Traffic with the infidels would be brought to an end, and those dreaded satellite dishes bringing the West's cultural "pollution" would be taken down. But for this to pass, the roots of the American presence in Arabia would have to be extirpated—and the Americans driven from the country.

The new unrest, avowedly religious, stemmed from the austerity that came to Saudi Arabia after Desert Storm. If the rulers could not subsidize as generously as they had in the past, the foreigner and his schemes and overcharges must be to blame. The dissidents were not cultists but men of their society, half-learned in Western sources and trends, picking foreign sources to illustrate the subjugation that America held in store for Arabia. Pamphleteering had come into the realm, and rebellion proved contagious. A dissident steps out of the shadows, then respectable critics, then others come forth. Xenophobic men were now agitating against the "crusaders" who had come to stay. "This has been a bigger calamity than I had expected, bigger than any threat the Arabian Peninsula had faced since God Almighty created it," wrote the religious scholar Safar al-Hawali, a master practitioner of the paranoid style in politics. The Americans, he warned, had come to dominate Arabia and unleash on it the West's dreaded morals.

Saudi Arabia had been free of the anticolonial complex seen in states such as Algeria, Egypt, Syria, and Iraq. But the simplicity of that Arabian-American encounter now belonged to the past. A *fatwa* (Islamic decree) of the senior religious jurist in the realm, Sheikh Abdelaziz ibn Baz, gave away the hazards of the U.S. presence in Arabia. Ibn Baz declared the Khobar bombing a "transgression against the teachings of Islam." The damage to lives and property befell many people, "Muslims and others alike," he wrote. These "non-Muslims" had been granted a pledge of safety. The sheikh found enough scripture and tradition to see a cruel end for those who pulled off the "criminal act." There was a saying attributed to the Prophet Muhammad: "He who killed an ally will never know the smell of paradise." And there was God's word in the Koran: "Those that make war against Allah and his apostle and spread disorder in the land shall be put to death or crucified or have their hands and feet cut off on alternate sides or be banished from the country. They shall be held to shame in this world and sternly punished in the next." The sheikh permitted himself a drapery of decency. There was no need to specify the identity of the victims or acknowledge that the Americans were in the land. There had remained in the jurist some scruples and restraints of the faith.

In ibn Baz's world, faith was about order and a dread of anarchy. But in the shadows, a different version of the faith was being sharpened as a weapon of war. Two years later, bin Laden issued an incendiary *fatwa* of his own—a call for murder and holy warfare that was interpreted in *Foreign Affairs* by the historian Bernard Lewis. Never mind that by the faith's strictures and practice, bin Laden had no standing to issue religious decrees. He had grabbed the faith and called on Muslims to kill "Americans and their allies . . . in any country in which it is possible to do so." A sacred realm apart, Arabia had been overrun by Americans, bin Laden said. "For more than seven years the United States has been occupying the lands of Islam in the holiest of its territories, Arabia, plundering its riches, overwhelming its rulers, humiliating its people, threatening its neighbors, and using its peninsula as a spearhead to fight the neighboring Islamic peoples." Xenophobia of a murderous kind had been dressed up in religious garb.

INTO THE SHADOWS

The attack on the *Cole* on October 12, 2000, was a case apart. Two men in a skiff crippled the *Cole* as it docked in Aden to refuel. Witnesses say that the assailants, who perished with their victims, were standing erect at the time of the blast, as if in some kind of salute. The United States controlled the sea lanes of that world, but the nemesis that stalked it on those shores lay beyond

America's reach. "The attack on the U.S.S. *Cole* . . . demonstrated a seam in the fabric of efforts to protect our forces, namely transit forces," a military commission said. But the official language could not describe or name the furies at play.

The attack on the *Cole* illuminated the U.S. security dilemma in the Persian Gulf. For the U.S. Navy, Yemen had not been a particularly easy or friendly setting. It had taken a ride with Saddam Hussein during the Gulf War. In 1994, a brutal war had been fought in Yemen between north and south, along lines of ideology and tribalism. The troubles of Yemen were bottomless. The government was barely in control of its territory and coastline. Aden was a place of drifters and smugglers. Moreover, the suspected paymaster of anti-American terror, bin Laden, had ancestral roots in Hadramawt, the southeastern part of Yemen, and he had many sympathizers there.

It would have been prudent to look at Yemen and Aden with a jaundiced eye. But by early 1999, American ships had begun calling there. U.S. officials had no brilliant options south of the Suez Canal, they would later concede. The ports of call in Sudan, Somalia, Djibouti, and Eritrea were places where the "threat conditions" were high, perhaps worse than in Yemen. The United States had a privileged position in Saudi Arabia, but there had been trouble there as well for U.S. forces: the terrorist attacks in 1995 and 1996, which took 24 American lives. American commanders and planners knew the hazards of Yemen, but the U.S. Navy had taken a chance on the country. Terrorists moved through Yemen at will, but American military planners could not find ideal refueling conditions in a region of great volatility. This was the imperial predicament put in stark, cruel terms.

John Burns of *The New York Times* sent a dispatch of unusual clarity from Aden about the *Cole* and the response on the ground to the terrible deed. In Yemen, the reporter saw "a halting, half-expressed sense of astonishment, sometimes of satisfaction and even pleasure, that a mighty power, the United States, should have its Navy humbled by two Arab men in a motorized skiff." Such was imperial presence, the Pax Americana in Arab and Muslim lands.

There were men in the shadows pulling off spectacular deeds.

But they fed off a free-floating anti-Americanism that blows at will and knows no bounds, among Islamists and secularists alike. For the crowds in Karachi, Cairo, and Amman, the great power could never get it right. A world lacking the tools and the political space for free inquiry fell back on anti-Americanism. "I talk to my daughter-in-law so my neighbor can hear me," goes an Arabic maxim. In the fury with which the intellectual and political class railed against the United States and Israel, the agitated were speaking to and of their own rulers. Sly and cunning men, the rulers knew and understood the game. There would be no open embrace of America, and no public defense of it. They would stay a step ahead of the crowd and give the public the safety valve it needed. The more pro-American the regime, the more anti-American the political class and the political tumult. The United States could grant generous aid to the Egyptian state, but there would be no dampening of the anti-American fury of the Egyptian political class. Its leading state-backed dailies crackled with the wildest theories of U.S.-Israeli conspiracies against their country.

On September 11, 2001, there was an unmistakable sense of glee and little sorrow among upper-class Egyptians for the distant power—only satisfaction that America had gotten its comeuppance. After nearly three decades of American solicitude of Egypt, after the steady traffic between the two lands, there were no genuine friends for America to be found in a curiously hostile, disgruntled land.

Egyptians have long been dissatisfied with their country's economic and military performance, a pain born of the gap between Egypt's exalted idea of itself and the poverty and foreign dependence that have marked its modern history. The rage against Israel and the United States stems from that history of lament and frustration. So much of Egypt's life lies beyond the scrutiny and the reach of its newspapers and pundits—the ruler's ways, the authoritarian state, the matter of succession to Mubarak, the joint military exercises with U.S. and Egyptian forces, and so on. The animus toward America and Israel gives away the frustration of a polity raging against the hard, disillusioning limits of its political life.

In the same vein, Jordan's enlightened, fragile monarchy was bound to the United States by the strategic ties that a skilled King Hussein had nurtured for decades. But a mood of anger and seething radicalism had settled on Jordan. The country was increasingly poorer, and the fault line between Palestinians and East Bankers was a steady source of mutual suspicion. If the rulers made peace with Israel, "civil society" and the professional syndicates would spurn it. Even though the late king had deep ties with the distant imperial power, the country would remain unreconciled to this pro-American stance. Jordan would be richer, it was loudly proclaimed, if only the sanctions on Iraq had been lifted, if only the place had been left to gravitate into Iraq's economic orbit. Jordan's new king, Abdullah II, could roll out the red carpet for Powell when the general turned up in Jordan recently on a visit that had the distinct sense of a victory lap by a soldier revisiting his early triumph. But the throngs were there with placards, and banners were aloft branding the visitor a "war criminal." This kind of fury a distant power can never overcome. Policy can never speak to wrath. Step into the thicket (as Bill Clinton did in the Israeli-Palestinian conflict) and the foreign power is damned for its reach. Step back, as George W. Bush did in the first months of his presidency, and Pax Americana is charged with abdication and indifference.

THE SIEGE

The power secured during Desert Storm was destined not to last. The United States could not indefinitely quarantine Iraq. It was idle to think that the broad coalition cobbled together during an unusually perilous moment in 1990–91 would stand as a permanent arrangement. The demographic and economic weight of Iraq and Iran meant that those countries were bound to reassert themselves. The United States had done well in the Persian Gulf by Iraq's brazen revisionism and the Iranian Revolution's assault on its neighboring states. It had been able to negotiate the terms of the U.S. presence—the positioning of equipment in the oil states, the establishment of a tripwire in Kuwait, the acceptance of an American troop presence on the Arabian Peninsula—at a time when both Iran and Iraq were on a rampage. Hence the popular concerns that had hindered the American presence in the Persian Gulf were brushed aside in the 1990s. But this lucky run was bound to come to an end. Iraq steadily chipped away at the sanctions, which over time were seen as nothing but an Anglo-American siege of a brutalized Iraqi population.

The campaign against Saddam Hussein had been waged during a unique moment in Arab politics. Some Muslim jurists in Saudi Arabia and Egypt even ruled that Saddam had run afoul of Islam's strictures, and that an alliance with foreign powers to check his aggression and tyranny was permissible under Islamic law. A part of the Arabian Peninsula that had hitherto wanted America "over the horizon" was eager to have American protection against a "brother" who had shredded all the pieties of pan-Arab solidarity. But the Iraqi dictator hunkered down, outlasting the foreign power's terrible campaign. He was from the neighborhood and knew its rules. He worked his way into the local order of things.

The Iraqi ruler knew well the distress that settled on the region after Pax Americana's swift war. All around Iraq, the region was poorer: oil prices had slumped, and the war had been expensive for the oil states that financed it. Oil states suspected they were being overbilled for military services and for weapons that they could not afford. The war's murky outcome fed the belief that the thing had been rigged all along, that Saddam Hussein had been lured into Kuwait by an American green light—and then kept in power and let off the hook—so that Pax Americana would have the pretext for stationing its forces in the region. The Iraqi ruler then set out to show the hollowness of the hegemony of a disinterested American imperium.

A crisis in 1996 laid bare the realities for the new imperium. Saddam Hussein brazenly sent his squads of assassins into the "safe haven" that the United States had marked out for the Kurds in northern Iraq after Desert Storm. He sacked that region and executed hundreds who had cast their fate with American power.

America was alone this time around. The two volleys of Toma-hawk missiles fired against Iraqi air-defense installations had to be launched from U.S. ships in the Persian Gulf and B-52 bombers that flew in from Guam. No one was fooled by the American re-sponse; no one believed that the foreign power would stay. U.S. officials wrote off that episode as an internal Kurdish fight, the doings of a fratricidal people. A subsequent air campaign—"fire and forget," skeptics dubbed it—gave the illusion of resolve and containment. But Clinton did not have his heart in that fight. He had put his finger to the wind and divined the mood in the land: there was no public tolerance for a major campaign against Sad-dam Hussein.

By the time the Bush administration stepped in, its leaders would find a checkered landscape. There was their old nemesis in Baghdad, wounded but not killed. There was a decade of Clinto-nianism that had invested its energy in the Israeli-Palestinian conflict but had paid the Persian Gulf scant attention. There was a pattern of half-hearted responses to terrorist attacks, pinpricks that fooled no one.

HAVING IT HIS WAY

It was into this witch's brew that Arafat launched the second *intifada* last year. In a rare alignment, there had come Arafat's way a U.S. president keen to do his best and an Israeli soldier-statesman eager to grant the Palestinian leader all the Israeli body politic could yield—and then some. Arafat turned away from what was offered and headed straight back into his people's fa-miliar history: the maximalism, the inability to read what can and cannot be had in a world of nations. He would wait for the "Arab street" to rise up in rebellion and force Pax Americana to redeem his claims. He would again let play on his people the old dream that they could have it all, from the river to the sea. He must know better, he must know the scales of power, it is reason-able to presume. But there still lurks in the Palestinian and Arab imagination a view, depicted by the Moroccan historian Abdallah

Laroui, that "on a certain day, everything would be obliterated and instantaneously reconstructed and the new inhabitants would leave, as if by magic, the land they had despoiled." Arafat knew the power of this redemptive idea. He must have reasoned that it is safer to ride that idea, and that there will always be another day and another offer.

For all the fury of this second *intifada,* a supreme irony hangs over Palestinian history. In the early 1990s, the Palestinians had nothing to lose. Pariahs in the Arab councils of power, they made their best historical decision—the peace of Oslo—only when they broke with the maximalism of their political tradition. It was then that they crossed from Arab politics into internal Israeli politics and, courtesy of Israel, into the orbit of Pax Americana. Their recent return into inter-Arab politics was the resumption of an old, failed history.

Better the fire of an insurrection than the risks of reconciling his people to a peace he had not prepared them for: this was Arafat's way. This is why he spurned the offer at Camp David in the summer of 2000. "Yasir Arafat rode home on a white horse" from Camp David, said one of his aides, Nabil Shaath. He had shown that he "still cared about Jerusalem and the refugees." He had stood up, so Shaath said, to the combined pressure of the Americans and the Israelis. A creature of his time and his world, Arafat had come into his own amid the recriminations that followed the Arab defeat in 1948. Palestine had become an Arab shame, and the hunt for demons and sacrificial lambs would shape Arab politics for many years.

A temporizer and a trimmer, Arafat did not have it in him to tell the 1948 refugees in Lebanon, Syria, and Jordan that they were no more likely to find political satisfaction than were the Jews of Alexandria, Fez, Baghdad, and Beirut who were banished from Arab lands following Israel's statehood. He lit the fuse of this second *intifada* in the hope that others would put out the flame. He had become a player in Israeli politics, and there came to him this peculiar satisfaction that he could topple Israeli prime ministers, wait them out, and force an outside diplomatic intervention that would tip the scales in his favor. He could not give his people a decent public order and employ and train the young, but he could launch a war in the streets that would break Israel's economic momentum and rob it of the normalcy brought by the peace of Oslo.

Arafat had waited for rain, but on September 11, 2001, there had come the floods. "This is a new kind of war, a new kind of battlefield, and the United States will need the help of Arab and Muslim countries," chief Palestinian negotiator Saeb Erekat announced. The Palestinian issue, he added, was "certainly one of the reasons" for the attacks against the United States. An American-led brigade against terrorism was being assembled. America was set to embark on another expedition into Arab-Muslim domains, and Arafat fell back on the old consolation that Arab assets would be traded on his people's behalf. A dowry would have to be offered to the Arab participants in this brigade: a U.S.-imposed settlement of the Israeli-Palestinian conflict. A cover would be needed for Arab regimes nervous about riding with the foreigner's posse, and it stood to reason that Arafat would claim that he could provide that kind of cover.

The terror that hit America sprang from entirely different sources. The plotters had been in American flight schools long before the "suicide martyrs" and the "children of the stones" had answered Arafat's call for an *intifada*. But the Palestinian leader and his lieutenants eagerly claimed that the fire raging in their midst had inspired the anti-American terror. A decade earlier, the Palestinians had hailed Saddam Hussein's bid for primacy in the Persian Gulf. Nonetheless, they had been given a claim on the peace—a role at the Madrid Conference of October 1991 and a solicitous U.S. policy. American diplomacy had arrived in the nick of time; the first *intifada* had burned out and degenerated into a hunt for demons and "collaborators." A similar fate lies in wait for the second *intifada*. It is reasonable to assume that Arafat expects rescue of a similar kind from the new American drive into Arab and Muslim lands.

No veto over national policies there will be given to Arafat. The states will cut their own deals. In the best of worlds, Pax Americana is doomed to a measure of solitude in the Middle East.

This time around, the American predicament is particularly acute. Deep down, the Arab regimes feel that the threat of political Islam to their own turfs has been checked, and that no good can come out of an explicit public alliance with an American campaign in their midst. Foreign powers come and go, and there is very little protection they can provide against the wrath of an angry crowd. It is a peculiarity of the Arab-Islamic political culture that a ruler's authoritarianism is more permissible than his identification with Western powers—think of the fates of Sadat and of the Pahlavis of Iran.

Ride with the foreigners at your own risk, the region's history has taught. Syria's dictator, Hafiz al-Assad, died a natural death at a ripe old age, and his life could be seen as a kind of success. He never set foot on American soil and had stayed within his world. In contrast, the flamboyant Sadat courted foreign countries and came to a solitary, cruel end; his land barely grieved for him. A foreign power that stands sentry in that world cannot spare its local allies the retribution of those who brand them "collaborators" and betrayers of the faith. A coalition is in the offing, America has come calling, urging the region's rulers to "choose sides." What these rulers truly dread has come to pass: they might have to make fateful choices under the gaze of populations in the throes of a malignant anti-Americanism. The ways of that world being what they are, the United States will get more cooperation from the ministers of interior and the secret services than it will from the foreign ministers and the diplomatic interlocutors. There will be allies in the shadows, but in broad daylight the rulers will mostly keep their distance. Pakistan's ruler, Pervez Musharraf, has made a brave choice. The rulers all around must be reading a good deal of their worries into his attempt to stay the course and keep his country intact.

A broad coalition may give America the comfort that it is not alone in the Muslim world. A strike against Afghanistan is the easiest of things—far away from the troubles in the Persian Gulf and Egypt, from the head of the trail in Arab lands. The Taliban are the Khmer Rouge of this era and thus easy to deal with. The frustrations to come lie in the more ambiguous and impenetrable realms of the Arab world. Those were not Afghans who flew into those towers of glass and steel and crashed into the Pentagon. They were from the Arab world, where anti-Americanism is fierce, where terror works with the hidden winks that men and women make at the perpetrators of the grimmest of deeds.

BRAVE OLD WORLD

"When those planes flew into those buildings, the luck of America ran out," Leon Wieseltier recently wrote in *The New Republic*. The 1990s were a lucky decade, a fool's paradise. But we had not arrived at the end of history, not by a long shot. Markets had not annulled historical passions, and a high-tech world's electronic age had not yet dawned. So in thwarted, resentful societies there was satisfaction on September 11 that the American bull run and the triumphalism that had awed the world had been battered, that there was soot and ruin in New York's streets. We know better now. Pax Americana is there to stay in the oil lands and in Israeli-Palestinian matters. No large-scale retreat from those zones of American primacy can be contemplated. American hegemony is sure to hold—and so, too, the resistance to it, the uneasy mix in those lands of the need for the foreigner's order, and the urge to lash out against it, to use it and rail against it all the same.

The first war of the twenty-first century is being fought not so far from where the last inconclusive war of the twentieth century was waged against Iraq. The war will not be easy for America in those lands. The setting will test it in ways it has not been tested before. There will be regimes asking for indulgence for their own terrible fights against Islamists and for logistical support. There will be rulers offering the bait of secrets that their security services have accumulated through means at odds with American norms. Conversely, friends and sympathizers of terror will pass themselves off as constitutionalists and men and women of "civil society." They will find shelter behind pluralist norms while aiding and abetting the forces of terror. There will be chameleons good at posing as America's friends but never turning up when needed. There will be one way of speaking to Americans, and another of letting one's population know that words are merely a pretense. There will step forth informers, hustlers of every shade, offering to guide the foreign power through the minefields and alleyways. America, which once held the world at a distance, will have to be willing to stick around eastern lands. It is both heartbreaking and ironic that so quintessentially American a figure as George W. Bush—a man who grew up in Midland, Texas, far removed from the complications of foreign places—must be the one to take his country on a journey into so alien, so difficult, a world.

SOMEBODY ELSE'S CIVIL WAR

IDEOLOGY, RAGE, AND THE ASSAULT ON AMERICA

■

MICHAEL SCOTT DORAN

> Call it a city on four legs
> heading for murder. . . .
> New York is a woman
> holding, according to history,
> a rag called liberty with one hand
> and strangling the earth with the other.
>
> Adonis [Ali Ahmed Said]
> "The Funeral of New York," 1971

In the weeks after the attacks of September 11, Americans repeatedly asked, "Why do they hate us?" To understand what happened, however, another question may be even more pertinent: "Why do they want to provoke us?"

David Fromkin suggested the answer in *Foreign Affairs* back in 1975. "Terrorism," he noted, "is violence used in order to create fear; but it is aimed at creating fear in order that the fear, in turn, will lead somebody else—not the terrorist—to embark on some quite different program of action that will accomplish whatever it is that the terrorist really desires." When a terrorist kills, the goal is not murder itself but something else—for example, a police crackdown that will create a rift between government and society that the terrorist can then exploit for revolutionary purposes. Osama bin Laden sought—and has received—an international military crackdown, one he wants to exploit for his particular brand of revolution.

Bin Laden has produced a piece of high political theater he hopes will reach the audience that concerns him the most: the *umma*, or universal Islamic community. The script is obvious: America, cast as the villain, is supposed to use its military might like a cartoon character trying to kill a fly with a shotgun. The media will see to it that any use of force against the civilian population of Afghanistan will be broadcast around the world, and the *umma* will find it shocking how Americans nonchalantly cause Muslims to suffer and die. The ensuing outrage will open a chasm between state and society in the Middle East, and the governments allied with the West—many of which are repressive, corrupt, and illegitimate—will find themselves adrift. It was to provoke such an outcome that bin Laden broadcast his statement following the start of the military campaign on October 7, in which he said, among other things, that the Americans and the British "have divided the entire world into two regions—one of faith, where there is no hypocrisy, and another of infidelity, from which we hope God will protect us."

Polarizing the Islamic world between the *umma* and the regimes allied with the United States will help achieve bin Laden's primary goal: furthering the cause of Islamic revolution within the Islamic world itself, in the Arab lands especially and in Saudi Arabia above all. He has no intention of defeating America. War with the United States is not a goal in and of itself but rather an instrument designed to help his brand of extremist Islam survive and flourish among the believers. Americans, in short, have been drawn into somebody else's civil war.

Washington had no choice but to take up the gauntlet, but it is not altogether clear that Americans understand fully this war's true dimensions. The response to bin Laden cannot be left to soldiers and police alone. He has embroiled the United States in an intra-Muslim ideological battle, a struggle for hearts and minds in which Al Qaeda has already scored a number of victories—as the reluctance of America's Middle Eastern allies to offer public support for the campaign against it demonstrates. The first step toward weakening the hold of bin Laden's ideology, therefore, must be to comprehend the symbolic universe into which he has dragged us.

AMERICA, THE HUBAL OF THE AGE

Bin Laden's October 7 statement offers a crucial window onto his conceptual world and repays careful attention. In it he states, "Hypocrisy stood behind the leader of global idolatry, behind the Hubal of the age—namely, America and its supporters." Because the symbolism is obscure to most Americans, this sentence was widely mistranslated in the press, but bin Laden's Muslim audience understood it immediately.

In the early seventh century, when the Prophet Muhammad began to preach Islam to the pagan Arab tribes in Mecca, Hubal was a stone idol that stood in the Kaaba—a structure that Abraham, according to Islamic tradition, originally built on orders from God as a sanctuary of Islam. In the years between Abraham and Muhammad, the tradition runs, the Arabs fell away from true belief and began to worship idols, with Hubal the most powerful of many. When bin Laden calls America "the Hubal of the age," he suggests that it is the primary focus of idol worship and that it is polluting the Kaaba, a symbol of Islamic purity. His imagery has a double resonance: it portrays American culture as a font of idolatry while rejecting the American military presence on the Arabian peninsula (which is, by his definition, the holy land of Islam, a place barred to infidels).

Muhammad's prophecy called the Arabs of Mecca back to their monotheistic birthright. The return to true belief, however, was not an easy one, because the reigning Meccan oligarchy persecuted the early Muslims. By calling for the destruction of Hubal, the Prophet's message threatened to undermine the special position that Mecca enjoyed in Arabia as a pagan shrine city. With much of their livelihood at stake, the oligarchs punished Muhammad's followers and conspired to kill him. The Muslims therefore fled from Mecca to Medina, where they established the *umma* as a political and religious community. They went on to fight and win a war against Mecca that ended with the destruction of Hubal and the spread of true Islam around the world.

Before the Prophet could achieve this success, however, he

encountered the *Munafiqun*, the Hypocrites of Medina. Muhammad's acceptance of leadership over the Medinese reduced the power of a number of local tribal leaders. These men outwardly accepted Islam in order to protect their worldly status, but in their hearts they bore malice toward both the Prophet and his message. Among other misdeeds, the treacherous *Munafiqun* abandoned Muhammad on the battlefield at a moment when he was already woefully outnumbered. The Hypocrites were apostates who accepted true belief but then rejected it, and as such they were regarded as worse than the infidels who had never embraced Islam to begin with. Islam can understand just how difficult it is for a pagan to leave behind all the beliefs and personal connections that he or she once held dear; it is less forgiving of those who accept the truth and then subvert it.

In bin Laden's imagery, the leaders of the Arab and Islamic world today are Hypocrites, idol worshipers cowering behind America, the Hubal of the age. His sword jabs simultaneously at the United States and the governments allied with it. His attack was designed to force those governments to choose: You are either with the idol-worshiping enemies of God or you are with the true believers.

The Al Qaeda organization grows out of an Islamic religious movement called the *Salafiyya*—a name derived from *al-Salaf al-Salih*, "the venerable forefathers," which refers to the generation of the Prophet Muhammad and his companions. *Salafi*s regard the Islam that most Muslims practice today as polluted by idolatry; they seek to reform the religion by emulating the first generation of Muslims, whose pristine society they consider to have best reflected God's wishes for humans. The *Salafiyya* is not a unified movement, and it expresses itself in many forms, most of which do not approach the extremism of Osama bin Laden or the Taliban. The Wahhabi ideology of the Saudi state, for example, and the religious doctrines of the Muslim Brotherhood in Egypt and a host of voluntary religious organizations around the Islamic world are all *Salafi*. These diverse movements share the belief that Muslims have deviated from God's plan and that matters can be returned to their proper state by emulating the Prophet Muhammad.

Like any other major religious figure, Muhammad left behind a legacy that his followers have channeled in different directions. An extremist current in the *Salafiyya* places great emphasis on *jihad*, or holy war. Among other things, the Prophet Muhammad fought in mortal combat against idolatry, and some of his followers today choose to accord this aspect of his career primary importance. The devoted members of Al Qaeda display an unsettling willingness to martyr themselves because they feel that, like the Prophet Muhammad, they are locked in a life-or-death struggle with the forces of unbelief that threaten from all sides. They consider themselves an island of true believers surrounded by a sea of iniquity and think the future of religion itself, and therefore the world, depends on them and their battle against idol worship.

In almost every Sunni Muslim country the *Salafiyya* has spawned Islamist political movements working to compel the state to apply the *shari'a*—that is, Islamic law. Extremist *Salafis* believe that strict application of the *shari'a* is necessary to ensure that Muslims walk on the path of the Prophet. The more extremist the party, the more insistent and violent the demand that the state must apply the *shari'a* exclusively. In the view of extremist *Salafis*, the *shari'a* is God's thunderous commandment to Muslims, and failure to adopt it constitutes idolatry. By removing God from the realm of law, a domain that He has clearly claimed for Himself alone, human legislation amounts to worshiping a pagan deity. Thus it was on the basis of failure to apply the *shari'a* that extremists branded Egyptian President Anwar al-Sadat an apostate and then killed him. His assassins came from a group often known as Egyptian Islamic Jihad, the remnants of which have in recent years merged with Al Qaeda. In fact, investigators believe that Egyptian Islamic Jihad's leaders, Ayman Zawahiri and Muhammad Atif, masterminded the attacks of September 11. In his 1996 "Declaration of War against the Americans," bin Laden showed that he and his Egyptian associates are cut from the same cloth. Just as Zawahiri and Atif consider the current regime of Hosni Mubarak in Egypt to be a nest of apostates, so bin Laden considers the Saudi monarchy (its Wahhabi doctrines notwithstanding) to have renounced Islam. According to bin Laden, his king has adopted "polytheism," which bin Laden defines as the acceptance of "laws fabricated by men . . . permitting that which God has forbidden." It is the height of human arrogance and irreligion to "share with God in His sole right of sovereignty and making the law."

Extremist *Salafis*, therefore, regard modern Western civilization as a font of evil, spreading idolatry around the globe in the form of secularism. Since the United States is the strongest Western nation, the main purveyor of pop culture, and the power most involved in the political and economic affairs of the Islamic world, it receives particularly harsh criticism. Only the apostate Middle Eastern regimes themselves fall under harsher condemnation.

It is worth remembering, in this regard, that the rise of Islam represents a miraculous case of the triumph of human will. With little more than their beliefs to gird them, the Prophet Muhammad and a small number of devoted followers started a movement that brought the most powerful empires of their day crashing to the ground. On September 11, the attackers undoubtedly imagined themselves to be retracing the Prophet's steps. As they boarded the planes with the intention of destroying the Pentagon and the World Trade Center, they recited battle prayers that contained the line "All of their equipment, and gates, and technology will not prevent [you from achieving your aim], nor harm [you] except by God's will." The hijackers' imaginations certainly needed nothing more than this sparse line to remind them that, as they attacked America, they rode right behind Muhammad, who in his day had unleashed forces that, shortly after his death, destroyed the Persian Empire and crippled Byzantium—the two superpowers of the age.

AMERICA, LAND OF THE CRUSADERS

When thinking about the world today and their place in it, the extremist *Salafis* do not reflect only on the story of the foundation of Islam. They also scour more than a millennium of Islamic history in search of parallels to the present predicament. In his "Declaration of War," for instance, bin Laden states that the stationing of American forces on the soil of the Arabian peninsula constitutes the greatest aggression committed against the Muslims since the death of the Prophet Muhammad in AD 632.

To put this claim in perspective, it is worth remembering that in the last 1,300 years Muslims have suffered a number significant defeats, including but not limited to the destruction of the Abbasid caliphate by the Mongols, an episode of which bin Laden is well aware. In 1258 the ruthless Mongol leader Hulegu sacked Baghdad, killed the caliph, and massacred hundreds of thousands of inhabitants, stacking their skulls, as legend has it, in a pyramid outside the city walls. Whatever one thinks about U.S. policy toward Iraq, few in America would argue that the use of Saudi bases to enforce the sanctions against Saddam Hussein's regime constitutes a world-historical event on a par with the Mongol invasion of the Middle East. Before September 11, one might have been tempted to pass off as nationalist hyperbole bin Laden's assumption that U.S. policy represents the pinnacle of human evil. Now we know he is deadly serious.

The magnitude of the attacks on New York and Washington make it clear that Al Qaeda does indeed believe itself to be fighting a war to save the *umma* from Satan, represented by secular Western culture. Extreme though they may be, these views extend far beyond Al Qaeda's immediate followers in Afghanistan. Even a quick glance at the Islamist press in Arabic demonstrates that many Muslims who do not belong to bin Laden's terrorist network consider the United States to be on a moral par with Genghis Khan. Take, for instance, Dr. Muhammad Abbas, an Egyptian Islamist who wrote the following in the newspaper *Al Shaab* on September 21:

> Look! There is the master of democracy whom they have so often sanctified but who causes criminal, barbaric, bloody oppression that abandons the moral standards of even the most savage empires in history. In my last column I listed for readers the five million killed (may God receive them as martyrs) because of the crimes committed by this American civilization that America leads. These five million were killed in the last few decades alone.

Similar feelings led another *Al Shaab* columnist that day, Khalid
al-Sharif, to describe the shock and delight that he felt while
watching the World Trade Center crumbling:

> Look at that! America, master of the world, is crashing down.
> Look at that! The Satan who rules the world, east and west, is
> burning. Look at that! The sponsor of terrorism is itself seared
> by its fire.

The fanatics of Al Qaeda see the world in black and white and
advance a particularly narrow view of Islam. This makes them a
tiny minority among Muslims. But the basic categories of their
thought flow directly from the mainstream of the *Salafiyya*, a perspective that has enjoyed a wide hearing over the last 50 years.
Familiarity thus ensures bin Laden's ideas a sympathetic reception
in many quarters.

In *Salafi* writings, the United States emerges as the senior member of a "Zionist-Crusader alliance" dedicated to subjugating
Muslims, killing them, and, most important, destroying Islam. A
careful reading reveals that this alliance represents more than just
close relations between the United States and Israel today. The international cooperation between Washington and Jerusalem is
but one nefarious manifestation of a greater evil of almost cosmic
proportions. Thus in his "Declaration of War" bin Laden lists
nearly a dozen world hot spots where Muslims have recently died
(including Bosnia, Chechnya, and Lebanon) and attributes all of
these deaths to a conspiracy led by the United States, even though
Americans actually played no role in pulling the trigger. And thus,
in another document, "Jihad Against Jews and Crusaders," bin
Laden describes U.S. policies toward the Middle East as "a clear
declaration of war on God, his messenger, and Muslims."

As strange as it may sound to an American audience, the idea
that the United States has taken an oath of enmity toward God
has deep roots in the *Salafi* tradition. It has been around for more
than 50 years and has reached a wide public through the works
of, among others, Sayyid Qutb, the most important *Salafi* thinker
of the last half-century and a popular author in the Muslim world

even today, nearly 40 years after his death. A sample passage taken from his writings in the early 1950s illustrates the point. Addressing the reasons why the Western powers had failed to support Muslims against their enemies in Pakistan, Palestine, and elsewhere, Qutb canvassed a number of common explanations such as Jewish financial influence and British imperial trickery but concluded,

> All of these opinions overlook one vital element in the question . . . the crusader spirit that runs in the blood of all Occidentals. It is this that colors all their thinking, which is responsible for their imperialistic fear of the spirit of Islam and for their efforts to crush the strength of Islam. For the instincts and the interests of all Occidentals are bound up together in the crushing of that strength. This is the common factor that links together communist Russia and capitalist America. We do not forget the role of international Zionism in plotting against Islam and in pooling the forces of the crusader imperialists and communist materialists alike. This is nothing other than a continuation of the role played by the Jews since the migration of the Prophet to Medina and the rise of the Islamic state.

Sayyid Qutb, Osama bin Laden, and the entire extremist *Salafiyya* see Western civilization, in all periods and in all guises, as innately hostile to Muslims and to Islam itself. The West and Islam are locked in a prolonged conflict. Islam will eventually triumph, of course, but only after enduring great hardship. Contemporary history, defined as it is by Western domination, constitutes the darkest era in the entire history of Islam.

AMERICA AND THE MONGOL THREAT

When attempting to come to grips with the nature of the threat the modern West poses, extremist *Salafis* fall back on the writings of ibn Taymiyya for guidance. A towering figure in the history of Islamic thought, he was born in Damascus in the thirteenth century, when Syria stood under the threat of invasion from the Mongols. Modern radicals find him attractive because he too faced the threat of a rival civilization. Ibn Taymiyya the firebrand exhorted his fellow Muslims to fight the Mongol foe, while ibn Taymiyya the intellectual guided his community through the problems Muslims face when their social order falls under the shadow of non-Muslim power. It is only natural that bin Laden himself looks to such a master in order to legitimate his policies. Using ibn Taymiyya to target America, however, marks an interesting turning point in the history of the radical *Salafiyya*.

Bin Laden's "Declaration of War" uses the logic of ibn Taymiyya to convince others in the *Salafiyya* to abandon old tactics for new ones. The first reference to him arises in connection with a discussion of the "Zionist-Crusader alliance," which according to bin Laden has been jailing and killing radical preachers—men such as Sheikh Omar Abdel Rahman, in prison for plotting a series of bombings in New York following the 1993 bombing of the World Trade Center. Bin Laden argues that the "iniquitous crusader movement under the leadership of the U.S.A." fears these preachers because they will successfully rally the Islamic community against the West, just as ibn Taymiyya did against the Mongols in his day. Having identified the United States as a threat to Islam equivalent to the Mongols, bin Laden then discusses what to do about it. Ibn Taymiyya provides the answer: "To fight in the defense of religion and belief is a collective duty; there is no other duty after belief than fighting the enemy who is corrupting the life and the religion." The next most important thing after accepting the word of God, in other words, is fighting for it.

By calling on the *umma* to fight the Americans as if they were the Mongols, bin Laden and his Egyptian lieutenants have taken the extremist *Salafiyya* down a radically new path. Militants have long identified the West as a pernicious evil on a par with the Mongols, but they have traditionally targeted the internal enemy, the Hypocrites and apostates, rather than Hubal itself. Aware that he is shifting the focus considerably, bin Laden quotes ibn Taymiyya at length to establish the basic point that "people of

Islam should join forces and support each other to get rid of the main infidel," even if that means that the true believers will be forced to fight alongside Muslims of dubious piety. In the grand scheme of things, he argues, God often uses the base motives of impious Muslims as a means of advancing the cause of religion. In effect, bin Laden calls upon his fellow Islamist radicals to postpone the Islamic revolution, to stop fighting Hypocrites and apostates: "An internal war is a great mistake, no matter what reasons there are for it," because discord among Muslims will only serve the United States and its goal of destroying Islam.

The shift of focus from the domestic enemy to the foreign power is all the more striking given the merger of Al Qaeda and Egyptian Islamic Jihad. The latter's decision to kill Sadat in 1981 arose directly from the principle that the cause of Islam would be served by targeting lax Muslim leaders rather than by fighting foreigners, and here, too, ibn Taymiyya provided the key doctrine. In his day Muslims often found themselves living under Mongol rulers who had absorbed Islam in one form or another. Ibn Taymiyya argued that such rulers—who outwardly pretended to be Muslims but who secretly followed non-Islamic, Mongol practices—must be considered infidels. Moreover, he claimed, by having accepted Islam but having also failed to observe key precepts of the religion, they had in effect committed apostasy and thereby written their own death sentences. In general, Islam prohibits fighting fellow Muslims and strongly restricts the right to rebel against the ruler; Ibn Taymiyya's doctrines, therefore, were crucial in the development of a modern Sunni Islamic revolutionary theory.

Egyptian Islamic Jihad views leaders such as Sadat as apostates. Although they may outwardly display signs of piety, they do not actually have Islam in their hearts, as their failure to enforce the *shari'a* proves. This non-Islamic behavior demonstrates that such leaders actually serve the secular West, precisely as an earlier generation of outwardly Muslim rulers had served the Mongols, and as the Hypocrites had served idolatry. Islamic Jihad explained itself back in the mid–1980s in a long, lucid statement titled "The Neglected Duty." Not a political manifesto like bin Laden's tracts,

it is a sustained and learned argument that targets the serious be-
liever rather than the angry, malleable crowd. Unlike bin Laden's
holy war, moreover, Islamic Jihad's doctrine, though violent, fits
clearly in the mainstream of *Salafi* consciousness, which historically has been concerned much more with the state of the Muslims themselves than with relations between Islam and the outside
world. The decision to target America, therefore, raises the question of whether, during the 1990s, Egyptian Islamic Jihad
changed its ideology entirely. Did its leaders decide that the foreign enemy was in fact the real enemy? Or was the attack on New
York and Washington tactical rather than strategic?

The answer would seem to be the latter. Bin Laden's "Declaration of War" itself testifies to the tactical nature of his campaign
against America. Unlike "The Neglected Duty," which presents a
focused argument, the "Declaration of War" meanders from
topic to topic, contradicting itself along the way. On the one
hand, it calls for unity in the face of external aggression and demands an end to internecine warfare; on the other, it calls in
essence for revolution in Saudi Arabia. By presenting a litany of
claims against the Saudi ruling family and by discussing the politics of Saudi Arabia at length and in minute detail, bin Laden
protests too much: he reveals that he has not, in fact, set aside the
internal war among the believers. Moreover, he also reveals that
the ideological basis for that internal war has not changed. The
members of the Saudi elite, like Sadat, have committed apostasy.
Like the Hypocrites of Medina, they serve the forces of irreligion
in order to harm the devotees of the Prophet and his message:

> You know more than anybody else about the size, intention,
> and the danger of the presence of the U.S. military bases in the
> area. The [Saudi] regime betrayed the *umma* and joined the in-
> fidels, assisting them . . . against the Muslims. It is well known
> that this is one of the ten "voiders" of Islam, deeds of de-Is-
> lamization. By opening the Arabian Peninsula to the crusaders,
> the regime disobeyed and acted against what has been enjoined
> by the messenger of God.

Osama bin Laden undoubtedly believes that Americans are

Crusader-Zionists, that they threaten his people even more than did the Mongols—in short, that they are the enemies of God Himself. But he also sees them as obstacles to his plans for his native land. The "Declaration of War" provides yet more testimony to the old saw that ultimately all politics is local.

THE FAILURE OF POLITICAL ISLAM

If the attacks on the United States represent a change in radical *Salafi* tactics, then one must wonder what prompted bin Laden and Zawahiri to make it. The answer is that the attacks are a response to the failure of extremist movements in the Muslim world in recent years, which have generally proved incapable of taking power (Sudan and Afghanistan being the major exceptions). In the last two decades, several violent groups have challenged regimes such as those in Egypt, Syria, and Algeria, but in every case the government has managed to crush, co-opt, or marginalize the radicals. In the words of the "Declaration of War,"

> the Zionist-Crusader alliance moves quickly to contain and abort any "corrective movement" appearing in Islamic countries. Different means and methods are used to achieve their target. Sometimes officials from the Ministry of the Interior, who are also graduates of the colleges of the *shari'a*, are [unleashed] to mislead and confuse the nation and the *umma* . . . and to circulate false information about the movement, wasting the energy of the nation in discussing minor issues and ignoring the main one that is the unification of people under the divine law of Allah.

Given that in Egypt, Algeria, and elsewhere regimes have resorted to extreme violence to protect themselves, it is striking that bin Laden emphasizes here not the brutality but rather the counterpropaganda designed to divide and rule. Consciously or not, he has put his finger on a serious problem for the extremist *Salafi*s: the limitations of their political and economic theories.

Apart from insisting on the implementation of the *shari'a*, demanding social justice, and turning the *umma* into the only legitimate political community, radical *Salafis* have precious little to offer in response to the mundane problems that people and governments face in the modern world. Extremist Islam is profoundly effective in mounting a protest movement: it can produce a cadre of activists whose devotion to the cause knows no bounds, it can galvanize people to fight against oppression. But it has serious difficulties when it comes to producing institutions and programs that can command the attention of diverse groups in society over the long haul. Its success relies mainly on the support of true believers, but they tend to fragment in disputes over doctrine, leadership, and agenda.

The limitations of extremist *Salafi* political theory and its divisive tendencies come to light clearly if one compares the goals of Al Qaeda with those of the Palestinian terrorist group Hamas, whose suicide bombers have also been in the headlines recently. The ideology of Hamas also evolved out of the Egyptian extremist *Salafiyya* milieu, and it shares with Al Qaeda a paranoid view of the world: the *umma* and true Islam are threatened with extinction by the spread of Western secularism, the policies of the crusading West, and the oppression of the Zionists. Both Hamas and Al Qaeda believe that the faithful must obliterate Israel. But looking more closely at Hamas and its agenda, one can see that it parts company with Al Qaeda in many significant ways. This is because Hamas operates in the midst of nationalistic Palestinians, a majority of whom fervently desire, among other things, an end to the Israeli occupation of the territories it gained in 1967 and the establishment of a Palestinian state in part of historic Palestine.

The nationalist outlook of Hamas's public presents the organization with a number of thorny problems. Nationalism, according to the extremist *Salafiyya*, constitutes *shirk*—that is, polytheism or idolatry. If politics and religion are not distinct categories, as extremist *Salafis* argue, then political life must be centered around God and His law. Sovereignty belongs not to the nation but to God alone, and the only legitimate political community is the *umma*. Pride in one's ethnic group is tolerable only so long as it does not divide the community of believers, who form an indivisible unit thanks to the sovereignty of the *shari'a*. One day, extremist *Salafis* believe, political boundaries will be erased and all Muslims will live in one polity devoted to God's will. At the moment, however, the priority is not to erase boundaries but to raise up the *shari'a* and abolish secular law. Nationalism is idolatry because it divides the *umma* and replaces a *shari'a*-centered consciousness with ethnic pride.

If Hamas were actually to denounce secular Palestinian nationalists as apostates, however, it would immediately consign itself to political irrelevance. To skirt this problem, the organization has developed an elaborate view of Islamic history that in effect elevates the Palestinian national struggle to a position of paramount importance for the *umma* as a whole. This allows Hamas activists to function in the day-to-day political world as fellow travelers with the nationalists. Thus one of the fascinating aspects of Palestinian extremist *Salafiyya* is a dog that hasn't barked: in contrast to its sibling movements in neighboring countries, Hamas has refrained from labeling the secular leaders in the Palestinian Authority as apostates. Even at the height of Yasir Arafat's crackdown against Hamas two years ago, the movement never openly branded him as an idolater.

Like Al Qaeda, Hamas argues that a conspiracy between Zionism and the West has dedicated itself to destroying Islam, but for obvious reasons it magnifies the role of Zionism in the alliance. The Hamas Covenant, for example, sees Zionism as, among other things, a force determining many of the greatest historical developments of the modern period:

> [Zionists] were behind the French Revolution, the communist revolution. . . . They were behind World War I, when they were able to destroy the Islamic caliphate [i.e., the Ottoman Empire]. . . . They obtained the Balfour Declaration [favoring establishment of a Jewish homeland in Palestine], [and] formed the League of Nations, through which they could rule the world. They were behind World War II, through which they made huge financial gains by trading in armaments, and paved the

way for the establishment of their state. It was they who insti-
gated the replacement of the League of Nations with the United
Nations and the Security Council. . . . There is no war going on
anywhere, without [them] having their finger in it.

Do a number of intelligent and educated people actually believe
this? Yes, because they must; their self-understanding hinges on it.
Since their political struggle must be for the greater good of the
umma and of Islam as a whole, their enemy must be much more
than just one part of the Jewish people with designs on one sliver
of Muslim territory. The enemy must be the embodiment of an
evil that transcends time and place.

Although the sanctity of Jerusalem works in Hamas's favor, in
Islam Jerusalem does not enjoy the status of Mecca and Medina
and is only a city, not an entire country. To reconcile its political
and religious concerns, therefore, Hamas must inflate the significance of Palestine in Islamic history: "The present Zionist onslaught," the covenant says, "has also been preceded by crusading
raids from the West and other Tatar [Mongol] raids from the
East." The references here are to Saladin, the Muslim leader who
defeated the crusaders in Palestine at the battle of Hattin in 1187,
and to the Muslim armies that defeated the Mongols at another
Palestinian site called Ayn Jalut in 1260. On this basis Hamas argues that Palestine has always been the bulwark against the enemies of Islam; the *umma*, therefore, must rally behind the
Palestinians to destroy Israel, which represents the third massive
onslaught against the true religion since the death of the Prophet.

Despite the similarities in their perspectives, therefore, Al
Qaeda and Hamas have quite different agendas. Al Qaeda justi-
fies its political goals on the basis of the holiness of Mecca and
Medina and on the claim that the presence of U.S. forces in Arabia constitutes the greatest aggression that the Muslims have ever
endured. Hamas sees its own struggle against Israel as the first
duty of the *umma*. The two organizations undoubtedly share
enough in common to facilitate political cooperation on many issues, but at some point their agendas diverge radically, a diver-
gence that stems from the different priorities inherent in their
respective Saudi and Palestinian backgrounds.

The differences between Al Qaeda and Hamas demonstrate how local conditions can mold the universal components of *Salafi* consciousness into distinct worldviews. They display the creativity of radical Islamists in addressing a practical problem similar to that faced by communists in the early twentieth century: how to build a universal political movement that can nevertheless function effectively at the local level. This explains why, when one looks at the political map of the extremist *Salafiyya*, one finds a large number of organizations all of which insist that they stand for the same principles. They do, in fact, all insist on the implementation of the *shari'a*, but the specific social and political forces fueling that insistence differ greatly from place to place. They all march to the beat of God's drummer, but the marchers tend to wander off in different directions.

The new tactic of targeting America is designed to overcome precisely this weakness of political Islam. Bin Laden succeeded in attacking Hubal, the universal enemy: he identified the only target that all of the *Salafiyya* submovements around the world can claim equally as their own, thereby reflecting and reinforcing the collective belief that the *umma* actually is the political community. He and his colleagues adopted this strategy not from choice but from desperation, a desperation born of the fact that in recent years the extremist *Salafis* had been defeated politically almost everywhere in the Arab and Muslim world. The new tactic, by tapping into the deepest emotions of the political community, smacks of brilliance, and—much to America's chagrin—will undoubtedly give political Islam a renewed burst of energy.

EXPLAINING THE ECHO

The decision to target the United States allows Al Qaeda to play the role of a radical "*Salafi* International." It resonates beyond the small community of committed extremists, however, reaching not just moderate *Salafis* but, in addition, a broad range of disaffected citizens experiencing poverty, oppression, and powerlessness across the Muslim world. This broader resonance of what appears to Americans as such a wild and hateful message is the dimension of the problem that many find most difficult to understand.

One reason for the welcoming echo is the extent to which *Salafi* political movements, while failing to capture state power, have nevertheless succeeded in capturing much cultural ground in Muslim countries. Many authoritarian regimes (such as Mubarak's Egypt) have cut a deal with the extremists: in return for an end to assassinations, the regime acquiesces in some of the demands regarding implementation of the *shari'a*. In addition, it permits the extremist groups to run networks of social welfare organizations that often deliver services more efficiently than does a state sector riddled with corruption and marred by decay. This powerful cultural presence of the *Salafi*s across the Islamic world means not only that their direct ranks have grown but also that their symbolism is more familiar than ever among a wider public.

But the attack on America also resonates deeply among secular groups in many countries. The immediate response in the secular Arab press, for example, fell broadly into three categories. A minority denounced the attacks forcefully and unconditionally, another minority attributed them to the Israelis or to American extremists like Timothy McVeigh, and a significant majority responded with a version of "Yes, but"—yes, the terrorist attacks against you were wrong, but you must understand that your own policies in the Middle East have for years sown the seeds of this kind of violence.

This rationalization amounts to a political protest against the perceived role of the United States in the Middle East. Arab and Islamic commentators, and a number of prominent analysts of the Middle East in this country, point in particular to U.S. enforcement of the sanctions on Iraq and U.S. support for Israel in its struggle against Palestinian nationalism. Both of these issues certainly cause outrage, and if the United States were to effect the removal of Israeli settlements from the West Bank and alleviate the suffering of the Iraqi people, some of that outrage would certainly subside. But although a change in those policies would dampen some of bin Laden's appeal, it would not solve the problem of the broader anger and despair that he taps, because the sources of those feelings lie beyond the realm of day-to-day diplomacy.

Indeed, secular political discourse in the Islamic world in general and the Arab world in particular bears a striking resemblance to the *Salafi* interpretation of international affairs, especially insofar as both speak in terms of Western conspiracies. The secular press does not make reference to crusaders and Mongols but rather to a string of "broken promises" dating back to World War I, when the European powers divided up the Ottoman Empire to suit their own interests. They planted Israel in the midst of the Middle East, so the analysis goes, in order to drive a wedge between Arab states, and the United States continues to support Israel for the same purpose. Bin Laden played to this sentiment in his October 7 statement when he said,

> What the United States tastes today is a very small thing compared to what we have tasted for tens of years. Our nation has been tasting this humiliation and contempt for more than eighty years. Its sons are being killed, its blood is being shed, its holy places are being attacked, and it is not being ruled according to what God has decreed.

For eighty years—that is, since the destruction of the Ottoman Empire—the Arabs and the Muslims have been humiliated. Although they do not share bin Laden's millenarian agenda, when secular commentators point to Palestine and Iraq today they do not see just two difficult political problems; they see what they consider the true intentions of the West unmasked.

Arab commentators often explain, for instance, that Saddam Hussein and Washington are actually allies. They ridicule the notion that the United States tried to depose the dictator. After all, it is said, the first Bush administration had the forces in place to remove the Baath Party and had called on the Iraqi populace to rise up against the tyrant. When the people actually rose, however, the Americans watched from the sidelines as the regime brutally suppressed them. Clearly, therefore, what the United States really wanted was to divide and rule the Arabs in order to secure easy access to Persian Gulf oil—a task that also involves propping up corrupt monarchies in Kuwait and Saudi Arabia. Keeping Saddam on a leash was the easiest way to ensure that Iran could not block the project.

Needless to say, this worldview is problematic. Since World War I, Arab societies have been deeply divided among themselves along ethnic, social, religious, and political lines. Regardless of what the dominant Arab discourse regarding broken promises has to say, most of these divisions were not created by the West. The European powers and the United States have sometimes worked to divide the Arabs, sometimes to unify them. Mostly they have pursued their own interests, as have all the other actors involved. Bin Laden is a participant in a profoundly serious civil war over Arab and Muslim identity in the modern world. The United States is also a participant in that war, because whether it realizes it or not, its policies affect the fortunes of the various belligerents. But Washington is not a primary actor, because it is an outsider in cultural affairs and has only a limited ability to define for believers the role of Islam in public life.

The war between extremist *Salafis* and the broader populations around them is only the tip of the iceberg. The fight over religion among Muslims is but one of a number of deep and enduring regional struggles that originally had nothing to do with the United States and even today involve it only indirectly. Nonetheless, U.S. policies can influence the balance of power among the protagonists in these struggles, sometimes to a considerable degree.

Until the Arab and Muslim worlds create political orders that do not disenfranchise huge segments of their own populations, the civil war will continue and will continue to touch the United States. The United States can play an important role in fostering authentic and inclusive polities, but ultimately, to live comfortably with outsiders, Arabs and Muslims more generally must learn to live in peace with one another. Whether they will do so is anybody's guess.

It is a stark political fact that in the Arab and Muslim worlds today economic globalization and the international balance of power both come with an American face, and neither gives much reason for optimism. Osama bin Laden's rhetoric dividing the world into two camps—the *umma* versus the United States and puppet regimes—has a deep resonance because on some levels it conforms, if not to reality, then at least to its appearances. This is why, for the first time in modern history, the extremist *Salafis* have managed to mobilize mass popular opinion.

This development is troubling, but the United States still has some cards to play. Its policies, for instance, on both West Bank settlements and Iraq are sorely in need of review—but only after bin Laden has been vanquished. These policy changes might help, but the root problem lies at a deeper level. Once Al Qaeda has been annihilated without sparking anti-American revolutions in the Islamic world, the United States should adopt a set of policies that ensure that significant numbers of Muslims—not Muslim regimes but Muslims—identify their own interests with those of the United States, so that demagogues like bin Laden cannot aspire to speak in the name of the entire *umma*. In 1991, millions of Iraqis constituted just such a reservoir of potential supporters, yet America turned its back on them. Washington had its reasons, but they were not the kind that can be justified in terms of the American values that we trumpet to the world. Today we are paying a price for that hypocrisy. This is not to say that we caused or deserved the attacks of September 11 in any way. It is to say, however, that we are to some extent responsible for the fact that so few in the Arab and Muslim worlds express vocal and unequivocal support for our cause, even when that cause is often their cause as well.

Since the events of September 11, innumerable articles have appeared in the press discussing America's loss of innocence. To foreigners, this view of Americans as naive bumpkins, a band of Forrest Gumps who just arrived in town, is difficult to fathom. Whether the MTV generation knows it or not, the United States has been deeply involved in other peoples' civil wars for a long time. A generation ago, for example, we supposedly lost our innocence in Vietnam. Back then, Adonis, the poet laureate of the Arab world, meditated on the ambivalence Arabs feel toward

America. In the aftermath of the September 11 attacks, his poem seems prophetic:

> New York, you will find in my land
> . . . the stone of Mecca and the waters of the Tigris.
> In spite of all this,
> you pant in Palestine and Hanoi.
> East and west you contend with people
> whose only history is fire.

These tormented people knew us before we were virgins.

WAS IT INEVITABLE?

ISLAM THROUGH HISTORY

■

KAREN ARMSTRONG

For many people in the Western world, the horrific events of September 11 simply confirmed a view of Islam that they had long held. The notion that Islam is an essentially violent and fanatical faith has become one of the tenets of the West, and this notion has been around for a long time. During the Crusades, scholarly monks in western Europe began to develop a hostile portrait of the religion of their Muslim enemies. With very little hard information, an extremely slender knowledge of the Koran, and a great deal of prejudice, they argued that the Prophet Muhammad had imposed his religion on an unwilling world by force of arms and that Islam was a religion dedicated to the concept of the holy war, or *jihad*. Islam was, therefore, the enemy of decent civilization. Muslims could not live at peace with people who adhered to another faith, since Islam was committed to the ideal of world conquest. This is still the popular view of Islam in some sectors of the news media, even though it bears little relation to the truth.

During the Crusades, the Western world was reinventing itself and finding its soul. When Pope Urban II summoned the expedition that would become known as the First Crusade in 1095, western Europe was beginning to recover from the long trauma of the Dark Ages, which had plunged its people into a period of barbarism after the collapse of the Roman Empire. The First Crusade was the first cooperative act of the new Europe in its struggle back onto the international stage. The Western world had to define itself anew, and it was helpful to have an enemy who could be portrayed as its opposite. Muslims and Jews, the two victims of the Crusaders, fit the bill, and the Islamophobia of Europe developed alongside its chronic anti-Semitism.

In both cases, the Europeans' distorted vision of Judaism and Islam seemed to reflect a buried worry about their own beliefs and behavior. Thus it was significant that the idea of the inherent violence and intolerance of Islam took root at a time when it was Christians who were fighting their own brutal holy wars against Muslims in the Middle East, committing atrocities that clearly violated the pacific message of Jesus. In the same way, at a time when the popes were trying to impose celibacy on the reluctant clergy, clerics described the Prophet Muhammad (with barely concealed envy) as a lecher and sexual pervert. At a time when feudal Europe was profoundly hierarchical, medieval scholars blamed Islam for giving too much power to menials and to women. It seemed that "Islam" was becoming the shadow self of Europe, an image of everything that Europeans believed they were not and everything that they feared they were.

The Christians of Europe were also puzzled about where Islam had come from. During the Middle Ages, there was a widespread belief that Muhammad was a charlatan, someone who had simply pretended to be inspired by God and had deceived the credulous Arabs. Some said that he had been influenced by a Christian heretic, who had imparted to him a bowdlerized version of the Christian religion. Europeans knew that Muslims venerated some of their own biblical heroes, such as Abraham, Moses, Noah, Solomon, and David. Muslims greatly revered Jesus and believed in his virgin birth, even though they did not think that he had been the Son of God. Everything seemed skewed. Where had Muhammad gotten these ideas? The medieval West could view Islam only as a distorted version of Christianity, and because Muhammad had received his revelations from God some six centuries after Jesus (the Last Word of God to humanity), he was undoubtedly guilty of blasphemy. There could be no further revelation, so the very existence of Islam was an outrage. Christians could only assume that in setting himself up as a prophet, Muhammad must have been determined to wipe out the true faith and replace it with his own, especially since—unlike the pacific Jesus—Muhammad had been a warrior. He must have imposed his faith by means of the sword.

Later, when European explorers were beginning to navigate the globe, nearly everywhere they went they found Islam: there were Muslims in the Middle East, in Africa, in India, in Southeast Asia, and even in China. "Islamdom" was collectively the greatest world power, and Europeans tended to resent it, in rather the same way as people in the developing world resent the United States today. In the sixteenth century, for example, when Europeans were beginning their scientific revolution and were developing a new kind of unified nation-state, the Ottoman Empire was probably the most up-to-date state in the world. It was difficult for Western people to consider Islam objectively and impartially, and the old Crusaders' notions about Muhammad and his religion persisted. People continued to take it for granted that Islam was a religion of *jihad*, that it was essentially incapable of respecting other faiths, and that it was the enemy of Western values. Even though Westerners are often impressed by such religions as Buddhism, they still tend to assume that there is something rather bogus about Islam. Today it is said that Islam is incapable of the tolerance, pluralism, and democracy that must characterize a modern society: it cannot separate "church" from "state"; it is misogynistic, incapable of change, and backward-looking. Muslims, it is imagined, are incapable of appreciating the West's free, democratic societies.

The reality of Islam, however, has always been very different from the Western stereotype. It is not an alien faith profoundly at odds with the Judeo-Christian tradition. It is certainly not addicted to violence and warfare. Nor is it fanatically opposed to all other religions.

THE EMBRACE OF ISLAM

When the Prophet Muhammad began to preach in Mecca in about AD 612, he did not believe that he was founding a new world religion to which all must submit in order to be saved. At the time, the Arabian Peninsula was in crisis. Mecca had developed a new market economy, and though this had made the Meccans rich beyond their wildest dreams, the new spirit of aggressive capitalism was incompatible with the old communal and egalitarian norms of the tribal system. Similarly, those tribes in Arabia who were still living the traditional, nomadic life were locked in a destructive cycle of war, in which vendetta was succeeded by countervendetta. Spiritual malaise and confusion reigned in Arabia. The Arabs were beginning to find that their old, pagan traditions, which had served them well for centuries, no longer spoke adequately to the changing conditions of their country. They knew about Christianity and Judaism, and were aware that these faiths were more advanced than their own. But the Jews and Christians whom they encountered would often pour scorn on the Arabs, pointing out that God had left them out of his divine plan, had sent them no prophet and no Arabic scripture. Some of the Arabs had become convinced that Allah (whose name simply means "The God"), the high god of Arabian pantheism, was the same as the deity worshipped by Jews and Christians. But there was a widespread feeling of inferiority and exclusion from this monotheistic faith.

That changed forever when Muhammad began to receive the revelations that would become the Koran, the inspired scripture that he brought to the Arabs. He was convinced that he was simply bringing the old religion of the Jews and the Christians to the Arabs, who had never been sent a prophet before. The Koran constantly insists that Muhammad had not come to cancel out the revelations delivered by Abraham, Moses, or Jesus. Muslims are commanded to speak with great courtesy to "the People of the Book": "Say to them: we believe what you believe—your God and our God is One." The message of the Koran is essentially pluralistic: God has sent prophets to every people on the face of the earth. His message is always the same. Men and women must make an act of existential surrender (*islam*) of their whole being to God. They must also share their wealth fairly and create a just and decent society where poor and vulnerable people are treated with respect. If they do this, their societies will prosper, because they will be conforming to the fundamental laws that govern human life. All rightly guided religion that conforms to this essential principle comes from God, although each people will express this divine teaching in its own language and its own cultural idiom. Muslim tradition says that God has sent 144,000 prophets to humanity—a symbolic number, suggesting infinity. The Koran endorses the teachings of the prophets of the Judeo-Christian tradition, because the Arabs were familiar with them. But today Muslim scholars argue that had Muhammad known about the Buddhists and the Hindus, the Native Americans and the Australian Aborigines, the Koran would have praised their religious sages, too. Thus Muhammad did not expect Christians and Jews to convert to Islam unless they particularly wished to do so. There was no need, because they had received perfectly valid revelations of their own.

The plural and tolerant vision of the Koran is beautifully expressed in the famous story of Muhammad's *miraj*, his mystical journey to Jerusalem and his ascent to heaven. This tale has become the archetype of Muslim spirituality, because it epitomizes the ascent that all Muslims must make to God—an ascent that is at the same time a return to the Source of Being. It was not intended to be taken literally: the early sources make it clear that this was a mystical event in the Prophet's life, which, like all discourse about God, could only be symbolic. We are told that one night Muhammad was miraculously conveyed by the Angel Gabriel, the Spirit of Revelation, from Mecca to the Temple Mount in Jerusalem. There he was greeted by all the great prophets of the past, who welcomed him into their midst, and Muhammad preached to them there. Then he and Gabriel began to ascend through the seven heavens to the Divine Throne, a journey that is remarkably similar to that experienced by the Jewish Throne Mystics. In each of the heavens, Muhammad met some of the major prophets: Moses, Aaron, Jesus, John the Baptist, Enoch, and Abraham. Moses even gave him advice on the number of times that Muslims should pray every day. This is a story of religious pluralism. It reflects the Prophet's yearning to bring the Arabs, who had seemed to be off the religious map, right into the heart of the monotheistic tradition. He is not shunned by the other prophets as a charlatan. They welcome him, listen to his insights, and he in turn takes advice from them. There is no competition, but rather a luminous acceptance and appreciation.

In passing, one might note that this spirit characterized Muslim behavior in Jerusalem, which plays such an important role in the story and which came under Muslim rule in AD 638, some six years after Muhammad's death. When the caliph Umar was being escorted around the holy city after the conquest, the Greek Orthodox patriarch took him to the Church of the Holy Sepulchre, built on the site where, it is believed, the body of Jesus was brought to be entombed after the Crucifixion. While he was there, the time for Muslim prayer came around, and the patriarch invited the caliph to pray beside the tomb of Jesus, but Umar refused and made the ritual prostrations in the street outside. He explained that had he prayed in the church, the Muslims would have wanted to build a mosque there to commemorate the first Islamic prayer made in the holy city. It was essential that the Christians keep their holy places, and Umar at once signed a decree to that effect. Until Jerusalem fell to the army of the First Crusade in 1099, the Christians remained in a majority under Muslim rule. They were never ejected from their holy places or from their homes on the Western Hill, in the healthiest and cooler part of town.

The Muslims used to call Jerusalem Bayt al-Maqdis, the City of the Temple, for the Koran mentions the great shrine built there by King Solomon. Not surprisingly, therefore, Umar was anxious to see the Temple, whose fame had reached the Arabs. But the Christians had left the Temple, which had been destroyed by the Romans in AD 70, in a ruined state, as a symbol of the defeat and degradation of Judaism. Jews had never been permitted to reside permanently in Christian Jerusalem. But the Muslims changed all this. When Umar was shown the ruined Temple, the site had been used for some years as the city garbage dump. He was horrified and immediately set to work to cleanse the great Temple platform, working alongside his men. When the holy place was purified, he built a simple wooden mosque there and invited the Jewish people back to the City of David. Seventy Jewish families migrated from the city of Tiberias to take up residence at the foot

of the Temple Mount, alongside the modest Muslim neighborhood. Today, many Jews feel that the mosques, oratories, and
shrines on the Temple Mount (which Muslims call the "Most
Holy Sanctuary" and revere as the third holiest site in the Muslim
world) are an abomination. But in the seventh century, Jews welcomed the Muslims into the holy city. At that time, Jews had no
ambition to rebuild their Temple: that was a task reserved for the
Messiah. Indeed, some Jews actually praised the Muslims as the
precursors of the Messiah, because they had purified this holy
place and paved the way for the coming of the Redeemer.

ONCE WERE WARRIORS?

So Muslim rule in Jerusalem conformed to the spirit of
Muhammad's *miraj*. But what were they doing there in the first
place? Does not the fact that they were not content to stay in their
own country but almost immediately began to occupy other lands
indicate an inherent thirst for *jihad* and world domination on religious grounds? This is what Westerners have believed for years,
but in fact the early Muslim conquests were not inspired by the
teachings of the Koran. After Muhammad's death in 632, the
Muslims of Arabia invaded the surrounding countries and a hundred years later they had a vast empire stretching from the Hi-
malayas to the Pyrenees. But although Muslims later put an
Islamic gloss on these wars of conquest, they had no religious significance. For centuries, the Arabs had supplemented the inadequate resources of Arabia by raiding the territories of their more
prosperous neighbors. But when in about 634 they began to in-
vade Syria, Iraq, Egypt, and Palestine, they encountered a political vacuum. The great empires of Persia and Byzantium had been
locked in a long, debilitating conflict with one another and were
exhausted. Much to their own astonishment, the Muslims defeated the Persian army in 637 and the Byzantine army in Syria,
Palestine, and Egypt by 641. They had had no dreams of world
conquest, yet found, rather to their surprise, that they were now
masters of a considerable empire. But they were not conquering

the world for Islam. None of the subject peoples were forced to convert to the Muslim faith, and indeed conversion was not encouraged at all until about 750. It was assumed that Islam was a religion for the Arabs, the sons of Ishmael, just as Judaism was a religion for the sons of Isaac and Jacob. Jews and Christians became *dhimmis*, the protected peoples of the empire. They had to acknowledge the political hegemony of the Muslim caliphs, but they were permitted full religious liberty and managed their own affairs.

So Muslims were not inspired by a passionate religious zeal to impose their faith at sword point. Nor was the *jihad* a pillar of their religion. The word "*jihad*" does not even primarily mean "holy war," as Westerners tend to define it. It means "struggle, effort." The Koran realizes that it is difficult to put the will of God into practice in a flawed, tragic world and demands a dedicated effort on all fronts: military, political, economic, intellectual, social, and ethical. Sometimes it may be necessary to fight in order to preserve decent values, but warfare is certainly not a major preoccupation. There is a very important and much quoted maxim attributed to Muhammad, which has him say to his companions while returning home after a battle, "We are returning from the lesser *Jihad* [the battle] to the greater *Jihad*," the far more significant, crucial, and demanding struggle to reform one's own society and to extirpate evil, greed, and malice from one's own heart.

The first Muslim community was fighting for its life. The powerful establishment of Mecca was determined to destroy Muhammad and his followers, and in pre-Islamic Arabia, that would almost certainly have meant that every Muslim man, woman, and child would have been exterminated. Because some parts of the Koran were revealed to the Prophet while the Muslims were fighting a desperate war, certain passages deal with the rules that should govern armed conflict. Basically, the Koran's view of warfare is very similar to the Western theory of the "just war." War is always "an awesome evil," but sometimes Muslims may have to fight to prevent persecution. They may never initiate hostilities, however, and aggressive warfare is always forbidden. The only permissible war, therefore, is a war of self-defense, but the moment the enemy sues for peace, hostilities must cease. Retaliation is permitted to avenge an attack, but it must be proportionate, and patience is the best option; it is better to refrain from any retaliation at all. This is the policy adopted by the Prophet himself. As soon as he realized that the tide had turned in his favor and that the Muslims were out of danger, he abandoned armed struggle, concentrated on building a peaceful coalition, and initiated an inspiring and courageous policy of nonviolence. In 630, Mecca opened its gates to him voluntarily, and he took the city without shedding a drop of blood and without forcing any of its inhabitants to convert from the old paganism to Islam.

Terrorists may quote some of the more ferocious passages of the Koran out of context, and, not surprisingly, Western people find these quotations extremely disturbing. They confirm the West's view of Islam as a violent religion. But the terrorists usually neglect the exhortations to peace and mercy that in almost every case immediately succeed the fierce passages. The whole tenor of the Koran is one of peace, not war. Above all, it says, "There must be no coercion in matters of religion." The Arabic here is extremely emphatic, and in general Muslims have been true to this principle. Until the twentieth century, Islam had a far better record of religious tolerance than did Western Christianity.

So Islam is clearly not an inherently violent religion and there is no reason to think that the mass slaughter of September 11 is an inevitable consequence of Muslim zeal. Muslims have never nurtured dreams of world conquest. They had no designs on Europe, for example, even though Europeans imagined that they did. Once Muslim rule had been established in Spain, it was recognized that the empire could not expand indefinitely. In fact, Muslims regarded the rest of Europe as a rather dismal, backward region. The weather was awful, there were no trade opportunities, and until the twelfth and thirteenth centuries the region showed very few signs of high civilization. Medieval Europeans tended to cower before the mighty Muslim giant, and when the army of Charles Martel managed to defeat a Muslim army at the Battle of Poitiers in 732, Europe breathed a collective sigh of

relief. But this Muslim expedition had been not a full-scale invasion, but only a minor raid (*ghazu*) into neighboring territory.
Muslim jurists may have divided the world into the *dar al-Islam*
(the abode of Islam) and the *dar al-Harb* (the abode of War), but
this was simply a legal way of expressing the difference that dis-
tinguishes "us" from "them"—as in "Jew" and "Gentile," or
"Greek" and "Barbarian."

So for the greater part of its history, Islam had no quarrel with
the West or with the Christian world. Nor are the ideals of Islam
incompatible with Western values. We have seen how similar are
the Western and Muslim notions of a just war. The Koran shares
the Judeo-Christian ideal of social justice and the vision of the
Koran is eminently fitted to guide Muslims in today's pluralistic
world. True, toward the end of the eighth century, Muslims
tended to imagine that Islam was the one true faith and that
Muhammad was the last and most important of the great
prophets, but this did not affect their treatment of religious minorities nor their relations with other faiths worldwide. The Sufi
mystics exhibited an outstanding appreciation of other religious
traditions. It was quite common for a mystic to cry in ecstasy that
he was neither a Jew, nor a Christian, nor a Muslim, or that he
was equally at home in a synagogue, a mosque, a temple, or a
church, because once one has glimpsed the reality of God, these
man-made distinctions were left far behind.

THE COMMUNAL IS POLITICAL

Muslim history has, of course, been scarred by war. There have
been Islamic rulers who have not lived up to the high ideals of the
Koran, and Muslims have often fought one another. But these
failures have been deeply troubling to Muslims. Politics is regarded as almost sacramental, to use a Christian term. The experience of creating and living in a just society would give devout
Muslims intimations of the divine, because they would be living
in accordance with God's will.

The political well-being of the Muslim community, the *umma*,
was therefore a matter of supreme importance, and if state insti-

tutions did not measure up to the Koranic ideal, if their political leaders were exploitative or immoral, or if their community was humiliated, Muslims could feel that their faith in life's ultimate purpose and value was imperiled. A Muslim would meditate on the current events of his time as a Christian might contemplate an icon, each using the creative imagination to discover the hidden divine presence there. Thus the discussions of the civil wars that scarred the first century of Muslim history were as decisive for Islam as were the great debates about the divinity of Jesus during the fourth and fifth centuries for Christianity. Muslims engaged in passionate discussions of political questions. Who was the rightful ruler of the *umma?* How could a society that killed its devout leaders claim to be guided by God? Should the caliph be the most pious Muslim or a direct descendent of the Prophet? Could rulers who lived in luxury and ignored the poverty of the vast majority of the population be true Muslims? It was from these debates that the religion and piety of Islam, as we know it today, began fully to emerge, as people asked what it really meant to follow the faith of the Koran. Muslims did not take the violence and injustice of their society for granted. They were filled with anguish by these lapses and used their distress to gain insight into the meaning of the Koranic revelation, and thus these political issues informed the spirituality, ethics, and intellectual life of the Muslim people.

If there came a time when Muslims saw the *umma* in a state of perpetual corruption or humiliated by foreign powers, some might take this as a devastating blow to the core of their faith. Muslims could feel as disturbed by the weakness or degradation of their *umma* as a Christian who saw somebody spitting on the Bible or desecrating the Eucharistic host. But this would not necessarily produce an atavistic, knee-jerk response. However overwhelming their distress, Muslims are always supposed to be constrained by the morality of the Koran and by Islamic law (the *shari'a*), which lays down precise rules concerning the declaration of war and the justification of force. Muslims may not take the initiative themselves in these grave matters, and Osama bin Laden has no legal authority to issue a *fatwa* summoning all Muslims to a holy war.

The importance attached to politics in Islam makes Westerners

uneasy, because they have separated church and state and take
their commitment to secularism very seriously. Does this mean
that Islam is inherently averse to the secular ideal? In theory, yes.
The mainspring of Muslim spirituality is the principle of *tawhid*,
or "making one": all things must be brought into the ambit of the
sacred, and society should reflect the unity of God. So putting religion and politics into separate spheres is not permissible. The demands of faith are all-encompassing; faith cannot be confined to
a limited sector of one's social or personal life.

But in practice, history shows that Muslims did effect a division between religion and politics. Running a large empire is
bound to be a messy and frequently bloody business; it is not easy
to live up to the high ideals of scripture when faced with the demands of realpolitik. This has been a universal experience, and
Muslims experienced this difficulty as acutely as did anybody else.
During the Abbasid caliphate (750–1258), whatever the grand
theory, there was a de facto separation of what would now be
called "church" and "state." The royal court had its own aristo-
cratic culture, known as the *adab,* and the elite did not live strictly
Islamic lives. The Abbasid caliphs, for example, had many more
wives than the mere four permitted by the Koran. The *shari'a* was
developed by the *ulama,* the religious scholars, largely as a coun-
tercultural protest against the inegalitarian and un-Islamic lifestyle
of the rulers. The people and the politicians led essentially different lives and were governed by different norms.

Periodically, at times of crisis, especially when the community
was threatened by an outside enemy, there were movements of
"reform" *(islah)* and "renewal" *(tajdid)* that were often quite revolutionary. These movements usually followed a similar pattern.
A reformer *(mujdadid)* would demand that Muslims use their
powers of independent reasoning *(ijtihad)* to find a new solution,
even if this contradicted the orthodoxy of the day. The emergency
demanded an entirely fresh solution and the old answers no
longer sufficed. The reformers tried to renew Islam by returning
to the pristine values of the Koran and the Prophet Muhammad;
as a result, they were often quite iconoclastic, throwing out all
later developments, especially those that had been influenced by

other religious traditions. These reform movements became a feature of Muslim life from the fourteenth century on, and many of the people we call "Muslim fundamentalists" today belong to this tradition of *islah* and *tajdid*.

The archetypal reformer was Ahmad ibn Taymiyya (1263–1328), a scholar of Damascus, which had suffered terribly during the Mongol invasions. Ibn Taymiyya declared that even though the Mongols had converted to Islam, they were in fact infidels and apostates, because they had promulgated their own law code instead of the *shari'a*. Muslims, therefore, owed them no allegiance. Today fundamentalists often quote this ruling when they declare independence of secularist rulers in Muslim countries. Like a true *mujdadid*, ibn Taymiyya condemned all Islamic developments since the time of the Prophet as inauthentic, including Shiism, Sufism, and Muslim philosophy. But he also had a positive program. He believed that Muslims must use *ijtihad* to bring the *shari'a* up to date in order to meet the new conditions in which Muslims found themselves under Mongol rule. Ibn Taymiyya was a worrying figure to the political establishment. He enraged the conservative *ulama*, who clung to the textbook answers, and he ended his life in jail. But the ordinary people of Damascus loved him, because they could see that his reforms had their interests at heart.

This type of reform, which tried to go back to the fundamentals, became known as the *Salafiyya*, because it looked back to *al-Salaf al-Salih*, "the venerable forefathers." It became very popular in the Arab world during the colonial period, when the *umma* was again threatened by a foreign foe. One of the most famous of these reform movements was Wahhabism, which developed in the Arabian Peninsula during the eighteenth century. At this time, the Ottoman Empire had begun its decline and was losing control in the peripheral provinces such as Arabia. To restore order, Muhammad ibn Abd al-Wahhab (1703–92) broke away from Istanbul and established an independent state in central Arabia and the Persian Gulf. He was a typical reformer in the tradition of ibn Taymiyya. He believed that the current crisis was best met by a strict return to the Koran and the practice of the Prophet and by a militant rejection of all later accretions, which included medieval jurisprudence, Sufi mysticism, and philosophy. Because the Ottoman sultans did not conform to his version of a purified Islam, Abd al-Wahhab declared that they were apostates and worthy of death. He tried to create an enclave of pure faith, based on his view of the first *umma* in the seventh century. Fundamentalists in the modern era, a period of even greater unrest and confusion for Muslims, sometimes resort to Abd al-Wahhab's aggressive techniques. Wahhabism is the form of Islam practiced today in Saudi Arabia; Osama bin Laden, therefore, grew up in a Wahhabi environment, even though he was more profoundly influenced by the twentieth century *mujdadid*, the Egyptian fundamentalist ideologue Sayyid Qutb, who was executed by President Gamal Abdel al-Nasser in 1966.

In Shi'a Islam, a minority form of Islam that is best described as pious protest against injustice and corruption in the mainstream Muslim community, religion and politics were separated as a matter of sacred principle. All government was regarded as illegitimate and corrupt, and Shi'a were instructed to withdraw from political life. Only when the Shi'a messiah, known as the "Hidden Imam," inaugurated a golden age of justice would it be permissible for a true Muslim to participate in government. When Ayatollah Ruhollah Khomeini of Iran decreed that a cleric should lead the *umma*, he was breaking with centuries of the most holy Shi'a tradition; this was as radical a step as would be the pope's abolition of the Mass. So even though in theory Muslims might find it difficult to separate church and state, in practice Muslims had found this to be every bit as necessary as the people of the West.

MODERN TIMES

It sometimes seems that such a profound gulf separates the Muslim world from the Western world today that the two will never truly understand one another. Some have spoken of a "clash of civilizations"; it is assumed that Muslims instinctively recoil from the modern, secular culture of the West and that their religion makes it impossible for them to understand Western values, ideals, and achievements. But this is not the case. It is important to realize that during the nineteenth century and at the beginning of the twentieth, almost every single leading Muslim intellectual was entranced by the West. They wanted their countries to become just like the United Kingdom and France. They seemed to "recognize" modern society and felt that it was an ideal that chimed perfectly with their own traditions and aspirations.

Thus we have the mid-nineteenth-century Egyptian writer Rifah al-Tahtawi, who served as an imam in the Egyptian army and had spent a year in Paris; when he returned home he published his diary. He had his reservations about the West, but he loved the efficiency of Paris, its clean streets, the careful education of French children, and the modern work ethic. He admired the rational spirit of French culture and noted approvingly that Parisians were "not prisoners of tradition but always love to know the origin of things and the proofs of them." He was impressed that even the common people could read and write and could discuss serious questions intelligently. He was also intrigued by the modern hunger for innovation, marveling that "everyone who is master of a craft wishes to invent something which was not known before or to complete something which has already been invented." He insisted that Muslim clerics acquaint themselves with these ways and bring their faith up to date. Modern science was no threat to Islam: scientists should enjoy the same status as the *ulama*. Education was key: the common people should be educated as they were in France, girls to the same standard as boys. Tahtawi seemed intoxicated by Western achievement: he wrote a poem in praise of the steam engine and saw the railway as an invention that would bring the peoples of the world closer together.

Similarly, the late-nineteenth-century Iranian intellectuals Mulkum Khan and Aqa Khan Kirmani urged their compatriots to acquire a Western education and replace the *shari'a* with a modern secular legal code, seeing this as the only route to progress. Secularist thinkers from their circles joined with the more liberal *ulama* in the Revolution of 1906, which forced the shah to inaugurate a constitution and a parliament. Most of the leading Iranian clerics supported this modern constitution. It would, argued Sheikh Muhammad Husain Naini, put some constraints on the tyranny of the ruler—and that was clearly a valid Muslim enterprise, since the Koran insisted on the paramount importance of social justice. Indeed, this Western style of constitutional government was the next best thing to the return of the Hidden Imam, who would inaugurate the perfect Muslim society. Many clerics and observers noted that the Europeans were in some ways better Muslims than the actual followers of the Prophet, because the new type of society that they had inaugurated was more fair and egalitarian than the traditional, imperfectly modernized Islamic countries.

Even after the Europeans had occupied Islamic countries and set up colonies there, some of this early enthusiasm persisted. Thus in Egypt, Muhammad Abdu, who in 1899 became the mufti (the leading interpreter of Islamic law), was greatly distressed by the British occupation of his country, but he had spent time in Paris, had studied Western science and philosophy, and felt quite at home with Westerners. He greatly respected the political, legal, and educational institutions of the modern West but did not believe that they could be transplanted wholesale into a deeply religious country such as Egypt, where the modernization process had been too rapid for the vast majority of the people to absorb. He feared that the country would be split into two camps: an elite who had received a Western education and understood the new ideas, and the rest, who did not. It was essential, he argued, to graft modern legal and constitutional innovations onto traditional Islamic ideas that the people could comprehend. Thus under Islamic law, the principle of *shurah* (consultation), which insisted that the people must be consulted in some way before a new piece of legislation was passed, was clearly quite compatible with democracy. So, too, was the principle of *ijmah* (consensus), which laid down that the consensus of the Muslim people as a whole gave validity to a Muslim law or practice. This precept would help the people to understand constitutional rule, whereby public opinion limited the power of the ruler. Abdu also wanted students to study science as well as Islamic law, so that future *ulama* could play a full role in modern society.

His younger contemporary, the journalist Rashid Rida, also believed that the *shari'a* must be reformed and brought into line with the new ideas of the West, but though he was convinced that this was possible, he realized that it would be a long, complex process. He wanted to see a fully modernized but also fully Islamic state and wanted to set up a special college at which students would study international law, sociology, world history, religion, and modern science alongside Islamic jurisprudence. In this way, it might be possible for future generations to wed the traditions of East and West.

The ideas of Rida and Abdu show that Muslims were beginning to move beyond their early uncritical enthusiasm for Europe and were starting to appreciate that modernization, according to the Western model, would not be easy. Muslims are not the only religious people to have had difficulty in adapting the traditions of their faith, which had evolved in the premodern world, to the radically altered conditions of modernity. None of us can be religious in the same way that our ancestors were. Christians have certainly found this to be true and are still engaged in a challenging and sometimes traumatic struggle to adapt the teachings of the Bible to the modern scientific and rational spirit. But neither Abdu nor Rida believed that Islamic norms were utterly incompatible with the new Western ethos. They admired Western society and wanted to find a way to reform their religious traditions to meet this new ideal.

So a hundred years ago, most Muslims had no quarrel with the West. They believed that Judaism and Christianity were valid revelations, and they revered Jesus and the Jewish prophets. In their empire, Jews and Christians were allowed full religious freedom; their society exhibited nothing comparable to the anti-Semitism of Christian Europe. In Muslim Jerusalem, Jews, Christians, and Muslims lived together in reasonable harmony—albeit not perfect—but with a coexistence that seems an impossible dream today. When Muslims began to appreciate the momentous fact that the West had developed a wholly new type of society, they were not horrified by these new institutions and ideals but were filled with admiration. During the last century something happened to this goodwill, and for many respect was transformed into hatred. Yet despite what many Muslims and non-Muslims alike may now believe, nothing in the history of Islam and its relations with the West made anything like the attacks of September 11 inevitable. The terrorists and their extremist cohorts hijacked not only several planes, but one of the world's great religions as well.

LEFT, RIGHT, AND BEYOND

THE CHANGING FACE OF TERROR

■

WALTER LAQUEUR

Over the centuries, terrorism has appeared in many guises. It is not an ideology or a political doctrine, but rather a method—the substate application of violence or the threat of violence to sow panic and bring about political change. Although it has rarely been absent from history, it has been more common in some ages and some civilizations than in others.

Those who try to understand terrorism in terms of the causes particular terrorists happen to support are bound to be baffled by the frequent and often extreme changes that have taken place in terrorists' political orientation over the years. Throughout the nineteenth and early twentieth centuries, terrorism came predominantly from the left, from anarchists and social revolutionaries, as well from nationalist separatists (as in Ireland). But during the interwar years, the main perpetrators of terrorism were on the extreme right and frequently had fascist sympathies.

Little or no terrorism erupted during World War II or its immediate aftermath, although there was a great deal of guerrilla warfare, which is something quite different. Then, in the late 1960s and 1970s, came a sudden upsurge of left-wing terrorism in Europe, Latin America, and elsewhere. This sudden resurgence had an unfortunate impact on terrorism studies, a field that emerged at about the same time. The news media, along with some in the academy, tended to take the slogans of contemporary terrorists at face value while ignoring terrorism's lengthy history. This led them to see terrorism as a new and unprecedented phenomenon, something that was essentially a response to injustice. If political, social, and economic justice could be achieved, the argument ran, there would be no terrorism, and so the way to deal with it was to address its "root causes": the grievances, stresses, and frustrations that lay behind the violence. Seen in this light, terrorists were fanatical believers driven to despair by intolerable conditions. They were poor and oppressed, or at least on the side of the poor and oppressed, and their inspiration was deeply ideological.

Left-wing terrorism also had a certain influence at this time on nationalist terrorism. The doctrine and the slogans of organizations such as the Basque separatist group ETA, sections of the Irish Republican Army, and the various Popular Fronts for the Liberation of Palestine clearly showed the impact of Marxism-Leninism. Subsequent events, however, would reveal that this ideological patina was merely a reflection of the zeitgeist, did not go very deep or last long, and hardly affected the staunch nationalism at these movements' cores.

Left-wing terrorism lasted for about a decade and then petered out or was suppressed, in Germany and Italy, Uruguay and Argentina—and in the United States. It was followed by a wave of terrorism that came from the extreme right, including attacks on refugees in various European countries and the rise of neofascist groups in Italy and elsewhere. Left-wing terrorist cells did not totally disappear, but they were no longer in the front rank.

Those who had sympathized with what they thought were the justified grievances behind terrorism found themselves in a quandary. The most devastating act of terrorism in American history before the attacks of September 11, for example, was carried out in 1995 in Oklahoma City. No one could deny that Timothy McVeigh had deeply felt grievances, but they were hardly the type with which people on the left wanted to sympathize. They were the grievances of *The Turner Diaries*, of America taken over by foreigners and degenerates, of the holy duty of all patriots to cleanse the country in a river of blood—in short, the worldview of a virulent form of fascism.

McVeigh was not unique, moreover. Similar descriptions could apply to the murderers of Anwar al-Sadat, Yitzhak Rabin, and Mohandas Gandhi. Their assassins belonged to fanatical nationalist and right-wing undergrounds firmly convinced that they were doing their patriotic duty by liquidating traitors. These terrorists could hardly be said to be engaging in "revolutionary violence," nor could poverty, oppression, or free-floating rage help to explain the torching of asylum-seekers' homes in Germany or the unspeakable atrocities perpetrated by Islamist terrorists in Algeria, where they were fighting not colonial rulers but their own compatriots.

THE NEW VULNERABILITY

Over the last two decades, changes in targets, weapons, and motives combined to make terrorists more dangerous than ever before. As the result of technical progress, developed societies became more vulnerable to attack. (So have the megacities of the developing world, for that matter, but the political repercussions of that vulnerability may take longer to unfold.) Traditional terrorist weapons such as explosives, meanwhile, became more lethal and efficient, and the technology and skills needed to make weapons of mass destruction diffused throughout the world. At the same time, there was also an upsurge of religious fundamentalism in many parts of the globe, and at the margins of this movement radical groups appeared that were prepared to engage in terrorist attacks.

This trend toward increased vulnerability was occurring even before the Internet sped it along. Until the middle of the nineteenth century, a group of people who wanted to kill their enemies had to go quite literally from house to house in order to locate and assassinate their victims. Whole cities could not be paralyzed until after the introduction of power plants, centralized water supplies, and other technical developments resulting in the centralization of services. It is true that even in the 1840s some philosophers of the bomb had already foreseen weapons of mass destruction. Karl Heinzen, a fiery if somewhat unbalanced German revolutionary, envisaged the use of poison gas, not to mention ballistic missiles. But at the time this was no more than terrorist science fiction. He and his followers did not pursue this course of action, and Heinzen went on to a more peaceable career as an editor of German-language newspapers in Louisville, Kentucky, and then Boston.

Many considered the invention of dynamite by Alfred Nobel several decades later to be a turning point in the history of terrorism. But the early bombs were still heavy, bulky, and dangerous to construct, and only with the miniaturization of explosives in the twentieth century did it become possible to launch terrorist bomb attacks on a large scale. Similarly, with the invention of the airplane, another dimension of terrorist attacks materialized, and even before World War I Russian revolutionaries were considering airplanes' terrorist potential, while Irish radicals were contemplating the submarine in similar terms. Both ideas were premature, however, and it would take decades for these fantasies to become realistic possibilities.

Traditional terrorists, whether left-wing, right-wing, or nationalist-separatist, were not greatly drawn to these opportunities for greater destruction. One reason was scruples. A hundred years ago, terrorists often would desist from an attack if their victim happened to be accompanied by family members or if there was a danger that innocents would be killed. Terrorism has become far more brutal and indiscriminate since then, and the terrorists of the second half of the twentieth century managed to persuade themselves that there were no innocents and that indiscriminate murder was permissible if it served the political aim. But even they tended to hesitate before carrying out true mass murder, partly because of the risk of a backlash against their cause, and partly because such actions were alien to their traditions and would repel their own supporters. They hated their enemies, but they had not been totally blinded by their hate. For the radical religious practitioners of the new terrorism, however, murder and destruction on an unprecedented scale did not pose much of a problem.

THE NEW TERRORISTS

Recent years have witnessed a growth of radical groups on the fringe of several religions. No one has yet fully determined why such processes should take place. In the Muslim world this development may have been connected with the declining attraction of other radical ideologies such as fascism and communism. But the trend was not limited to Islam. It could be found, for example, among certain millenarian Christian sects. As the century drew to a close, these latter groups caused security officers in various places to worry about attacks in conjunction with the turn of the new millennium. Much to the officers' relief, such attacks did not materialize. But the fear had not been unjustified, for it is only one step from believing that the world is deeply corrupt and sinful, and that only massive destruction in a final battle between good and evil will bring about redemption, to deciding to take an active hand in catalyzing the process. Among small extremist Jewish groups in Israel, in fact, could be found the same belief in a final battle between the forces of good and evil (Gog and Magog), and some even thought that acts such as the destruction of the Muslim shrines on the Temple Mount would give history a little push.

Radical religious groups have been particularly strong and particularly prone to turn violent in the Muslim world. Scanning the present world map of terrorism shows that Muslim states or Muslim minorities are involved in almost 90 percent of all substate terrorist conflicts, from the Philippines to the Middle East, from Nigeria to the Balkans. This has not always been the case, nor is there reason to believe that it will always remain so, but about the present state of affairs there can be no two opinions. Other, non-Muslim terrorist groups are continuing the struggles in which they have been engaged, such as those in Ireland, in the Basque country, in Greece, and in Sri Lanka. But these terrorists are relatively small, localized, and unimportant in comparison with the terrorism of radical Islamist groups.

How to explain this upsurge of terrorist violence? It has been argued that wherever Muslims live they have been the subject of oppression and persecution and that terrorism is the natural response to such conditions. This might have been a persuasive explanation prior to World War I, or even World War II, when only a handful of independent Islamic states existed. There are still a few Muslim minorities in the world that have not yet achieved autonomy or independence, but this is true for many non-Muslim minorities as well. Since 1948, many dozens of Muslim states have come into being and the great majority of Muslims now live in states of their own; if there is oppression, it is mainly by their own kind.

Can the frequency of violence be explained as the result of a "clash of civilizations"? No, because the bloodiest conflicts have occurred not between Muslim groups or states and the West but within the Muslim world itself. This holds true for both interstate conflicts (such as the Iran-Iraq War and the Iraqi invasion of Kuwait) as well as intrastate conflict (such as the terrorism of the Algerian Islamists against their fellow citizens, as a result of which some 70,000 people are believed to have been killed). It applies also to the persecution of the Kurds, as well as to the civil war in Afghanistan. It applies to the many assassination attempts, successful and unsuccessful, against Arab and Muslim leaders.

This pattern of events has led to speculation about the possibility of some particularly aggressive element in Islam that inspires terrorism, and it is not difficult to point to various historical examples, such as the notorious sect of the Assassins. Yet although there was Muslim terrorism in the age of imperialism in both India and Egypt, these instances were rare, terrorism was never in the mainstream, and the inspiration was probably more nationalistic than religious.

The recent rise of Islamist radicalism can more usefully be explained as the result of the decline of other political doctrines and the emergence of an intellectual and spiritual vacuum waiting to be filled. Here the adoption of Islamist doctrine by once-Marxist Arab intellectuals is most illuminating. During the 1990s, Horst Mahler, a former leading member and ideologist of the Baader-Meinhof Gang, Germany's left-wing terrorist group, became a spokesperson for extreme right-wing views. There were many

Mahlers in the Middle East. This change in the zeitgeist led to a rejection of the Western way of life and Western values, a revolt against modernity in general, and, in extreme cases, a call for *jihad*, or holy war.

Similar trends were by no means wholly unknown to Western civilization. The concept of a crusade, after all, is not Islamic: Christianity has also carried out holy wars. European fascism was also a revolt against the West, the Enlightenment, and humanism, and illuminating parallels can be discovered by comparing certain European fascist movements (for instance, those in Romania and the early Falange in Spain) with the radical Islamists. The Romanian and Spanish fascist movements were mystical and religious in inspiration, in contrast to Nazi Germany and fascist Italy, and their attitudes toward martyrdom and death were similar to that of the radical Islamists. But in Europe the idea of crusades went out fashion many centuries ago and the clerical-fascist cult has also disappeared, whereas in the Muslim world the concept of *jihad* has had a revival. In other places the general trend has been toward multiculturalism and the coexistence of religions, but this has not been the case in the contemporary Muslim world.

IDEAS AND POLITICS

Still, the connection between this radical fundamentalist revival and terrorism is not as straightforward as it might appear. Islamist fundamentalism comes in a variety of forms and is often quietist. Saudi Arabia finances Islamist activities in scores of countries, benefiting mosques and cultural institutions that serve as recruiting ground for the terrorists, but the Saudis do not allow any such activities within their own country. One of the guiding lights of modern Islamist radicalism, the Egyptian dissident Sayyid Qutb, argued that existing Arab regimes should be overthrown first because only then would a *jihad* be successful. Some of Qutb's disciples continued the struggle in the spirit of their master, but other militants established a different order of priorities, directing their attacks at the unbelievers of the West instead.

Furthermore, it is unclear whether the upsurge of terrorism can be explained mainly, let alone exclusively, by the history of ideas. In all probability it has as much to do with Muslims' feelings of frustration with their own countries' recent track records, compared to both West and East. These non-Muslim regions have made considerable economic progress, whereas the countries of the Middle East have generally stagnated or shown negative growth. This stagnation has resulted in growing poverty and unemployment, increased numbers of educated young people who have not found jobs in their professions, and growing resentment against those who have been more successful. It has also produced a wish to blame foreigners for the misery—self-criticism being too painful and too dangerous.

The frustration also stems from the lack of progress in much of the Muslim world toward anything resembling democratic institutions. The demand for political democracy may not be overwhelming: according to public-opinion polls only about 10 percent of respondents favor a political system of this kind. But little freedom exists even on the local level, and even Arab critics have conceded the lamentable state of affairs on the cultural and intellectual scene. More important yet, militarily these societies have not been able to assert themselves (witness the repeated defeat of Pakistan by India, the victories of Israel over its Arab neighbors). All these frustrations have created a climate that acts as a breeding ground for terrorist activities. To what extent the prevailing ideology that developed in response to this unhappy state of affairs is radical Islamist, nationalist, or a mixture of the two may be difficult to establish, and generalizations are impossible because the situation varies from place to place and from time to time. But what is common is the feeling that the misery must have been caused by an outside enemy, and hence a resentment and a hate not felt in countries that have made progress.

KNOW THINE ENEMY

The new terrorism is a fanaticism that expresses itself in, among other things, suicide bombing and the willingness to cause indiscriminate slaughter. In contrast to widespread belief, however, suicide bombing is not a recent phenomenon. On the contrary, until fairly recently terrorism was more or less synonymous with a suicide mission. The main weapon of the attack was the dagger, and unless the victim could be found alone and defenseless, the *sicarii* of Jewish history and the Assassins of Muslim history were unlikely to return from their missions. This was true even for much of the nineteenth century, as the makeshift bombs of the anarchists and the Russian revolutionaries were so unstable that they had to be thrown from a short distance (that is, if they did not explode first in the hands of the attacker). Those who went on an attack of this kind were fully aware of the risk, and many of them wrote farewell letters to their friends and families. Only with the advent of more sophisticated weapons in the twentieth century and the growing conviction among terrorists that it was permissible to kill the innocent did terrorism become less risky.

Even in our age, suicide bombing has by no means been limited to terrorists in Islamic countries. It has been a favorite form of attack by the Liberation Tigers of Tamil Eelam in Sri Lanka, members of which have carried out some 180 such attacks over the years in their country and in India. (The former Indian prime minister Rajiv Gandhi was one of their victims.) In Sri Lanka, the total number of Tamils—who are not Muslim and are not religiously motivated—is only a few million, and their per capita rate of suicide terrorists is thus far higher than that among either Muslims or Arabs. And suicide bombing has occurred, albeit on a smaller scale, in many terrorist movements during the last decade.

Muslim suicide bombers have tended to be young and deeply indoctrinated, led to believe that it is their duty to make the ultimate sacrifice for their group, country, or religion and that a far more enjoyable form of existence awaits them in the hereafter. But the world has also experienced many secular terrorist bombers who had no paradise awaiting them, such as the 4,000 young Japanese who volunteered for kamikaze actions at the end of World War II and the members of elite German SS units asked to undertake suicide missions when the Nazi war effort was approaching final defeat.

It is easier to trace the psychological and cultural sources of terrorist suicide missions than to trace the phenomenon of fanaticism that plays such a central role in the new terrorism. Fanaticism has existed in every civilization and at almost all times, but it has not necessarily expressed itself in terrorist action. At present, fanaticism can be found far more often in certain societies and cultures than in others, and psychiatry has not been of much help in explaining this phenomenon. Psychiatrists have shied away from confronting this subject, doubting whether it was part of their discipline; criminologists have been reluctant to discuss evil, for even if it is real it is a theological concept rather than a social science one. Madness, especially paranoia, plays a role in contemporary terrorism. Not all paranoiacs are terrorists, but all terrorists believe in conspiracies by powerful, hostile forces and suffer from some form of delusion and persecution mania.

Although a disturbed childhood and other forms of deprivation can explain the mind-set of some violent criminals, this profile by no means fits most serial murderers. Similarly, it is a hopeless exercise to try to explain terrorists, individually or collectively, wholly in social categories such as national or social oppression, messianic belief, or protest against injustice. In the bloodiest terrorist campaigns the element of crime and madness plays an important role, even if many are reluctant to acknowledge it.

WHAT COMES NEXT

Some terrorist campaigns have lasted longer than others, but all have come sooner or later to an end, and the present one will be no exception. Radical Islamist groups are in the forefront of terrorism today, but this is unlikely to remain the case forever. It is precisely in those countries where the population has been exposed to fundamentalist regimes or violence, such as Afghanistan, Iran, or Algeria, that enthusiasm for violent action is least prevalent. The candidates for terrorism have come mainly from *madrassas* (Islamic schools) in Pakistan or similar institutions in Europe. It is futile to speculate from where the terrorists of the future will emerge. Terrorism can appear on the extreme fringe of almost any ideology or cult. As weapons of mass destruction will give unprecedented power to small groups of individuals, and as there is no accounting for the mental sanity of a handful of people, the element of madness will probably play an even greater role in the future than is does at present or has in the past.

Are weapons of mass destruction likely to be used soon, and if so by whom? This depends, in part, on the success of the present operations against those responsible for the attacks of September 11 and those responsible for the anthrax mailings. If the operations succeed, terrorist movements—although not all individuals or small groups, whose behavior is unpredictable—will think twice before using nuclear, biological, or chemical weapons in a major way. The recent attacks, moreover, have shown that even conventional weapons can have devastating results if used creatively. Still, we know that the use of weapons of mass destruction has been contemplated by certain radical terrorist groups, and that the barrier to using biological weapons has been broken, and so preparations for such eventualities are imperative.

Today's world has no Clausewitz or Machiavelli to serve as our guide to terrorism and counterterrorism. But certain basic observations can be made based on past experience and common sense. No society can protect all its members from terrorist attack, but all societies can reduce the risk by taking the offensive, by keeping terrorists on the run rather than concentrating on defense alone. Terrorism in previous periods of history was little more than a nuisance, but as a result of the technological and other trends mentioned above, the danger is now much greater. In past ages, state and society could face terrorists with some equanimity. If one plane was hijacked, all others continued to fly; if one bank was robbed, all others continued to function; if one politician was killed, others were only too willing to take his place. But in an age of weapons of mass destruction this is no longer the case; even one attack can be overwhelmingly devastating.

It is difficult to imagine a world without terrorism in the foreseeable future, for it would imply a world without conflict and tension. There will always be groups, small and not so small, with grievances against other groups and an inclination toward violence. Some of these grievances will be justified and will also be open to a political solution. Others will be justified but may collide with the equally justified claims of another group. And still others may simply be beyond rational discourse and any known approach of conflict resolution.

Even with all that is going on today, therefore, it would be a mistake to focus only on the present threat. Movements inspired by religious and radical fanaticism do not last forever. Past experience shows that the original fanaticism tends to peter out, whether because of internal quarrels, external setbacks, or the rise of a new generation with different priorities. The main future danger to civilization, in other words, could well come from different quarters than those that generated the present one. But this does not offer much comfort, because even if the political and religious orientation of terrorists changes, the capacity to inflict unacceptable damage will not. For this reason, one must conclude that the world is now entering a new phase in its history, more dangerous than any before.

GRAVEYARD OF EMPIRES
AFGHANISTAN'S TREACHEROUS PEAKS

■

MILTON BEARDEN

Michni Point, Pakistan's last outpost at the western end of the barren, winding Khyber Pass, stands sentinel over Torkham Gate, the deceptively orderly border crossing into Afghanistan. Frontier Scouts in gray *shalwar kameezes* (traditional tunics and loose pants) and black berets patrol the lonely station commanded by a major of the legendary Khyber Rifles, the militia force that has been guarding the border with Afghanistan since the nineteenth century, first for British India and then for Pakistan. This spot, perhaps more than any other, has witnessed the traverse of the world's great armies on campaigns of conquest to and from South and Central Asia. All eventually ran into trouble in their encounters with the unruly Afghan tribes.

Alexander the Great sent his supply trains through the Khyber, then skirted northward with his army to the Konar Valley on his campaign in 327 BC. There he ran into fierce resistance and, struck by an Afghan archer's arrow, barely made it to the Indus River with his life. Genghis Khan and the great Mughal emperors began passing through the Khyber a millennium and a half later and ultimately established the greatest of empires—but only after reaching painful accommodations with the Afghans. From Michni Point, a trained eye can still see the ruins of the Mughal signal towers used to relay complex torch-light messages 1,500 miles from Calcutta to Bukhara in less than an hour.

In the nineteenth century the Khyber became the fulcrum of the Great Game, the contest between Great Britain and Russia for control of Central Asia and India. The first Afghan War (1839–42) began when British commanders sent a huge army of

British and Indian troops into Afghanistan to secure it against
Russian incursions, replacing the ruling emir with a British pro-
tégé. Facing Afghan opposition, by January 1842 the British were
forced to withdraw from Kabul with a column of 16,500 soldiers
and civilians, heading east to the garrison at Jalalabad, 110 miles
away. Only a single survivor of that group ever made it to Jalalabad safely, though the British forces did recover some prisoners
many months later.

According to the late Louis Dupree, the premier historian of
Afghanistan, four factors contributed to the British disaster: the
occupation of Afghan territory by foreign troops, the placing of
an unpopular emir on the throne, the harsh acts of the British-
supported Afghans against their local enemies, and the reduction
of the subsidies paid to the tribal chiefs by British political agents.
The British would repeat these mistakes in the second Afghan
War (1878–81), as would the Soviets a century later; Americans
and others would be wise to consider them today.

In the aftermath of the second British misadventure in Afghanistan, Rudyard Kipling penned his immortal lines on the role of
the local women in tidying up the battlefields:

> When you're wounded and left on Afghanistan's plains
> And the women come out to cut up what remains
> Jest roll to your rifle an' blow out your brains
> An' go to your Gawd like a soldier.

The British fought yet a third war with Afghanistan in 1917, an
encounter that neither burnished British martial history nor sub-
dued the Afghan people. But by the end of World War I, that
phase of the Great Game was over. During World War II, Afghanistan flirted with Aryanism and the Third Reich, becoming, fleetingly, "the Switzerland of Central Asia" in a new game of
intrigue, as Allied and Axis coalitions jockeyed for position in the
region. But after the war the country settled back into its natural
state of ethnic and factional squabbling. The Soviet Union joined
in from the sidelines, but Afghanistan was so remote from the
consciousness of the West that scant attention was paid to it until

the last king, Mohammed Zahir Shah, was deposed in 1973. Then began the cycle of conflict that continues to the present.

THE SOVIET EXPERIENCE

Afghanistan festered through the 1970s, but with the seizure of power in Kabul by Nur Mohammed Taraki in 1978, the country began a rapid spiral into anarchy. Washington's ambassador in Kabul, Adolph Dubs, was kidnapped in February 1979 and then killed during a failed rescue attempt; the next month, Hafizullah Amin seized the prime ministership along with much of Taraki's power; and eight months later, on December 27, after watching the disintegration of order for much of a decade, the Kremlin decided to try its hand at military adventure.

The Soviets began with a modern repetition of the fatal British error of installing an unpopular "emir" on the Afghan "throne." The operation was marked by a brutal efficiency: Hafizullah Amin was killed under mysterious circumstances, Kabul was secured, and the Soviets put their man, Babrak Karmal, at the helm of the Afghan government. It looked initially as if the Soviets' optimistic prediction that they would be in and out of Afghanistan almost before anyone noticed might prove correct. Certainly, President Jimmy Carter was too preoccupied with the hostage crisis in Iran to give much thought to Afghanistan, or so the Kremlin believed.

To Moscow's surprise, however, Carter reacted quickly and decisively. He cancelled a number of pending agreements with the Soviet Union, ranging from wheat sales to consular exchanges; he set in motion the boycott of the 1980 Olympic games in Moscow; and, much more quietly and decisively, he signed a presidential finding that tasked the Central Intelligence Agency (CIA) with the organization of aid, including arms and military support, to the Afghan people in their resistance to the Soviet occupation. In January 1980, Carter sent his national security adviser, Zbigniew Brzezinski, for consultations with Pakistani leaders, who were already supporting the Afghan resistance. On a side trip from

Islamabad, Brzezinski traveled the length of the Khyber Pass to the outpost at Michni Point, where he was photographed squinting along the sights of a Soviet AK–47 assault rifle, its muzzle elevated and pointing into Afghanistan. In that moment, the president's national security adviser became the symbol of the impending phase of U.S. involvement in Afghanistan's endless martial history.

The CIA had to scramble to comply with the president's order. But within weeks it had organized its first weapons delivery—a shipment of several thousand venerable Enfield .303 rifles—to the resistance fighters, who were already beginning to snipe at the Soviet invaders. During the 1980s, the agency would deliver several hundred thousand tons of weapons and ordnance to Pakistan for distribution to the Afghan fighters known to the world as *mujahideen* ("soldiers of God"). The coalition of countries supporting the resistance grew to an impressive collection that included the United States, the United Kingdom, Pakistan, Saudi Arabia, Egypt, and China. Lining up behind seven separate and fractious Afghan resistance leaders based in Peshawar, the capital of Pakistan's Northwest Frontier Province, the *mujahideen* field commanders were allotted their supplies and sent off to face the Soviet forces.

For the first five years of its covert war, the CIA attempted to maintain "plausible deniability," trying to ensure that the aid it provided to the resistance was not obviously identifiable as having come from the United States. The CIA's officers in Pakistan kept a low profile, and the weapons they supplied to the *mujahideen*, with the exception of the British-made Enfields, were models manufactured in Warsaw Pact countries. An additional advantage of using Soviet-bloc weapons was that the *mujahideen* could use any ammunition they could capture from army garrisons of the puppet Democratic Republic of Afghanistan (DRA)—or buy, with American dollars, from corrupt DRA quartermasters or even Red Army supply officers.

By 1985, the Soviet 40th Army had grown from its original, limited expeditionary force to an occupation force of around 120,000 troops, widely dispersed at garrisons around the country. But as the Soviet forces grew, so did the Afghan resistance. By the mid–1980s the *mujahideen* had more than 250,000 full- or part-time fighters in the field, and though they and the civilian population had suffered horrendous losses—a million dead and 1.5 million injured, plus 6 million more driven into internal and external exile—the Soviet forces were also beginning to suffer.

As the CIA became more deeply involved in its covert proxy war with the Soviet Union, it became clear to President Ronald Reagan's new CIA director, William Casey, that the conflict had stalemated. The United States was fighting the Soviets to the last Afghan in a confrontation that could run on indefinitely. By 1985 Soviet air tactics had been refined, and the *mujahideen* suffered increasing casualties from the growing Soviet fleet of heavily armored MI–24D attack helicopters. The Afghans had nothing in their arsenals adequate to defend against this equipment and so, after a heated debate and heavy pressure from Congress, the White House decided to provide them with Stinger antiaircraft missiles. The Stingers entered the war a month after Mikhail Gorbachev's August 1986 speech in Vladivostok, where he described the conflict, now in its seventh year, as a "bleeding wound." U.S. intelligence at the time, however, indicated that as he uttered those first words of disengagement, he also gave his generals one year to bring the Afghans under control, using whatever force necessary. Three months earlier the Soviets had replaced the failing Babrak Karmal with the brutal, sadistic secret-police chief Mohammed Najibullah, a move that only stiffened *mujahideen* resistance and set the scene for the endgame of the Soviets' Afghan adventure.

Two events in the late summer of 1986 changed the course of the war. On August 20 a lucky shot by the *mujahideen* sent a 107 mm rocket into a DRA supply dump on the outskirts of Kabul, setting off secondary explosions that destroyed tens of thousands of tons of ordnance, lighting up the skies of the Afghan capital by night and smoldering during the day. A month later, on September 26, a team led by a resistance commander with the unlikely name of Ghaffar ("the forgiver," one of the 99 names of Allah) brought down three MI–24 helicopters in the first Stinger ambush of the war. The effect of these events on the *mujahideen* was electric, and within days the setbacks for the Soviet forces were snow-balling, with one or two aircraft per day falling from the skies at the end of the Stingers' telltale white plumes.

When the snows melted in the high passes for the new fighting season of 1987, diplomatic activity intensified, with the United States represented by the exceptionally able Michael Armacost, then the undersecretary of state for political affairs. It had become clear not only to Gorbachev and his negotiators but also to his generals in the field that there would be no letup in Afghanistan, and that the time to consider disengagement had come. On April 14, 1988, after agonized negotiations over such tortured concepts as "negative symmetry" in drawing down supplies to the com-batants, the Geneva accords ending Soviet involvement in Afghanistan were signed. The date for the final withdrawal of all Soviet forces was set at February 15, 1989, a timetable that was also to mark the end of outside military support to both sides in the war, at least in theory.

The commander of the Soviet 40th Army in Afghanistan, Gen-eral Boris Gromov, choreographed the Soviet departure to the last moment of the last day. On February 15 the international press was shuttled from nearby Termez, in the Soviet republic of Uzbekistan, to a special press center, complete with a new, cov-ered pavilion. The body of a hapless minesweeper had been qui-etly carried across the Friendship Bridge over the Amu Dar'ya (the river that forms the border between Afghanistan and Uzbek-istan) before the press had time to reason that his blanket-wrapped form was the last Russian soldier killed in the ten-year war. The cameras of several dozen news services zoomed in on the center of the bridge, where a lone Soviet tank had pulled to a halt. The diminutive Soviet general jumped from the turret, pulled his battle-dress tunic into place, and strode purposefully over the last hundred yards toward the Soviet side of the river. Just before he reached the end of the bridge, his son Maksim, a slim, awk-ward 14-year-old, greeted his father with a stiff embrace and pre-sented him with a bouquet of red carnations. Son and father marched the last 50 yards out of Afghanistan together.

THE AFGHAN ARABS

In ten years of war, the Soviet Union admitted to having had about 15,000 troops killed in action, several hundred thousand wounded, and tens of thousands dead from disease. The true numbers might be higher, but they are not worth debating. What followed Gromov's exit grew rapidly into a cataclysm for the Soviets and a national disaster for the Afghans.

The first signs came in May 1989, when an already emboldened Hungarian government correctly concluded it could open its border with Austria without fear of Soviet intervention. That signal act was followed a month later by the stunning election of a Solidarity majority in Poland's parliament, ending that country's nearly half-century of communist rule. Throughout the summer of 1989, the people of East Germany took to the streets, first in small numbers, then gaining strength and courage in the tens and hundreds of thousands until, on the night of November 9, in a comedy of errors and miscues, the Berlin Wall was breached and Germans surged from east to west. The world had hardly digested these events when the Czech playwright Vaclav Havel and his band of dissidents from the Magic Lantern theater carried out their own Velvet Revolution a month later.

With the world's eyes focused almost exclusively on the historic events in Eastern Europe, or on the vivid image of a young demonstrator staring down a Chinese tank in Beijing's Tiananmen Square, the drama unfolding in Afghanistan received scant attention. Though there were heroic efforts by relief agencies to provide humanitarian aid, the senior officials of President George H.W. Bush's administration did not look back to that former war zone, their energies instead consumed by the stunning denouement of the Cold War. As the 1990s began with great hope elsewhere in the world, in Afghanistan a new post–Cold War construct started taking shape: the failed state. And as it failed and spun into anarchy, Afghanistan became home to a new and little-understood threat: the aggrieved Arab extremist.

The role of the so-called Afghan Arabs in the ten-year war

against the Soviet occupation is the subject of much debate and misinformed commentary. By early 1980 the call to *jihad* ("holy war") had reached all corners of the Islamic world, attracting Arabs young and old and with a variety of motivations to travel to Pakistan to take up arms and cross the border to fight against the Soviet invaders in Afghanistan. Some were genuine volunteers on missions of humanitarian value, others were adventure-seekers looking for paths to glory, and still others were psychopaths. As the war dragged on, a number of Arab states discreetly emptied their prisons of homegrown troublemakers and sent them off to the *jihad* with the hope that they might never return. Over the ten years of war as many as 25,000 Arabs may have passed through Pakistan and Afghanistan. At one time the CIA considered having volunteer Arab legions take part in the war, but the idea was scrapped as unwise and unworkable. Despite what has often been written, the CIA never recruited, trained, or otherwise used the Arab volunteers who arrived in Pakistan. Moreover, the Arabs who did travel to Afghanistan from Peshawar were generally considered nuisances by *mujahideen* commanders, some of whom viewed them as only slightly less bothersome than the Soviets. As fund-raisers, however, the Arabs from the Persian Gulf played a positive, often critical role in the background of the war. During some months in 1987 and 1988, Arab fund-raisers in Pakistan and in their home countries raised as much as $25 million for their largely humanitarian and construction projects. Among the more prominent of these Arab fund-raisers was a young man named Osama bin Laden, the son of a billionaire from the construction industry in Saudi Arabia.

Active in Afghanistan since the early 1980s, having previously worked in the Persian Gulf to recruit Arabs for the *jihad*, bin Laden focused his early energies on construction projects, building orphanages and homes for widows as well as roads and bunker systems in the eastern part of the country. He and a few of his Saudi followers saw some combat in 1987 while associated with the Islamic Unity Party of Abdul Rasul Sayaf, an Egyptian-trained Afghan member of the Muslim Brotherhood who would later embrace Saudi Wahhabism (an austere form of Islam that

developed in Saudi Arabia in the eighteenth century). At the crucial battles of Jaji and Ali Khel, Sayaf and his Saudis acquitted
themselves well by stopping a Soviet and DRA advance that
could have resulted in large-scale destruction of *mujahideen* supply dumps and staging areas in the province of Paktia. More than
two dozen Saudis died in those engagements, and the military legend of Osama bin Laden was born.

But at this point in the war, few were concerned about the role
of the Afghan Arabs, with the exception of growing criticism by
Western humanitarian organizations of the harsh fundamentalism
of the Saudi Wahhabis and Deobandis (members of another austere school of Islam that developed in India in the nineteenth century and that had close links to Wahhabism), whose influence in
the refugee camps in Pakistan, now bursting with about three million Afghans, was pervasive. In these squalid camps an entire generation of young Afghan males was born into and raised in the
strictest fundamentalism of the Deobandi *madrassas* (Islamic
schools). It was here that the seeds of the Taliban were sown.

THE RISE OF THE TALIBAN

Although the Soviets left Afghanistan in 1989, it was not until
April 1992 that the *mujahideen* finally took the capital, Kabul,
and declared what passed for victory. Their triumph would be
short-lived. Old hatreds and ethnic rivalries once again drove
events, and without the unifying presence of foreign armies on
Afghan soil, the state of Afghanistan simply fell apart. The civil
war resumed with horrendous brutality until the population was
ready for any path to peace, and soon one presented itself.

Rising almost mystically from the sheer chaos, the Taliban
(their name refers to students of Islam), began to form under the
leadership of Mullah Mohammad Omar, a one-eyed cleric from
Oruzgan province in central Afghanistan. More as a result of timing than of military might, they swept through the Pashtun region
of eastern Afghanistan, a welcome relief from the brigands controlling the valleys and mountain passes. By 1996 the Taliban had

seized Kabul and killed Najibullah, and the Afghan people seemed to accept their deliverance. The West fleetingly saw the Taliban as the source of a new order and a possible tool in yet another replay of the Great Game: the race for the energy riches of Central Asia. U.S. and foreign oil firms were looking for ways to pipe the vast natural-gas reserves of Turkmenistan to energy-starved markets in Pakistan. By 1996, most of the route of the proposed pipeline was loosely under Taliban control, and the match of politics, power, and energy seemed attractive. But this optimism would not last long. In 1997 plans for the Afghan pipeline were shelved and the country began an even sharper downward spiral, as the Taliban overreached in their quest to take control of the country. Their atrocious human-rights record and treatment of women drew international scorn, and with the exception of diplomatic recognition from Saudi Arabia, the United Arab Emirates, and Pakistan, Afghanistan was in total isolation. Its failure as a state of any recognizable form was now complete.

Against this backdrop, the Afghan Arab troublemakers began to drift back to Afghanistan. Many of them, including Osama bin Laden, had left after the Soviet defeat, full of determination to bring about radical societal change in their home countries. All failed, and many began roaming among the few remaining states in the world that served as safe havens for their kind. But with the collapse of the Soviet Union, the would-be terrorists of the world had fallen on hard times. They lost their playgrounds in Eastern Europe and the Soviet Union, and even the redoubtable 1970s Latin American–born terrorist Carlos (nicknamed "the Jackal") had wound up in the Sudanese capital, Khartoum—where, coincidentally, bin Laden had also settled after a failed attempt to bring about change in his Saudi homeland. Bin Laden engaged in a number of agricultural, construction, and business ventures, but most of his consciousness was consumed by a brooding hatred of the United States. This passion grew during the 1991 Gulf War, and five years later, with U.S. troops still stationed in Saudi Arabia, bin Laden's rage found its final form. It would be the United States against which he would concentrate his energies.

By 1995, however, bin Laden's presence in Sudan had become an issue both for the United States and for Saudi Arabia, which by this time had stripped bin Laden of his citizenship. The Sudanese were quietly told that bin Laden was a major obstacle to improved relations, and that Khartoum would be wise to ask him to leave. Sudan had already begun ridding itself of undesirables. In a dramatic setup, Carlos, stretched out on a Khartoum hospital operating table having a vasectomy reversed, was abruptly bundled up by French security officers and spirited off to Paris to stand trial for his earlier crimes. According to a PBS *Frontline* television interview with Sudanese president Umar Hassan al-Bashir, the Sudanese government offered to keep bin Laden on a tight leash, or even hand him over to the Saudis or to the Americans. The Saudis reportedly declined the offer, for fear that his presence would only cause more trouble in the kingdom, and the United States reportedly passed because it had no indictable complaints against him at the time. In 1996, then, on U.S. and Saudi instructions, bin Laden was expelled from Sudan, and he moved to the last stop on the terror line, Afghanistan.

Still relatively unknown to the public, bin Laden came into view through a CNN interview in 1997, when he claimed that his disciples had been behind the killing of 18 American soldiers in Somalia in 1993. The next year he issued a *fatwa* (an Islamic decree) of questionable authenticity, calling for all-out war against all Americans. But it was in August 1998 that he was indelibly etched into the world's consciousness, when terrorists thought to have links to his Al Qaeda organization struck simultaneously at American embassies in Kenya and Tanzania, killing 224 people, including 12 Americans, and wounding 5,000. The U.S. response was quick but futile: 75 cruise missiles were launched at bin Laden's training camps in Afghanistan and at a pharmaceutical factory suspected of producing precursors for chemical weapons in Sudan. Bin Laden escaped unharmed, and the attack on the Sudanese pharmaceutical factory remains a smoldering controversy to this day.

BACK TO THE FUTURE?

Since 1998, the hunt for bin Laden has been the driving force behind U.S. policy toward Afghanistan. Although the Taliban have repeatedly claimed that bin Laden has been under their control and incapable of fomenting the various attacks with which he is charged—including that against the U.S.S. *Cole* in the Yemeni port of Aden in October 2000 and the recent attacks on the World Trade Center and the Pentagon—the U.S. government has little doubt that bin Laden is the culprit.

It probably could not be otherwise, but how this first engagement in the new U.S. war on terrorism is conducted will be crucial to all that follows. If the terror network is to be dismantled, it will be with help from the security services of Pakistan, Egypt, Jordan, Sudan, and a few others, not from the exclusive efforts of the United States or its European allies. So the tale ends where it began, at Michni Point. As the George W. Bush administration balances its military and political goals, plans to send U.S. troops into Afghanistan to seize bin Laden will surely be weighed carefully for their practicality and political implications. Strident calls to add the overthrow of the Taliban regime to the list of American objectives may be attractive in terms of human rights, but that objective, too, must be weighed against the goal of making certain that the events of September 11 are not repeated.

Some have called for an explicit alliance with Afghanistan's now-leaderless Northern Alliance. This grouping of commanders, meticulously pulled together in shifting alliances by the late Ahmed Shah Masoud, held about 10 percent of Afghan territory before the U.S. air strikes began on October 7. Already the recipient of military and financial support from Russia and Iran, it seems a logical partner in the U.S. quest to locate and neutralize the bin Laden network and replace the Taliban regime. But that is not a wise course—not simply because of the cold irony of allying ourselves with the Russians in any fight in Afghanistan, but because it is not likely to achieve either goal. The likely consequences of a U.S. alliance with the late Masoud's fighters—themselves largely drawn from among Afghanistan's Tajik and Uzbek ethnic minorities—would be the coalescing of Afghanistan's majority Pashtun tribes around their Taliban leaders and the rekindling of a brutal, general civil war that would continue until the United States simply gave up. The provision of assistance to the Northern Alliance might be a useful short-term strategy to pressure the Taliban, if it is handled delicately, but any real military alliance with Masoud's successors is likely to backfire.

The Bush administration would do better to try to draw off those segments of the Pashtun population that are only loosely allied with the Taliban regime. Many of the Pashtuns who have signed on with the Taliban since 1996 did so because the Taliban seemed to offer a fair chance for peace after decades of indescribably brutal war. They did not sign on to fight the United States, whose military might many of them will recall from the struggle against the Soviet occupation. The administration seems to realize this, and it is now moving quietly, gathering resources in the land of the Pashtun. If anyone is to replace the Taliban and choose a new emir for Afghanistan, it will have to be the people of Afghanistan themselves. Any doubters should ask the British and the Russians.

THE RESTLESS REGION

THE BRITTLE STATES OF CENTRAL AND SOUTH ASIA

■

RAJAN MENON

By directing its initial military efforts against terrorists hiding in Afghanistan, the United States is making a high-stakes gamble. The war on terrorism, if it goes badly, risks intensifying the civil war in that country while further destabilizing adjacent states and dramatically altering relations with Russia and China in unintended and unanticipated ways.

The Taliban, now controlling 90 percent of Afghanistan, came to prominence in the resistance to an unpopular Marxist government that finally collapsed in 1992. In the succession war that followed, the Taliban prevailed, aided by outside support from Pakistan, Saudi Arabia, and the United States. Initial greetings of the war-weary Afghan people evaporated under the Taliban's puritanical and oppressive rule that pushed an already shell-shocked, hard scrabble people into starvation. Among Afghanistan's neighbors, excepting Pakistan, the rise of the Taliban was viewed with consternation. By 1998, aid to the anti-Taliban Northern Alliance within Afghanistan was flowing from Russia, Uzbekistan, Iran, and India.

In Russia's eyes, the Taliban supported the Islamists in Tajikistan (where Russian forces have been based since 1992 to prevent the establishment of an Islamist regime) and fostered radical Islam elsewhere in Central Asia and in Chechnya. Uzbekistan's authoritarian leader, Islam Karimov, saw the Taliban as an ally of the banned Islamic Movement of Uzbekistan (IMU) and therefore supported the anti-Taliban coalition's Uzbek wing. For India, the rise of a pro-Pakistani regime in a traditionally friendly country was a strategic setback. India also feared (rightly, as it turned out) that armed Islamist separatist groups in the contested region of

Kashmir, already supported by Pakistan, would gain a new patron. Iran also supported the Northern Alliance, for Iranians have close historical ties with the Hazaras of central Afghanistan, who are fellow Shi'a Muslims and have received particularly rough treatment from the Taliban. Given this array of powerful enemies, bin Laden, with his money and Arab fighters, became invaluable to the Taliban's war against the Northern Alliance. But he also became a major force unto himself.

Pakistan's leader, Pervez Musharraf, has made it clear that he does not want the Northern Alliance to govern post-Taliban Afghanistan. Rather, he has warned, Islamabad will insist on a friendly government in Kabul.

Unlike Pakistan, Iran sees the Taliban as a threatening, puritanical Sunni regime that sits on its flanks and was, until September 11, bankrolled by Saudi Arabia, another unfriendly Sunni state. But aiding, even cheering, an American attack on Afghanistan is a different matter given the tensions that still exist between Iran and the United States and the struggles between proponents and opponents of reform that now mark Iran's politics.

Furthermore, the Iranians have not forgotten that the United States once regarded a Taliban-controlled Afghanistan as a good outcome that would replace anarchy with stability and allow the construction of a Unocal natural-gas pipeline from Turkmenistan to Pakistan via Afghanistan. The strategic value of the pipeline project for Washington was its contribution to the further isolation of Iran: Turkmenistan was considering an alternative pipeline corridor across Iran's territory, which the United States strongly opposed. Yet Iran is supporting the Northern Alliance, tacitly putting it on the same side as the United States.

Tajikistan, Turkmenistan, and Uzbekistan all share borders with Afghanistan. The Turkmen have no wish to be the springboard for an American invasion of Afghanistan (which could create a wave of Afghan-Turkmen refugees), not least because Iran, through which Turkmenistan exports natural gas to Turkey, would not want it to. Unlike Uzbekistan and Tajikistan, Turkmenistan does not face the threat of homegrown Islamist insurgencies, but it fears that supporting a war against Afghanistan could create one.

For its part, nearby Tajikistan has struggled with a civil war of its own against other Islamist groups. A power-sharing agreement brokered by Russia and Iran in 1997 has reduced friction between the factions vying for power. But American use of Tajik air bases could tear apart the fractured society that has since been on the mend.

Uzbekistan's own Islamic rebel group, the IMU, operates in the Ferghana Valley (which slices through Kyrgyzstan and Tajikistan, as well) and has also carried out attacks in and around the capital, Tashkent. President Karimov has sought strategic links with the United States, not only to better fight the IMU, but also to check what he sees as Russia's hegemonic designs. For these reasons, Uzbekistan, which shares a 110-mile-long border with Afghanistan, has proven to be the most cooperative Central Asian state in the U.S. military campaign. Even though the United States may envisage a short-term use of Uzbek military installations, however, a quick exit may prove tricky because of unanticipated developments there and within Afghanistan that result from the war against the Taliban.

THE CREEPING MISSION

One danger, then, that attends American involvement in Afghanistan is that the United States will find itself drawn inexorably into Central Asia, a region laced with political minefields. It is a land of authoritarian polities and brittle governing institutions. Laws and institutions matter less in this region than do strongmen, whose tight grip on power ensures that succession struggles will erupt once they depart.

Islamist and ethnic insurgencies have affected Kyrgyzstan, Tajikistan, and Uzbekistan in varying degrees. Corruption, organized crime, and the narcotics trade are rampant. So are poverty, high population-growth rates, and sweeping social changes produced by the Soviet Union's implosion. Together, these conditions produce plenty of anomic, disgruntled young men, the ideal raw materials for radical movements.

There are also suspicions that divide the Uzbeks from the other peoples of the region. The Kyrgyz and Tajik governments, for example, see the IMU as a threat. But these smaller states are also wary of Uzbekistan's irredentist and territorial ambitions. They would not want an alignment between the United States and Uzbekistan to increase the already pronounced disparities in power between them and Uzbekistan or to increase the Uzbeks' freedom of maneuver in Central Asia.

The war against the Taliban and the creation of a stable post-Taliban Afghanistan, then, could well prove to be protracted missions, requiring a far longer presence in Central Asia than Washington now envisages. This kind of entanglement could lead to a messy case of "mission creep." And the chances of that occurring will increase if the United States accepts the view of local leaders, and of Russia, that Islamist radicalism is terrorism supported from abroad, pure and simple. For that assessment, though not totally false, is incomplete.

Consider the IMU: although it does have links to the Taliban (each supports the other, albeit in different ways), its rise since the late 1990s cannot be separated from Karimov's systematic throttling of democratic and moderate Islamist parties and the festering problems in the Ferghana Valley caused by poverty, unemployment, and demographic pressures. The United States could unwittingly promote Islamic extremism by underwriting the security of a regime that equates dissent with subversion.

Karimov has offered Uzbekistan's airspace and bases for U.S. search-and-rescue missions and has granted American helicopters and transport planes use of its airfields. But going beyond that to allow a substantial U.S. troop deployment in Uzbekistan and provide bases for ground and air attacks against Afghanistan will provoke Russia and perhaps strengthen the IMU. Karimov may take these additional risks, but they will come at a price for Washington: a long-term partnership that brings U.S. military and economic assistance and commits the United States to remain in Uzbekistan long after its operations against the Taliban have ended.

PAKISTAN'S HIGH-WIRE ACT

America's war against terrorism offers countries a mix of opportunity and danger. Nowhere is this clearer than in Pakistan. In the years preceding September 11, and particularly since the election of President George W. Bush, Pakistan has seen its once-special relationship with the United States steadily erode. America's rationale for an alliance with Islamabad in the 1970s and 1980s had been predicated on the containment of the Soviet Union, a rationale that disappeared in the 1990s. Worse for Pakistan, the longtime estrangement of India and the United States (based on strategic differences during the Cold War) was replaced by a growing sense of mutual admiration. Shared democratic ideals, the lure of India's large market (made more accessible by the country's economic liberalization) and common suspicions about China drove a realignment of relations between the two giant democracies. The momentum driving them together seemed unstoppable. Pakistan, feeling bypassed, saw a strategic nightmare in the making.

The events of September 11 gave Pakistan a chance to reverse its marginalization, to move closer to America's inner circle and to escape the dishonor and sanctions that came from being stamped as a state that supports terrorism. The United States has since lifted the economic sanctions imposed on India and Pakistan when the two countries tested nuclear weapons in the spring of 1998. Had terrorism not struck, India alone was slated to enjoy such a waiver.

The irony of what has happened is compelling. Pakistan, ruled by a man who seized power from an elected government, is the state most responsible for the Taliban's rise; Pakistan's financial institutions have been used extensively by terrorist groups to move funds worldwide; Pakistan had been one of only three countries that had diplomatic relations with the Taliban prior to September 11 and is the only one that still does. Yet now Pakistan, which has yet to hold the free elections that Musharraf has promised, is one of America's principal partners against the

Taliban in a campaign that British prime minister Tony Blair has described as a cause for all democracies.

This transformation is not an unalloyed blessing for Pakistan, which is taking a dangerous risk by joining the war against the Taliban. Its status in the U.S.-led coalition stems from its location adjacent to Afghanistan. But the government of Pervez Musharraf could well collapse under the weight of protest demonstrations organized by Islamist organizations. In late September, prior to any major U.S. strikes against Afghanistan, these protesters took to the streets of Quetta, Karachi, and Islamabad. The turnout was smaller than expected, and the government contrived counterdemonstrations (which was telling in itself), but the Islamists succeed in firing a shot across the bow.

Pakistani society is split in its opinion of the American war against the Taliban. The country's social fabric is already under enormous stress from the many divisions between different classes, ethnic groups, Sunni and Shi'a, and the native-born *mohajirs* (Muslim immigrants from the other parts of British India). To make matters worse, two million Afghan refugees already live in the country and more are arriving as the war progresses.

This is a combustible mix, and the concussions from an explosion in Pakistan will prove powerful and travel far. This country of 140 million has a violent history of internal strife and has fought several wars with India. Pakistan's Islamists have sympathizers within the military and the ISI; Musharraf, who made a series of personnel changes in both institutions in October, is well aware of this. How secure will Pakistan's nuclear weapons be if civil war erupts? How will India react to a disintegrating Pakistan? These uncertainties hang in the air as Washington moves to destroy Osama bin Laden's Al Qaeda organization and to unseat the Taliban and reconstitute Afghanistan's politics.

The Taliban understands how dicey the Musharraf government's position is, and its calls for a *jihad* to resist the United States are meant to make it even more tenuous. Musharraf wants to reap the benefits of cooperation with the United States while avoiding the whirlwind that could result from the nature of that cooperation. His is a delicate balance. To pull it off, he has provided two military bases and agreed to share intelligence and to allow overflights of Pakistani territory by U.S. military aircraft. He has, however, stopped short of allowing air and ground attacks from Pakistan's bases.

INDIA'S STAKE

September's bloodshed has made it harder for India to push its nascent strategic convergence with Washington at Pakistan's expense. Until September, everything seemed on course. Top officials in the Bush administration were known to favor an alignment with India, a democracy that belatedly is undertaking economic reform. With its population, land area, military power, and economic potential far exceeding Pakistan's, India was seen as having greater strategic heft, especially as a counterweight to the rising power of China. Pakistan, by contrast, seemed a troublesome mess. Terrorist groups and radical Islamists were prominent in its political arena, its economy was a shambles, its viability as a state was in doubt, and it was ruled by a coup maker. But Pakistan's adjacency to Afghanistan now gives it opportunities to support U.S. operations against the Taliban in ways that India cannot.

India's leaders are of two minds about these new circumstances. They resent being upstaged—and for reasons of geography, at that—by a state they consider strategically inferior. They worry that the United States or the United Kingdom may resume arms sales to Pakistan to reward its courage and to bolster its security. At the same time, the Indian government, led by the nationalist Bharatiya Janata Party, sees India as an emerging power whose strategic significance will make it the preferred U.S. partner in the long run.

India regards the Taliban as a Pakistani client that also trains and funds separatist guerillas operating in Kashmir, the disputed region over which India and Pakistan have fought several wars and innumerable skirmishes. India wrongly defines the nub of the problem in Kashmir as Pakistani-supported terrorism. In fact, the upheaval there results from many other issues, some left over from history, and others created by India's heavy-handed policies. Now that the United States is focused on terrorism, India hopes that Washington will goad Pakistan to liquidate the militant Islamist groups that operate freely on its territory and receive its support in infiltrating the portion of Kashmir controlled by India. Pakistan is already being urged by Washington to clamp down. But although terrorism is indeed part of the problem in Kashmir, the United States must not, on account of September 11, come to see it as the essence.

If Pakistan disintegrates, Indians on the far right will celebrate. But the more thoughtful ones realize that anarchy in an adjoining state with close religious and ethnic links with India could produce many dangerous outcomes, among them greater disorder in Kashmir, refugee flows into the Indian state of Punjab, and Pakistan's replacement by a gaggle of unruly, quarrelsome statelets. Apart from the risks of civil strife in a neighboring country, the disintegration of a multiethnic state along its border cannot be good for India, an even more diverse society that has seen its share of ethnic and communal violence.

RUSSIAN OPPORTUNITIES

For Russia, the September attacks provide an opportunity to improve ties with the United States and to increase its bargaining position. Russian president Vladimir Putin offered Russian airspace for U.S. search-and-rescue missions in Afghanistan and, after some debate within his government, chose not to block the Uzbek and Tajik governments from offering the United States access to their military bases. Russia has also agreed to share intelligence on Afghanistan and to increase its support for the Northern Alliance.

The reasons behind these actions are straightforward. Moscow regards the Taliban as a menace in Central Asia and Chechnya, but it has been able to do little to combat the Taliban's influence, beyond arming the Northern Alliance. With the conflict in

Chechnya on their hands and the memories of the Soviet war in Afghanistan fresh in their minds, the Russians have been in no mood to take on the Taliban directly. Russia's leaders would applaud the Taliban's fall, even if it results from a use of American power near the Russian border. But they do not want that outcome to pave the way for a sustained American strategic presence in Central Asia, one of the few regions where Russia exercises great influence and sees vital interests at stake. This makes Russia's armed forces and intelligence services ambivalent about helping America's war on terrorism. The difficulties in garnering Moscow's support will mount if Russia begins to suspect that the by-product of its cooperation will be an American beachhead on its southern border.

Putin portrays the basic problem in Chechnya as Islamic fundamentalism and terrorism—often in combination, and invariably financed from the outside, including by the Taliban. Chechnya certainly contains both of these elements, but the war there cannot be explained solely as the product of marauding fanatics and terrorists. Its origins, long and complex, lie in the tsarist conquests of the northern Caucasus, the brutal Soviet policies that nearly destroyed the Chechen people, a Russian war waged with disregard for Chechen civilians, and the Chechens' own determination, demonstrated for well over a century, to break free.

The United States seems fated to be engaged in a long war on terrorism that will require support in many ways from many countries, a number of them in the Muslim world. Accepting the Russian position on Chechnya will subvert coalition-building, identify the United States with Russia's ruinous war, and feed the canard that America cares little about Muslim lives. Prior to September 11, some prominent figures in Russia's establishment were launching trial balloons, suggesting that the time was nigh for a political solution in Chechnya. They have since done an about-face and now champion a more vigorous war, undoubtedly convinced that the West will accept tougher policies in Chechnya. By trading silence on Chechnya for Russia's support against terrorism, the United States will encourage such thinking. It will then not just have misread the reality in Chechnya, it will have ill served Russia's democratic consolidation and economic recovery by backing a failed policy.

CHINA'S SELF-INTEREST

China's position on America's war against Al Qaeda is similar to Russia's in substance and motivation. Beijing supports global cooperation on terrorism and, in sharp contrast to its behavior during the North Atlantic Treaty Organization's war in Kosovo, has not castigated the United States for using military power. Consistent with its opposition to the unilateral use of American force, however, China stresses the need to work through the United Nations.

Beijing sees the Taliban as a guru, paymaster, and trainer of separatists in its western province of Xinjiang, which borders Afghanistan and whose indigenous Turkic-Muslim Uighurs only sullenly accept Chinese rule. China does not face armed resistance in Xinjiang as Russia does in Chechnya, though, and it has reined in separatism by mixing repression with co-optation and a policy of Han Chinese immigration that has recast the province's ethnic composition. Even by Beijing's account, however, Xinjiang's secessionists have become bolder since the Soviet Union fell and the Taliban has risen. China is also concerned that the spread of radical Islam in Central Asia will spill into Xinjiang or buoy Uighur nationalists.

That said, the solidity of China's support for a prolonged American campaign against terrorism remains in doubt. Among the developments that could reduce it are a crisis over Taiwan (or even a sharp disagreement concerning U.S. arms sales to the island); an American use of force that is uncontrolled by international, or at least multilateral, mechanisms and that creates disorder in Muslim regions in and around China; and suspicions that the United States is out to increase its military presence in Central Asia, whose states are hoping to be an important source of China's energy imports.

AN AMERICAN BALANCING ACT

Identifying the nature and ramifications of what happened on September 11 is the easy, if cheerless, part. Crafting and implementing a policy toward terrorism that includes the use of military power and also minimizes the strategic ill effects stemming from its use is harder. That is the Bush administration's unenviable responsibility. There are hazards attached to particular choices. But knowing what they are does not guarantee success. Using force against the particular threat of terrorism may wind up destabilizing important countries and regions.

Unintended consequences could be most acute in Afghanistan and Pakistan. The former is likely to experience continued civil war; the latter could be convulsed by disorder. The United States has gathered much support; an administration led by individuals who once sniffed at multilateralism is now its fervent advocate. Yet once the United States begins to use force, cooperation will be harder to come by—partly because of time's passage, but also because states that once proclaimed their solidarity will realize that America's use of military power creates immediate and long-range costs that they all fear.

President Bush faces a Hobson's choice. He must meet Americans' expectation that those responsible for September 11 be punished and convey to those planning more attacks that there is a price to be paid for killing innocent Americans. The multilateral cooperation he needs to combat terrorism on other fronts (sharing intelligence, closing off terrorists' funding) has been hard to arrange. It will be harder still to maintain now that military force is being applied, particularly if its use is seen to be unilateral.

THE KINGDOM IN THE MIDDLE

SAUDI ARABIA'S DOUBLE GAME

■

F. GREGORY GAUSE III

Of all the countries linked to the tragic events of September 11, few have played as central—or as complicated—a role as Saudi Arabia. After all, it is where Osama bin Laden was born and raised, and although his views may be extreme, he remains very much a product of its educational and cultural milieu. It was in Saudi Arabia, moreover—a country known for its official adherence to a particularly strict strain of Sunni Islam—that bin Laden recruited many of the henchmen who carried out the attacks on the United States.

And yet Saudi Arabia is also a longtime ally of the United States and a country that, shortly after the attacks, became the command center from which the American military coordinated some of its regional responses to the subsequent crisis. Saudi Arabia today is home to a large number of U.S. fighter aircraft and troops, and is the staging ground for U.S. air patrols over southern Iraq.

Saudi Arabia thus finds itself in a startlingly ambivalent role: the country is both a source, however indirect, of terror against the United States and a key American ally in the battle against that terror. Still other contradictions exist: the kingdom has long been a close American security partner, yet it has only reluctantly agreed to cooperate with Washington's military and political responses to the September 11 attacks. Saudi Arabia is the world's largest producer and exporter of oil and has played a major role in stabilizing oil markets in times of crisis, yet it has also worked hard over the past three years to double the price of that oil.

The country's ruling family, the House of Saud, has managed

these contradictions for decades and shows no sign of losing its grip on the country any time soon, despite the serious domestic political problems that plague it. Nonetheless, the events of September 11 have made the kingdom's balancing act even more delicate than it was before. Just as the current crisis has highlighted both the tensions and enduring interests in the Saudi relationship with the United States, so should it now force the kingdom's rulers to confront the contradictions in the society they govern—contradictions so dangerous they have already produced a number of citizens willing to immolate themselves in order to kill innocent Americans.

RESTRAINED RADICALS

Since the middle of the eighteenth century, when the rulers of a small emirate in central Arabia made a pact with a Muslim preacher and reformer named Muhammad ibn Abd al-Wahhab, the political fortunes of the Al Saud family have been tied to his austere and puritanical interpretation of Islam. Wahhabism, as it became known to its enemies (its adherents describe themselves as *muwahhidun*, believers in the absolute oneness of God), provided the ideological justification the House of Saud needed to extended its rule throughout Arabia, cutting across tribal and regional differences. The Wahhabi *ulama* (clergy) also helped staff the early Saudi state, acting as judges, tax collectors, and military recruiters for the regime. With the advent of oil wealth in the second half of the twentieth century, the role of the *ulama* expanded still further, and the clergy began to run new state-sponsored schools and universities, to staff newly expanded government bureaucracies (especially the ministries of Justice and Pilgrimage Affairs and the women's educational system), and to direct international nongovernmental organizations established to promote the spread of their brand of Islam.

Throughout the lifetime of this partnership, the *ulama* have remained extremely supportive of House of Saud rule, even when the country's oil wealth reduced the clerics' political importance by providing the Saudi rulers with a new means to attract the support, or buy the acquiescence, of their population. Wahhabism mandates obedience to one's Muslim rulers and offers little support to those who would seek to overturn the political order. The higher ranks of the *ulama* have regularly issued *fatwas* (religious judgments) condemning the Al Saud family's domestic enemies, ratifying transfers of power within the family, and supporting the rulers' policies—from the modernization of the 1950s and 1960s to the complicated foreign policy of the 1990s, which included the invitation of U.S. and other foreign forces into the kingdom in 1990, the attack on Iraq in 1991, and the subsequent Saudi participation in multilateral Arab-Israeli peace talks.

Official support from Wahhabi clerics, however, has not precluded serious challenges to the Saudi regime from emerging. In the late 1920s, the founder of the modern Saudi kingdom, Abdelaziz ibn Saud, had to rally loyal tribesmen and townspeople to put down a revolt among his Wahhabi shock troops. The rebels objected to the king's pragmatic declaration that the British mandates of Iraq and Transjordan were off limits to military attack; they advocated instead an unlimited *jihad* (holy war) to spread Wahhabi doctrine, a *jihad* that the king, anxious to avoid provoking the powerful British, was intent on avoiding.

Although that rebellion was ultimately crushed, the spirit of these religiously inspired rebels has continued to animate some in Saudi society. Such zealots have found both material and ideological sustenance on the fringes of the vast religious bureaucracies built by the Saudi government. Over the years, violent opposition has periodically flared up in the face of innovations such as women's education or the introduction of radio and television. In 1979, on the eve of the Muslim year 1400, a group of extremists took over the Grand Mosque in Mecca, the holiest site in Islam, calling for a general revolt and accusing the Al Saud family of abandoning the principles of Islam. It took three weeks for government forces, assisted by French special military units, to retake the Mosque.

THE ORIGINS OF A TERRORIST

It is from this tradition of religious-based rebellion, and not from more formal and politically quiescent mainstream Wahhabism, that bin Laden emerged. His life story is now well known to many observers, but it is useful to point out several facts. First, bin Laden is largely self-taught on religious matters. He did not attend any of the Islamic colleges in Saudi Arabia, but instead received a degree in public administration from one of the kingdom's "secular" (the term is relative in Saudi Arabia) universities.

Bin Laden's intense antipathy toward the United States and the Saudi regime, therefore, was not the result of any kind of Wahhabi indoctrination. Instead, it was the product, ironically, of the two greatest foreign policy successes to emerge from U.S.-Saudi cooperation: the Afghan battle against the Soviet Union and the Persian Gulf War. It was during the first conflict that bin Laden cut his teeth as a holy warrior, starting out as a financial contributor to the cause but then becoming a recruiter and organizer of volunteer Arab fighters and eventually becoming a fighter himself. The success of the Afghan *jihad*, seen by many of those involved as a literal miracle from God, convinced bin Laden that spiritual strength and an uncompromising commitment could bring down a superpower. The subsequent U.S. military deployment to the Persian Gulf in 1990 provided him with a new target by persuading him that, like the Soviets before them, the Americans were now intent on dominating the Muslim world—and that the Saudi regime had become complicit in this American plan.

The Gulf War also led to a brief expansion of political freedom in Saudi Arabia, one of the most closed countries in the world. Islamist activists, unhappy both with what they considered the regime's drift away from strict Islamic norms and its inability to protect the country without recourse to foreign, non-Muslim help, took advantage of this new freedom to press the government for political change. Bin Laden, fresh from his successes in Afghanistan, fell in with this spontaneous, grassroots movement. In 1992, more than a hundred Islamist activists sent a detailed,

46-page critique and policy program, known as the "Memorandum of Advice," to the Saudi regime. Although bin Laden did not sign the document, he has referred to it frequently in his writings as representing his agenda for political change in the kingdom.

Although the memorandum was sharply worded and highly critical of the Saudi government, it did not challenge the basic right of the Al Saud family to rule. It did, however, call for a more thorough Islamization of public life in the kingdom, accusing the government of allowing secular laws and practices to dominate politics and economics. It blasted the government for what its authors saw as a lack of commitment to Islamic causes in the country's foreign policy. And it questioned why Saudi Arabia, having spent billions of dollars on sophisticated weapons, had been forced to call on the United States to protect it after Iraq's invasion of Kuwait.

The year after the publication of the memorandum, a number of the regime's more strident critics left Saudi Arabia for London, where they established the Committee for the Defense of Legitimate Rights. This group, which began sending faxes attacking the government back to Saudi Arabia, soon attracted the attention of the Western news media. So, too, did the public demonstrations against the government that broke out in September 1994 in Burayda, a town in central Saudi Arabia known for its religious conservatism. Such levels of dissent had not been seen in the kingdom for decades, and they proved to be the last straw for the Saudi rulers, who had already begun warning their critics not to overstep their bounds. Islamist activists were arrested and the government established new committees to more closely monitor the religious bureaucracies, Islamic charities, and fund-raisers in the country.

As part of this general crackdown, in April 1994 bin Laden was stripped of his Saudi citizenship and passport. For three years, he had already been spending increasing amounts of time in Sudan, "encouraged" by Saudi authorities to absent himself from the kingdom. For its part, Sudan's Islamist government welcomed both the ideological fervor and the capital that bin Laden brought with him. In exchange for these contributions, Sudan provided bin Laden a base for his first efforts to organize military activities against the United States—specifically, against the U.S. campaign in Somalia in 1992–93.

The subsequent Saudi decision to formally expel bin Laden was probably triggered by his decision in early 1994 to follow the lead of other Saudi dissidents and set up an office in London. Bin Laden's Committee on Advice and Reform had, like the other dissident groups, issued a series of faxes commenting on Saudi politics. But bin Laden quickly became more radical in his language and more extreme in his stated goals. After the 1994 crackdown, bin Laden dropped what little restraint he had left. He accused the Saudi regime of declaring war on Islam and called on Saudi citizens to liberate their homeland. He openly linked what he saw as the ruling family's un-Islamic behavior to pressure from the United States and speculated that the Americans hoped to force Saudi Arabia to make peace with Israel.

Rather than calming the country, the Saudi crackdown made the Islamist opposition—bin Laden included—more violent. In November 1995, a car bomb exploded at the offices of a U.S. military training mission in Riyadh, killing six Americans and a number of third-country employees; in their televised confessions, the perpetrators admitted to having been influenced by bin Laden's ideas. In June 1996, a more powerful car bomb exploded outside the Khobar Towers apartment complex in Saudi Arabia's Eastern Province, killing 19 American soldiers who had been involved with the U.S. air patrols over southern Iraq and wounding hundreds of Americans and Saudis. It has never been established whether bin Laden was involved in this attack. The Clinton administration identified an Iranian connection, and there is no evidence that bin Laden and the Shi'a government of Iran have cooperated. (The 1998 U.S. indictment of bin Laden for the embassy bombings in East Africa accused him of "forging an alliance" with the government of Iran. But given the antipathy between Iran and bin Laden's Taliban allies in Afghanistan, it seems unlikely that such an alliance developed very far beyond the talking stage.)

Despite the uncertainty over his responsibility for the Khobar

Towers bombing, however, bin Laden's increasingly high profile in radical circles and the increasing violence in Saudi Arabia soon led Riyadh and Washington to pressure the Sudanese government to cut its ties with him. Bin Laden left Sudan, however, and reestablished his headquarters in Afghanistan. Shortly thereafter, in September 1996, he issued a *fatwa* against what he called the "Crusader-Zionist alliance" and the Al Saud family. Given his lack of formal religious training, the *fatwa* was an audacious presumption. In it, he called on Saudis and other Muslims to attack Americans in Saudi Arabia, the presence of whom he considered the most serious threat to Islam in the entire world. In February 1998, he followed this up by announcing the creation of the "International Islamic Front for *Jihad* against Jews and Crusaders," a union of his movement with like-minded Sunni radicals from Egypt, Pakistan, and Bangladesh. This was accompanied by another *fatwa*, which condemned the U.S. "occupation" of the Arabian Peninsula, the devastation inflicted on the Iraqi people by economic sanctions, and U.S. support for Israel, and called on Muslims everywhere to "kill the Americans and their allies, civilians and military . . . in any country in which it is possible to do it."

In August 1998, the U.S. embassies in Kenya and Tanzania were destroyed by car bombs, and bin Laden was indicted four months later for participating in these attacks. Neither the indictment nor the American missile strikes on his bases in Afghanistan and on a pharmaceutical plant in Sudan proved a deterrent, however. In December 1999, authorities in the United States and Jordan arrested confederates of bin Laden for planning explosions to coincide with millennium celebrations. In October 2000, still other affiliates of bin Laden's Al Qaeda organization attacked the U.S.S. *Cole*, an American destroyer, in the Yemeni port of Aden. And in June 2001, in response to reported threats from bin Laden, American forces in the Persian Gulf area were put on high alert, joint U.S.-Jordanian military exercises were cut short, and the U.S. Navy fleet in the Gulf left port. Three months later, this escalating sequence concluded with the attacks on the World Trade Center and the Pentagon.

Although expelling American troops from Saudi Arabia remained bin Laden's primary goal throughout this period, it is worth noting that he has not managed to attack any American personnel or assets in Saudi Arabia itself since at least 1996. This is probably because, after the bombings of that year, the Saudi government began aggressively breaking up networks of domestic opposition. By June 1999, Riyadh felt so confident about the success of this campaign that it released from prison Salman al-Awda and Safar al-Hawali—two of the major leaders of the Islamist agitation of the early 1990s. It would be a mistake, however, to assume that these internal security operations have eradicated sympathy for, or sympathizers with, bin Laden in the kingdom. As late as 1996, Riyadh rejected a Sudanese-American plan to turn bin Laden over to Saudi authorities for trial, fearing a domestic backlash. And the fact that bin Laden was able to recruit a number of Saudis into the September 11 operation strongly suggests that his message still resonates in some of the darker corners of the kingdom. On October 7, another bomb went off on a commercial street frequented by foreigners in Khobar, killing an American and a British citizen—yet another indication, perhaps, of bin Laden's ongoing appeal in the country.

CAUGHT IN THE MIDDLE

Saudi Arabia's reluctance to be publicly linked with any U.S. military action against Afghanistan must puzzle Americans who remember the kingdom's open alliance with the United States during the Gulf War. Bin Laden today is as much an enemy of the Saudi government as he is of Washington. Why the Saudi hesitation, then?

The answer is that in 1990, a hostile army marched all the way up to the Saudi border, having gobbled up one Arab monarchy in its path and seeming capable of doing the same thing to the Al Saud. Saddam Hussein posed a real and immediate threat to the stability of the royal family's rule—such a threat, in fact, that the Saudis were willing to run the risk of incurring a public-opinion backlash by inviting American forces into the kingdom.

The Saudi rulers view today's crisis in very different terms. Tough internal security policies have squelched the antigovernment and anti-American violence that threatened the kingdom in the mid-1990s. Although he remains popular in some circles, bin Laden has been isolated from Saudi society and seems unable to launch operations within the country. The Saudis would still like to see him disappear, of course, as quickly and as quietly as possible. But he no longer represents an immediate threat to the regime's security, certainly not in the way that Saddam Hussein did in 1990. And the attacks of September 11 have not changed this fact.

The current American military campaign against bin Laden, his infrastructure, and the Taliban therefore places the Saudis in a difficult position, for it raises the profile of bin Laden in Saudi Arabia and the rest of the Muslim world. As long as he evades punishment, bin Laden's popular support will grow, causing problems for those governments aligned with the United States. Only when bin Laden is brought to justice—or justice is brought to him—will his popular following begin to dwindle.

Another problem is that the U.S. military campaign in Afghanistan has implicated the Saudi regime, as an American ally, in an attack on a fellow Muslim country. Riyadh had soured on the Taliban even before it formally broke relations with Kabul after the September 11 attacks. The Saudi ambassador had been withdrawn years earlier. Afghanistan retains a positive place in the Saudi popular imagination, however, as a poor country that suffered greatly but, by staying true to its faith, liberated itself from superpower occupation. Although the United States continually emphasizes that its current battle is being fought against bin Laden and the Taliban—and not against Afghan society—many in Saudi Arabia and the Arab and Muslim world see it as simply another great power picking on Afghanistan.

Furthermore, the crisis could not have come at a worse time for the American public image in the Arab world. Two issues, both emphasized in bin Laden's recent propaganda, explain the recent erosion of the generally positive reputation with which the United States emerged from its victory in the Gulf War. The first is the Palestinian question. The resumption of Israeli-Palestinian violence in the fall of 2000 has had a profound impact on Arab public opinion. Important questions, such as why the peace process broke down and what responsibility Yasir Arafat bears for that breakdown, have been drowned out by broadcast images of Palestinians deaths. As a result, this crisis has once again become the central theme preoccupying and uniting Arab populations. And in this conflict, the United States, thanks to its close ties to Israel and the "hands-off" stance taken by the Bush administration in its first months in office, has been implicated in the Israeli military response.

This is not to say that the Palestinian conflict somehow caused the events of September 11. Nothing could be further from the truth. Bin Laden does not want a two-state solution to the Israeli-Palestinian conflict, or a more balanced U.S. policy toward Palestinians, or a more active U.S. diplomatic role in negotiations there. He wants Israel out of the Middle East, just as he wants the United States out of the Middle East. Had the Camp David summit between Arafat and Israeli prime minister Ehud Barak in the summer of 2000 succeeded, would bin Laden have called off the attacks? Of course not.

U.S. policy on the Palestinian issue is relevant, however, to the larger question of Arab public opinion, especially for those Arabs who would never use violence against the United States but who would like to see justice for the Palestinians. When the "Arab street" sees the United States as being opposed to the Palestinians, it makes it hard for moderate Arab governments to cooperate with Washington. The Bush administration recognizes these constraints and has tried to reassure Arab governments and citizens that, like the Clinton administration before it, it sees Palestinian statehood as the goal of the peace process. This may be too little too late, however; the 11 months of violence between Israelis and Palestinians that preceded the September attacks have soured the Arab public mood and made it very hard for countries like Saudi Arabia to support American military moves against Afghanistan wholeheartedly.

The second factor that has damaged the U.S. standing in the Arab world is Iraq. This is even the case in those countries that were the most threatened by Saddam Hussein in 1990. Washington has lost the propaganda war surrounding its economic sanctions on Saddam's regime, and this has had a damaging impact on the U.S. image in the region. The vast majority of Arabs view the sanctions as being aimed not at Baghdad's rulers, who have withstood them for ten years, but at Iraqi society. This perception holds true despite the changes that have been made to the sanctions policy to allow more food and consumer goods to get into the country, and despite the rising price of oil in the last few years, which has increased the money available for such supplies. The sanctions continue to strengthen many Arabs' belief that the United States opposes not just Arab dictators, but rather Arab and Muslim populations in general. And this belief has further constrained the ability of the Saudis and other Arab governments to publicly support the United States in its antiterror campaign.

And so the Saudi regime is forced to walk a tightrope. Riyadh needs Washington to guarantee its security, but it is unwilling to risk the domestic political problems that would come from being publicly associated with the U.S. military campaign in Afghanistan. Thus the Saudi government allows the United States to use bases in Saudi Arabia for logistical purposes, and does not look too closely at what those missions actually entail. At the same time, it assures its own public that it has forbidden the United States to use those bases for direct military strikes against Afghanistan. Riyadh has broken relations with the Taliban government and begun to cooperate with Washington's efforts to cut off financial resources to terrorist networks. But it assures Saudi citizens that it has extracted promises from Washington not to extend the military campaign to Arab states such as Iraq.

On only one issue, in fact, have the Saudis been unreservedly helpful to the United States since the crisis began: oil. As the world's largest petroleum producer, the Saudis dominate the Organization of Petroleum Exporting Countries (OPEC) and the world oil market. Oil prices have fallen precipitously since the September 11 attacks, as projections of recession in the United States and an economic slowdown worldwide have reduced expectations of future oil demand. In response, some OPEC members have called for production cuts to push the price of oil back up. The Saudis, however, have resisted those calls—so far. Nonetheless, oil could still become an irritant in Saudi-American relations in the near future. The United States will need to keep oil prices down if it hopes to regain its economic footing. The Saudis, with a growing population and serious strains on their budget, are likely to want oil prices—and thus, oil revenues—to rise. Washington and Riyadh should waste no time in struggling to balance these competing interests as soon as the immediate military campaign ends.

FRIENDS IN DEED?

Despite the drop in oil prices, Saudi Arabia remains a rich country, one that has managed surprisingly well to maintain political stability. But although Riyadh has succeed in controlling the many tensions in its relations with the United States for more than six decades, this does not mean that the regime's future is guaranteed. The kingdom built an extensive welfare state in the 1970s, when its population was very small and oil revenues seemed unlimited. Now oil revenues have become less bountiful. With one of the fastest-growing populations in the world, Saudi Arabia must somehow manage to find jobs for its people and maintain the high level of services that are now straining its infrastructure.

Crown Prince Abdallah, who exercises day-to-day control of the government in place of his brother, the ailing King Fahd, has made some tentative attempts to reform the Saudi economy. And recognizing the increasing level of education among many Saudis and a public desire to have a greater say in governance, in 1993 the regime established an appointed Consultative Council. Whether this modest innovation will defuse public dissatisfaction, however, remains uncertain. So, too, do plans for succession. The Al Saud family has grown exponentially over the years, and exactly what role the more than 5,000 Al Saud princes will play in the government and the economy remains difficult to predict, especially once the current generation of senior princes, the sons of ibn Saud, pass from the scene.

Washington can help Riyadh manage some of these vexing issues by prodding the Saudis to take the economic and political steps necessary to help ensure stability. Indeed, the United States cannot afford not to do this; the fact that Saudi Arabia sits on 25 percent of the world's known oil reserves, in a region that contains over 60 percent of those reserves, makes stability there a key U.S. interest.

Washington must move carefully, however. In the months since September 11, some have looked at the large number of Saudis involved in the attacks and concluded that the United States should respond by pushing the Saudi government to democratize. According to this logic, a more open political process would deflect opposition into institutionalized channels and reduce the appeal of terrorism. Heavy U.S. pressure in this direction could, however, have just the opposite effect. Were elections to be held today in Saudi Arabia, they would be won by candidates whose worldview is closer to that of Osama bin Laden than to that of Thomas Jefferson. Moreover, the kinds of economic change that Saudi Arabia needs will, in the short term, increase public dissatisfaction. The Saudi government, therefore, needs some time and political space to take the necessary hard economic steps.

Other observers have argued that Wahhabism is responsible not just for bin Laden but for political violence throughout the Muslim world. This is a superficial and specious argument, however. Wahhabism is no more responsible for bin Laden than fundamentalist Christianity is for Timothy McVeigh. Political violence in the Muslim world has much more to do with immediate political circumstances than with theological debates. Doctrinaire Wahhabis would never violently seek to overthrow their governments, since their creed forbids it; disorder in the Muslim community is considered more dangerous than unjust rulers. And for Washington to take a public stand against a particular school of Islamic interpretation would only feed the beliefs of those who already think that the United States is engaged in a general clash with Islamic civilization.

That being said, the Saudis do have some soul-searching to do, even if it cannot be imposed on them from outside. Official Wahhabism may not encourage antistate violence, but it is a particularly severe and intolerant interpretation of Islam. It encourages the view that even fellow Muslims who do not meet its strict standards should not be considered members of the community. This viewpoint is dangerously divisive. The Saudi elites should consider just what role such a severe doctrine and the vast religious infrastructure they have built around it played in bin Laden's rise. If some fine-tuning of doctrine would reduce the risk of extremist violence, they should have the courage to consider it before it's too late.

COMMANDEERING THE PALESTINIAN CAUSE
BIN LADEN'S BELATED CONCERN

■

SAMUEL R. BERGER AND MONA SUTPHEN

A French newspaper recently described President George W. Bush as "responsible" for the September 11 assault on the United States because he had turned his back on negotiations in the Middle East. One does not need to browse widely through the Middle Eastern press, or indeed read the comments of many of the region's leaders, to hear the argument that, in some fashion, the attacks on America were the cruel but somehow inevitable consequence of Muslim rage over unfulfilled Palestinian aspirations, U.S. support for Israel, and the failure of the peace process.

To truly understand the brutal attacks on the United States and the motivation of the attackers, however, it is important to untangle the Israeli-Palestinian conflict and other sources of anti-American sentiment in the region from the strategic objectives of Osama bin Laden and his operatives—and to distinguish sharply between the purpose he seeks to achieve and the grievances he seeks to exploit.

With theological roots in a rigid strain of Wahhabism, bred by a growing antipathy against the elite regimes that rule the states of the Arab world, and hardened by anti-imperialist fervor during the ten-year battle to repel the Soviet invasion of Afghanistan, bin Laden's *jihad* took shape with the deployment of troops to the Arabian Peninsula by the United States and its allies during the Persian Gulf War. "Occupying the lands of Islam in the holiest of places" is at the core of bin Laden's indictment against us. His vitriolic screeds have defined his purpose: imposition of his radical, fundamentalist vision in a Muslim domain stretching from Central Asia through the Persian Gulf and beyond, starting with the expulsion of the United States from the region.

Along the way, ideology crossed over into fanaticism—"the violent transformation of an irremediably sinful and unjust world," in the words of Harvard University professor Michael Ignatieff. If Saddam Hussein is a traditional pursuer of hegemony, seeking to assert his personal control over the region, bin Laden is an ideological one, seeking a radical Islamic revolution. In many ways, bin Laden's ultimate "twin towers" are Pakistan and Saudi Arabia, and the United States is as much his instrument as his object, as he seeks not only to harm our country grievously but also to provoke Washington into the kind of polarizing response that wraps us around the necks of those governments, pulls them down, and replaces them with revolutionary regimes.

So at the outset, one must separate bin Laden's agenda from the distinct but relevant identification of the sources of sympathy for him and resentment in the Arab and Muslim worlds. Indeed, until it served his larger purposes after the September 11 attacks, bin Laden had been no champion of the Palestinian cause, although conflict in the Middle East has allowed him to more easily coalesce a wide range of terrorist groups under the Al Qaeda umbrella. Nor is bin Laden's cause social equity; he is not some distorted reflection of the "anti-globalization" movement, although despair, inequity, and corruption provide him camouflage. If any evidence of this is needed, five million starving Afghans are poignant testimony to his passion for social justice.

Unquestionably, the cycle of violence in the Middle East over the past year, which from the Arab perspective is driven by Israel's occupation and its American-supplied power (without regard to Palestinian provocations), has provided resonance for bin Laden in the region. Moreover, America is a magnet for a range of frustrations—some derived from our power and some from our policies. But it is important to lay flatly to rest the notion that September 11 somehow is payback for American support of Israel or for the failure of American Middle East policy. The United States must make this point forcefully, even as it recognizes that the long-term strategy for destroying bin Laden and Al Qaeda requires the extremists be marginalized rather than glorified. To do so will, in part, involve defusing the Middle East conflict, providing security for Israel and dignity for the Palestinians. This goal is not likely to be achieved without active U.S. engagement.

Success in the peace process would not deflect bin Laden any more than the failure of the negotiations at Camp David in the summer of 2000 would have contributed to the September 11 terrorist attacks. Bin Laden's first efforts to target the United States—attacking U.S. troops in Yemen and Somalia in 1992 and 1993—came with the birth of the Israeli-Palestinian peace process in Oslo. His brutal assault on the U.S. embassies in Tanzania and Kenya in 1998 came well before the start of the *intifada* that has so roiled the waters in the region. Planning for the latest attacks appears to have been well under way by the time of Camp David and continued simultaneously with the quieter negotiations in the months that followed.

These plans were laid at a time when the outlines of a peace agreement could be seen that involved the return of at least 95 percent of the West Bank to the Palestinians, with further offsets from Israeli land; a Palestinian state with its capital in East Jerusalem; some form of divided sovereignty on the Temple Mount; and the opportunity for a decent life for Palestinian refugees, if not the right of return to Israel that they desired. Ultimately, there was no agreement, but these contours, advanced by the United States after eight years of intense effort, hardly reflect a lack of American sympathy to Palestinian aspirations. None of that was relevant to bin Laden's equation.

Indeed, a peaceful resolution of the Israeli-Palestinian conflict is inimical to bin Laden's interests and objectives. In many respects, the situation there is the last remaining unresolved question as to whether a state system within the Arab world will prevail or whether bin Laden's vision of a theocratic Islamist empire will gain ground. A Palestinian state, co-existing alongside Israel, would be a serious blow to bin Laden and Al Qaeda. Not only would it stabilize and solidify the Arab state system, it would demonstrate acceptance of pluralism in the region—a concept antithetical to bin Laden's interpretation of Islam.

Nor is it true that the failure of the Camp David negotiations created the *intifada* that has so changed the landscape of the region. If anything, the peace process in the Middle East was undercut because it went too slowly, not too fast. The promise of Oslo and the Interim Agreement of 1993 was the expectation that five years of self-rule and confidence-building would lay the groundwork for tackling the hard issue of a final peace. As that timeline slipped—a victim of Yitzhak Rabin's assassination, the terrorism of Hamas, a falling rather than rising standard of living for the Palestinian people, a loss of confidence among Israelis and Palestinians alike, a Palestinian Authority that did not prepare its people for peace or inspire the world with trust, and three years of Binyamin Netanyahu's government in Israel, which turned its back to the peace process—trust and momentum eroded. Frustration on both sides mounted.

Not long after Rabin's funeral, as the process slowed and hope on both sides became harder to sustain, President Bill Clinton reflected one evening that "Rabin's assassin knew exactly what he was doing." President Clinton called the sides to Camp David in the summer of 2000 because he and his advisers foresaw exactly what could happen if the opportunity for a breakthrough for peace was not seized. Indeed, violence already had broken out during the "days of rage" earlier in May. The future without peace was painfully clear: a deadly cycle of violence that would threaten Israel's future, devastate the Palestinian people, and radicalize the region in a way that now provides ideological sanctuary for bin Laden, just as the mountains of Afghanistan provide him physical sanctuary.

America's long-term strategy against terrorism must incorporate several elements if it is to marginalize the extremists in the Muslim world. First, we must dismantle and destroy the terror groups arrayed against us, and their support systems, using every tool at our disposal, including military force. In so doing, we must use that force in a way that isolates the extremists without isolating us. We must be unrelenting in our pursuit of an enemy that thinks it can outlast us; our staying power is as important as our firepower. And our actions must be justifiable to the world as destroying those who attack us and those who support them—

not less and not more. To sustain what will necessarily be a long-term effort, we must preserve international support, assistance, and stability, particularly among Afghanistan's neighbors. Our use of force must be strategic, intelligence-driven, and targeted, avoiding civilian casualties as much as possible. The terrible images of planes shattering buildings and lives on September 11 must remain etched in the world's consciousness. They should not be replaced with images that only confuse the distinction between perpetrator and victim.

Second, we must bring more of our diplomatic, political, intellectual, and economic energy to the Islamic world, with more knowledge and broader vision. This requires sustained, informed, and high-level engagement. We must lift the veil of ignorance that separates us from the diverse one-fourth of the world that is Muslim. Our own society provides an important resource: nearly ten million Muslim Americans, including millions of Arab Americans, can be a bridge, not a target.

Third, we must actively seek to reverse the spiral of violence in the Middle East by creating a political process that at least can offer breathing space for the Palestinians and the Israelis. Without such actions on our part, the conflict will continue to be a cauldron of bitterness that will drive the center of gravity in the region in a radical direction. We should be intransigent about terror in the region, but not intransigent in exploring ways to end the violence.

The challenge for both Israel and the Palestinians is to confront terrorism under the current circumstances. For Yasir Arafat, this means he cannot continue to use Hamas and Islamic Jihad to fight his political struggle, because doing so destroys his own moral and political credibility and that of the Palestinian Authority. For Israel, it means there are risks to categorically equating Arafat with Hamas and Islamic Jihad, because doing so legitimizes the very fundamentalists that must be marginalized in order to achieve peace.

The essential political dimension of the struggle against Al Qaeda and the extremists will not succeed over the long term if the leaders of the Arab world do not come to grips with their own weaknesses and vulnerabilities. For the most part, they have deferred the hard decisions on modernization and openness by deflecting popular disaffection in their own countries toward the United States and toward Israel. To survive, leaders in the region must create and present to their peoples a viable alternative to radicalism and repression: modern Islamic states that respect individual rights, fight corruption, and prove that modernization and Islam are not incompatible. Pluralism and development in the region are the enemies of extremism, not Islam.

With all of this, some level of anti-Americanism will persist. Our power, wealth, and culture make us an inevitable target for resentment, both related and unrelated to our policies. Our histories and circumstances are very different. But so long as the United States brings firmness, wisdom, and a broader vision to its efforts, it is not inevitable that our futures must diverge.

STRANGLING THE HYDRA

TARGETING AL QAEDA'S FINANCES

■

WILLIAM F. WECHSLER

Days after the devastating attack on the United States, the president addressed Americans still reeling from the violence. Speaking from the White House, he assured his fellow citizens that the U.S. response would not be limited to military retaliation or a law-enforcement investigation: Washington would also target the financial network that facilitated and supported the operations of Osama bin Laden's henchmen and terrorism more generally. "I have just signed an executive order directing the Treasury to block all financial transactions between the bin Laden terrorist group and American persons and companies," the president said. "It puts the financial world on notice: if you do business with terrorists, if you support or sponsor them, you will not do business with the United States of America."

Actually, it was two presidents who said that. The first half of the quote came from Bill Clinton and was uttered on August 22, 1998, shortly after the bombings of the U.S. embassies in Kenya and Tanzania. The second half was said by George W. Bush on September 24, 2001, following the strikes on the World Trade Center and the Pentagon. Two presidents, two terrorist attacks, two executive orders, two calls to target Al Qaeda's global financial network. And yet Al Qaeda still has all the money it needs to carry out its operations.

In the aftermath of both attacks, many in Congress and the news media argued that Washington could easily cripple the terrorists by shutting down Al Qaeda's financial network. That the United States had not already done so, they claimed, was evidence of official nonchalance, capitulation to the desires of the domestic banking lobby, or simple incompetence. But others argued the exact opposite, saying that the presidential threats had been public relations stunts; the measures described would be useless in the war against terrorism, since sophisticated criminals could hide dirty money easily and do so routinely despite extensive efforts to stop them.

Both of these arguments are wrong. The truth is that Clinton and Bush did the right thing when they targeted Al Qaeda's financial network, and their concern has already led to significant progress in the war on terrorism. It is a mistake, however, to think that such measures alone can produce a quick victory. Following the money is no substitute for a broader counterterrorism strategy involving complementary actions in the military, intelligence, diplomatic, and legal spheres. Continuing to target Al Qaeda's financial network remains vital, however, if Washington hopes to disrupt the terrorists in the short term, reduce their reach over the long term, and eventually take them down entirely.

MAKING MONEY

Osama bin Laden is unusual for a terrorist. He did not become famous by leading an army into battle, through personal acts of valor in combat, or by running a local terrorist cell. Instead, bin Laden's claim to fame was his ability to raise, manage, and move money for the Afghan armies that fought the invading Soviet troops in the 1980s. This fact is central to understanding the Al Qaeda organization today, for its Saudi leader still derives much of his authority and influence from the cash he controls.

When reporting on Al Qaeda's finances over the years, American journalists have generally focused on the $300 million that bin Laden is alleged to have inherited from his family's construction business. This assumes, however, that Al Qaeda's budget comes from bin Laden's personal checkbook. In fact, although his own money has undoubtedly been helpful to his cause, of far greater value has been the complex global financial network that he first helped develop to fund the Afghan *mujahideen*. Bin Laden carefully maintained this network when he returned to Saudi Arabia after the Soviet withdrawal, during his subsequent sojourn to Sudan, and after he decamped to Afghanistan. It was this money-raising and money-moving system, in fact, that helped him ingratiate himself with his new hosts, the Taliban. The shape of this financial network may have changed slightly over the years, but it remains essentially similar to the one that helped fund the *mujahideen* two decades ago.

Al Qaeda raises money in four basic ways. First are its legal businesses and investments. Bin Laden's assets in Sudan, for instance, have been well reported, and include a holding company, construction firms, agricultural businesses, investment firms, tanneries, and transportation companies. Honey exporters in Yemen associated with Al Qaeda have recently received attention from U.S. authorities. There has also long been speculation that Al Qaeda is involved in more extensive commerce and investments around the world, although evidence for this remains shaky. Some now speculate that bin Laden was involved with the massive short-selling of stocks in airlines, insurance, and reinsurance companies shortly before the September 11 attacks. Investigations of these claims are underway in Europe, Japan, and the United States. Although these allegations remain uncertain, if they are proved it will demonstrate that Al Qaeda possesses an extremely high (and previously unappreciated) degree of financial sophistication. Before September 11, most terrorism experts would have regarded the notion that Al Qaeda was capable of massive global stock manipulations as theoretically possible but highly improbable. But then again, they would have said the same about the notion that Al Qaeda could simultaneously hijack several commercial airliners and use them to destroy the World Trade Center.

The second way Al Qaeda makes money is through criminal schemes, both petty and grand. Afghanistan is the world's leading producer of opium, and virtually all of it comes from Taliban-controlled territory, despite the fact that the Taliban claim to oppose drug production on religious grounds. Given Al Qaeda's key role in financing the Taliban, there is reason to suspect that it, too, may be involved with drug smuggling. On a smaller scale, local

Al Qaeda cells also are taught to commit petty crimes to help support their operations. These activities include cigarette smuggling and financial fraud, and they are widespread despite the wealth of the organization as a whole.

Al Qaeda also solicits donations from rich Muslims who share its goals. Such donations were vital to the *mujahideen* in their war against the Soviets and remain an important source of income for Islamist extremists today. And the donors are surprisingly numerous. Conventional wisdom dictates that terrorists or their supporters are very poor and have no real options in life. But a significant percentage of terrorists and their backers in fact come from middle-class and wealthy families. Such is the case with bin Laden himself and many of the September 11 hijackers. Unfortunately, the identities of most of the wealthy donors remain a matter of mere speculation; this area requires further investigation.

The fourth and perhaps most important source of Al Qaeda's budget is the mass fund-raising it conducts through charitable and nongovernmental organizations. Raising money through such channels presents several advantages. First, millions of Muslims around the world with no sympathy for terrorism believe that donating money to charity is a basic requirement of their religion, and offer billions of dollars each year. Second, these funds are raised predominantly in cash—the easiest kind of transactions for criminals to conceal and the hardest for law enforcement and intelligence to trace. Third, since many of these charities are associated with Islam, they generally attract less oversight from regulatory authorities in predominately Muslim states. The religious nature of these charities also can make it easier for Al Qaeda to recruit individuals from within the charities to siphon off funds. Finally, since many of these charities operate openly around the world (and on the Internet), they offer excellent cover for transnational movements of terrorist personnel, material, and funds.

One should take care, however, to distinguish the various ways in which individual charitable and nongovernmental organizations relate to terrorists. Some charities are little more than fronts for terrorist fund-raising. People within these organizations, and most of those who give to them, know very well where the money they raise goes. The existence of these fronts does not mean, however, that everyone whose money goes to Al Qaeda knows that they are contributing to terrorism. Many legitimate charities have been infiltrated by Al Qaeda associates who then steal money that they direct to terrorism. Still other charities support both Al Qaeda and legitimate projects. Hamas and Hezbollah have demonstrated how advantageous it is for terrorist groups to offer social services to the poor and weak. Among other things, it makes fundraising much easier. The Irish Republican Army used the same model for decades to raise money in Boston and New York.

ON THE MOVE

Once Al Qaeda has raised the money, of course, it then needs to send it where it will be most useful. Al Qaeda maintains a decentralized, loose confederation of cells to which it sends cash for use as seed money—what some have called "venture capital" for entrepreneurial terrorists. Al Qaeda moves this money using four primary mechanisms, a diversification that explains bin Laden's remark to a Pakistani newspaper that the U.S. crackdown on his finances would "not make any difference" because "by the grace of God, al-Qaeda has more than three different alternative financial networks."

The first of these methods is basic cash smuggling. Such smuggling remains the simplest and, in many circumstances, still the best way to move dirty money. Moreover, most Middle Eastern economies are still much more cash-intensive than those of the United States, Europe, and other developed countries. Many law-abiding people in the Middle East routinely carry and use much more cash than Americans would ever dream of, even for purchases as large as automobiles. As a result, the large cash movements that signal criminal activity in the West are not nearly as likely to stand out in the Middle East.

Al Qaeda also uses the global banking system—especially underregulated banking havens—to hold and launder its money.

Such havens offer numerous advantages to terrorists: strict bank secrecy, poor customer identification, anonymous company incorporation, hidden trust formation, no supervision or examination of banks or their transactions, no reporting of suspicious activity, and little or no cooperation with foreign law enforcement. And such havens have proliferated in recent years as a by-product of globalization. Advances in technology have meant that many places around the globe that were previously too physically remote to participate in the international banking system can now use the Internet to provide financial services to anyone, anywhere, at any time—often in complete secrecy. Al Qaeda operatives are as "aware of the cracks inside the Western financial system as they are of the lines in their hands," bin Laden boasted in that same Pakistani newspaper interview, continuing, "these are the very flaws of the Western financial system that are become a noose for it."

In addition to such havens, Al Qaeda also uses the formal Islamic banking system. This is an entirely legitimate parallel system that was established for those who feel their religion prohibits them from being involved in the charging or payment of interest. There is nothing inherently wrong with this system. But due in part to its religious affiliation, this system generally includes even less regulation than Western banks.

Even if the formal Islamic banking system were highly regulated, Al Qaeda could always fall back on its fourth means of moving money: the *hawala* underground banking system. *Hawala*, the name of which comes from the Arabic word for "change" and the Hindi word meaning "in trust," is particularly valuable to Al Qaeda because it allows for cash transfers that leave little or no paper trail, involve no government regulation or oversight, and do not require the actual physical movement of banknotes across borders. Again, there is nothing inherently illegitimate or criminal about the *hawala* system; it originally developed to protect travelling merchants from bandits and has functioned in South Asia and the Middle East for centuries (a similar system exists among the Chinese diaspora). And in some remote areas *hawala* is the only banking system available; there are no Citibank branches in Jalalabad.

Moving money through the *hawala* system requires only a phone call, fax, or e-mail from one *hawaladar* to another. A client gives cash to an agent in, say, Pakistan, and asks that it be delivered to someone else in New York. The Pakistani *hawaladar* then calls a colleague in New York, who disburses the proper amount to the intended recipient. No actual wire transfers or contacts with formal banks are involved. The advantages of this system to terrorists are obvious. Pakistani bankers estimate that the *hawala* system brings between $2.5 billion and $3 billion into the country each year, compared to only $1 billion that enters through the formal banking system. Over one thousand *hawaladars* ply their trade in Pakistan, and although most *hawala* transactions represent small amounts, some individual deals have reportedly involved as much as $10 million.

WHAT HAS BEEN DONE?

The diversity of Al Qaeda's fund-raising sources and money-movement mechanisms has made it very difficult for the United States and its allies to shut them down. Moreover, even if they succeeded, financial measures could achieve only so much. Such actions will not, by themselves, strike a death blow to Al Qaeda.

Consider, by analogy, Washington's efforts to stop organized crime at home. Ever since Al Capone was sent to prison for tax evasion, U.S. law-enforcement officials have focused on attacking perpetrators' financial networks. Such efforts have succeeded in diminishing the power and influence of the Mafia in American society. But organized crime remains a problem, even in a nation with good law enforcement, strong regulation of the financial-services industry, and no shortage of political will to combat it.

After the 1998 bombings of the U.S. embassies in Kenya and Tanzania, the Clinton administration adopted a new strategy towards Al Qaeda's financial components, going beyond conventional law enforcement and trying to trace funds associated with specific terrorist acts. Washington has recognized that there are limits to what law-enforcement agencies can achieve, particularly in the near term. Moreover, policymakers often have legitimate reasons for not putting their primary focus on bringing a given individual to trial. The highest goal is to protect American lives, and tactical considerations must often give way if they impede larger strategic aims.

Washington therefore needed to learn how to temporarily disrupt and, whenever possible, permanently destroy key institutions that help Al Qaeda raise, hold, and move funds. This meant rounding up key people, shutting down front companies, and targeting the banks that provide laundering services and help transfer funds. It meant isolating Al Qaeda's holdings from the legitimate financial world, and forcing those who would donate money to terrorists to think twice before they do so.

Disruption has not always been as satisfying as destruction, but it has proved an appropriate short-term goal. Every time one of Al Qaeda's financial components is interfered with it forces the group to take time, money, and personnel to rebuild or replace it. This, in turn, delays it from pursuing individual terrorist acts. And over the long term, if combined with additional military, diplomatic, intelligence, and law-enforcement actions, such efforts can seriously weaken Al Qaeda's capability for mischief.

Some of the disruptive actions taken since 1998 have been covert and must remain so. But much has been, and can still be, done in the open. Shortly after the embassy bombings, for example, President Clinton signed executive orders invoking the International Emergency Economic Powers Act (IEEPA), first against bin Laden and Al Qaeda, and then against the Taliban. This move instantly blocked any bank accounts in the United States that were linked to these groups and made it a crime for any American to do business with them. It also allowed Washington to bring sanctions against businesses anywhere in the world that have dealings with operations that were later determined to be "controlled by" or "acting on behalf of" or "providing support for" Al Qaeda or the Taliban.

Many observers focus on the first provision and ask why more funds have not been frozen in the intervening years. Although U.S. investigators did turn up $255 million of Taliban-controlled assets in U.S. accounts, this was not the most important target of

Clinton's executive order. The second measure, which allowed Washington to threaten other actors with sanctions, has proved far more significant. This fact is not properly appreciated, even by many inside government. The second measure allows U.S. officials to approach foreign governments or institutions quietly, behind the scenes, and force them to make a decision: either help Washington track down terrorists' funds or risk being cut off entirely from the U.S. economy. Banks in the Middle East can be threatened with losing invaluable access to banks and other financial institutions in New York City. Important donors can be threatened with being cut off from the American marketplace.

This approach has at times worked well. In 1999, for instance, Washington was able to use this leverage to quietly pressure other governments to ban the flights of Ariana airlines, a key element in the network used to ferry terrorist money, materiel and personnel to and from Afghanistan. Later these sanctions were overtly internationalized through a U.N. Security Council resolution. And, by way of further illustration, in one unrelated but parallel case, a similar executive order allowed Washington to bring tremendous pressure to bear on a Cypriot bank used by the former Yugoslav president Slobodan Milosevic, eventually forcing it to cut off Milosevic financially and disclose key details of his financial dealings to the West.

U.S. actions against the Al Qaeda financial network should continue to follow a similar, quiet approach. But other, higher-profile measures have been helpful as well, such as President George W. Bush's open condemnation of Muslim charities linked to bin Laden—including one that, until recently, included Pakistani President Musharraf on its board. The recent public action to impose sanctions on a specific Pakistani *hawaladar* and a wealthy, well-connected Saudi businessman are also important steps that send the right signal throughout the region.

The Clinton administration also recognized that even as it took specific measures against bin Laden and his allies, it also had to change the environment that facilitated the movement of terrorist finances. The United States and its allies in the G-7 group of highly industrialized countries began working to limit the proliferation of unregulated banks worldwide. Three multilateral organizations were charged with investigating three different but related aspects of this problem. The Financial Stability Forum—a group of important national finance ministries, central banks, and international banking organizations—was charged with investigating how underregulated offshore centers contribute to global macroeconomic instability. The Organization for Economic Cooperation and Development, a group of developed countries, started investigating how underregulated financial centers facilitate global tax evasion. And the Financial Action Task Force, the forum that sets international standards to fight money laundering, was asked to identify countries and territories that are "non-cooperative with the global fight against money laundering."

All three organizations successfully completed their work in 2000 and released reports to "name and shame" those countries that were the worst offenders. As hoped, this reporting sparked a market reaction. Some of the targeted countries were told they could no longer issue bonds on favorable terms; some of their banks saw their relationships with banks in New York, London, and other centers of finance eliminated; and some institutions saw their Standard & Poor's rating drop. The reactions to these measures were swift. After denying for years that there was any problem at all, a great number of the "named and shamed" countries suddenly decided to completely rewrite their banking laws and regulations. Other countries, particularly some in the Middle East, saw what had happened to their neighbors and started to change their own laws preemptively.

BARRIERS TO SUCCESS

Notwithstanding these accomplishments, however, the United States has managed only limited and incremental success in the fight to shut down the Al Qaeda financial network. This is due partly to the difficulties inherent in targeting such a diverse and diffuse terrorist organization. But there have been other reasons as well.

Most important, Washington has often been stymied by a lack of political will on the part of key states in the Middle East and South Asia. American accusations have been met with denials and American requests for cooperation have been met with delays. Sometimes it seemed as if certain governments feared Al Qaeda's terrorists less than they feared public revelations of their citizens' complicity in financing them.

Even some governments that wanted to help had trouble doing so because of loopholes and weaknesses in their own laws. Most countries in the Middle East and South Asia have few or no effective regulations to combat money laundering. Many of their banks evade examinations for years at a time. Some have strict secrecy rules and "see-no-evil" financial cultures. And most of these countries do not routinely audit their charities.

For its part, the United States has had its own problems. Too many American diplomats are unfamiliar with financial and banking issues, a deficiency that obviously limits their ability to help combat international criminal and terrorist financial networks. Few intelligence officials who understand the nuances of the global banking system are also fluent in Arabic. The Central Intelligence Agency has done a reasonably good job at analysis but a poor job at developing human intelligence within Al Qaeda's financial network. Moreover, despite the tripling of the Federal Bureau of Investigation's counterterrorism budget during the Clinton administration, there remained some subjects that law enforcement did not investigate fully, such as Web sites that solicit funds for terrorists, and other matters that were barely investigated at all, such as the *hawala* network that still operates in the United States.

Another difficulty is achieving interagency coordination. Targeting Al Qaeda's financial network requires the active cooperation of a great number of diverse federal departments and agencies, each with different goals and perspectives. The law enforcement, intelligence, diplomatic, and regulatory agencies all must work together. Yet, quite often, bureaucrats within these organizations find it difficult to cooperate among themselves, much less with others.

Even when agencies have managed to work effectively they

have sometimes found themselves hamstrung by inadequacies in American laws and regulations. Despite a great amount of effort at the end of the Clinton administration, key federal measures to combat money laundering, which have long been applied to the banking industry, have still not been extended to nondepository institutions. Unlike in Europe, American securities brokers, casinos, insurance companies, wire transmitters, and other money services are not now widely required to report suspicious activities.

U.S. officials have also confronted inadequacies in the legal authorities that underlie U.S. international initiatives. In some cases, IEEPA authority was too blunt an instrument, its sanctions too sweeping. There are times when it would be more effective to raise the penalty for noncooperation in a more incremental fashion, such as by imposing new information-sharing requirements if foreign banks are to be allowed to do business with U.S. institutions. In still other cases, the IEEPA has proven too feeble. Washington does not have a free hand to impose sanctions if foreign governments ignore U.S. threats. Quite often U.S. government lawyers have raised legitimate but frustrating barriers against designating a foreign bank or company under IEEPA, for fear of having to defend the government against anticipated lawsuits—for example, when the intelligence community must act on information that is compelling but fails to meet the standard of proof that would be required in a U.S. court. At other times Washington has had sufficient evidence but has been unable to risk exposing that evidence, and thus possibly endangering a valuable intelligence source, in open court.

THE WORK THAT REMAINS

In the wake of the September 11 terrorist attacks, the international political environment has changed markedly. Many predominantly Arab and Muslim states are now much more willing to cooperate with U.S. counterterrorism efforts. This new consensus will not last, however; Washington has a rare window of opportunity in which to make progress against Al Qaeda's financial network, but it may soon start to close.

President Bush's initial step of once again invoking IEEPA was the right one. It clearly indicated that his administration has adopted its predecessor's strategy of moving beyond law enforcement in targeting Al Qaeda's money channels. Meanwhile, Bush also took two additional steps that bear noting. His executive order put additional focus on charities, a good step that should be followed up. The language of the executive order also called for measures against those whom Bush referred to as "associates" of Al Qaeda, an intentionally vague standard that should strengthen U.S. leverage.

Bush should now take full advantage of this additional power to demand that key Muslim countries—particularly Saudi Arabia, Egypt, Pakistan, the United Arab Emirates, and all generally friendly nations along the Persian Gulf—fully cooperate with U.S. efforts to crack down on the Al Qaeda network, no matter where the money trail leads. This is not a subject that can be left to subordinates in the national security community or to Treasury Secretary Paul O'Neill. Despite their brave rhetoric, many of the countries in question will find it hard to take the necessary steps to combat terrorist financing. But without them, U.S. efforts to combat Al Qaeda will continue to be only marginally effective.

More generally, the United States and its European allies should urge moderate Muslim states to bring their anti-money-laundering regimes up to international standards and fully audit their domestic charitable organizations, using outside auditors if necessary. This may require a change in policy for the Bush administration, since one of O'Neill's first decisions in office was to greatly undermine existing multilateral efforts against underregulated, noncooperating jurisdictions that facilitate tax evasion. But it would be a reversal well worth making.

The United States should also unilaterally identify and disrupt the activities of individual foreign banks that are found to be safe havens for terrorist funds. This might be done covertly through information warfare, by hacking into banks' computers and disrupting their operations. Or it might be done overtly if the administration can, using Bush's executive order, get enough publicly releasable information to show that a specific foreign bank is indeed moving money for Al Qaeda.

The U.S. government needs new powers to more easily and effectively cut rogue banks off from the legitimate international financial system. The United States must be able to approach suspected foreign rogue banks—again, often quietly, behind the scenes—and threaten them with sanctions not because a direct connection to Al Qaeda can be openly proved, but on the basis of general concerns that the bank has become a money-laundering haven. This could mean that the bank has no internal compliance system, that it has a pattern of illegal activities, or that it operates under strict secrecy.

In 2000 a bipartisan bill that would have granted these powers to the U.S. government was put forward by the Clinton administration. Unfortunately, even after being passed overwhelmingly by the House Banking Committee, it was killed in the Senate without a vote by Senator Phil Gramm, then the chairman of the Senate Banking Committee. Fortunately, the bill has once again been taken up and, in the new political environment, is likely to be passed soon. Officials in the Treasury Department as well as in the diplomatic and intelligence communities should begin work now to identify which specific foreign banks will be approached immediately after this measure becomes law.

Finally, the Bush administration and Congress should also make all efforts to prevent terrorist fund-raising within U.S. borders. Attorney General John Ashcroft has made a series of useful legislative proposals to help law enforcement better target money laundering in general and terrorist financing in particular. These proposals also appear likely to be passed by Congress.

The Treasury Department and bank regulators should also give U.S. financial institutions specific guidance on how to identify suspicious transactions. And all domestic financial institutions should finally be brought under anti-money-laundering laws and regulations, including the American *hawala* system. This again may require a change in policy for the Bush administration. Unfortunately, prior to September 11, O'Neill and White House economic adviser Lawrence Lindsey spent a lot of time publicly questioning many fundamental elements of the U.S. anti-money-laundering regime. O'Neill started the year by diverting regulatory resources to begin a "cost-benefit" analysis of these regulations. Since September 11, however, his rhetoric has changed. It seems now that he is beginning to recognize that any assessments of the costs have to focus not on the relatively insignificant, internationally accepted, and long-standing regulatory requirements on banks, but on the devastating effects of terrorism and other crimes and the financial networks that support them.

Even if all of these steps are taken, the road ahead remains a long one. Accounts must be blocked, charities will shut down, and banks will have their business disrupted. Some of this will occur with loud public fanfare, some with only quiet congratulations among intelligence officials. But Al Qaeda's financial network will survive and adapt, at least in the short term. Over a longer period, as the network is further isolated from the legitimate banking system, as key cells are taken down for good, as risk-averse donors start to find alternative ways to further their political causes, as the governments of the Middle East and South Asia bring their money-laundering rules up to international standards, and as the *hawala* system is brought above ground, the Al Qaeda financial network should be reduced to a shadow of what it is today. Such a victory may well be a quiet one, unheralded by any ticker-tape parade. But it will be a victory nonetheless.

INTELLIGENCE TEST

THE LIMITS OF PREVENTION

■

RICHARD K. BETTS

As the dust from the attacks on the World Trade Center and the Pentagon was still settling, the chants began: The CIA was asleep at the switch! The intelligence system is broken! Reorganize top to bottom! The biggest intelligence system in the world, spending upward of $30 billion a year, could not prevent a group of fanatics from carrying out devastating terrorist attacks. Drastic change must be overdue. The new conventional wisdom was typified by Tim Weiner, writing in *The New York Times* on October 7: "What will the nation's intelligence services have to change to fight this war? The short answer is: almost everything."

Yes and no. A lot can, must, and will be done to shore up U.S. intelligence collection and analysis. Reforms that should have been made long ago will now go through. New ideas will get more attention and good ones will be adopted more readily than in normal times. There is no shortage of proposals and initiatives to shake the system up. There is, however, a shortage of perspective on the limitations of improved performance that we can expect. Some of the changes will substitute new problems for old ones. The only thing worse than business as usual would be naive assumptions about what reform can accomplish.

Paradoxically, the news is worse than the angriest critics think, because the intelligence community has worked much better than they assume. Contrary to the image left by the destruction of September 11, U.S. intelligence and associated services have generally done very well at protecting the country. In the aftermath of a catastrophe, great successes in thwarting previous terrorist attacks are too easily forgotten—successes such as the foiling of plots to bomb New York City's Lincoln and Holland tunnels in 1993, to bring down eleven American airliners in Asia in 1995, to mount attacks on the West Coast and in Jordan around the millennium, and to strike U.S. forces in the Middle East in the summer of 2001.

The awful truth is that even the best intelligence systems will have big failures. The terrorists that intelligence must uncover and track are not inert objects; they are living, conniving strategists. They, too, fail frequently and are sometimes caught before they can strike. But once in a while they will inevitably get through. Counterterrorism is a competitive game. Even Barry Bonds could be struck out at times by a minor-league pitcher, but when a strikeout means people die, a batting average of less than 1.000 looks very bad indeed.

It will be some time before the real story of the September 11 intelligence failure is known, and longer still before a reliable public account is available. Rather than recap the rumors and fragmentary evidence of exactly what intelligence did and did not do before September 11, at this point it is more appropriate to focus on the merits of proposals for reform and the larger question about what intelligence agencies can reasonably be expected to accomplish.

SPEND A LOT TO GET A LITTLE

One way to improve intelligence is to raise the overall level of effort by throwing money at the problem. This means accepting additional waste, but that price is paid more easily in wartime than in peacetime. Unfortunately, although there have certainly been misallocations of effort in the past, there are no silver bullets that were left unused before September 11, no crucial area of intelligence that was neglected altogether and that a few well-targeted investments can conquer. There is no evidence, at least in public, that more spending on any particular program would have averted the September 11 attacks. The group that carried them out had formidable operational security, and the most critical deficiencies making their success possible were in airport security and in legal limitations on domestic surveillance. There are nevertheless several areas in which intelligence can be improved, areas where previous efforts were extensive but spread too thinly or slowed down too much.

It will take large investments to make even marginal reductions in the probability of future disasters. Marginal improvements, however, can spell the difference between success and failure in some individual cases. If effective intelligence collection increases by only five percent a year, but the critical warning indicator of an attack turns up in that five percent, gaining a little information would yield a lot of protection. Streamlining intelligence operations and collection is a nice idea in principle but risky unless it is clear what is not needed. When threats are numerous and complex, it is easier to know what additional capabilities we want than to know what we can safely cut.

After the Cold War, intelligence resources went down as requirements went up (since the country faced a new set of high-priority issues and regions). At the end of the 1990s there was an uptick in the intelligence budget, but the system was still spread thinner over its targets than it had been when focused on the Soviet Union. Three weeks before September 11, the director of central intelligence (DCI), George Tenet, gave an interview to *Signal* magazine that now seems tragically prescient. He agonized about the prospect of a catastrophic intelligence failure: "Then the country will want to know why we didn't make those investments; why we didn't pay the price; why we didn't develop the capability."

The sluice gates for intelligence spending will open for a while. The challenge is not buying some essential element of capability that was ignored before but helping the system do more of everything and do it better. That will increase the odds that bits and pieces of critical information will be acquired and noticed rather than falling through the sieve.

Another way to improve intelligence is to do better at collecting important information. Here, what can be improved easily will help marginally, whereas what could help more than marginally cannot be improved easily. The National Security Agency (NSA), the National Imagery and Mapping Agency (NIMA), and associated organizations can increase "technical" collection—satellite and aerial reconnaissance, signals intelligence, communications monitoring—by buying more platforms, devices, and personnel to exploit them. But increasing useful human intelligence, which everyone agrees is the most critical ingredient for rooting out secretive terrorist groups, is not done easily or through quick infusions of money.

Technical collection is invaluable and has undoubtedly figured in previous counterterrorist successes in ways that are not publicized. But obtaining this kind of information has been getting harder. For one thing, so much has been revealed over the years about U.S. technical collection capabilities that the targets now understand better what they have to evade. State sponsors of terrorism may know satellite overflight schedules and arrange activities that might be observable accordingly. They can utilize more fiber-optic communications, which are much harder to tap than transmissions over the airwaves. Competent terrorists know not to use cell phones for sensitive messages, and even small groups have access to impressive new encryption technologies.

Human intelligence is key because the essence of the terrorist threat is the capacity to conspire. The best way to intercept attacks is to penetrate the organizations, learn their plans, and identify perpetrators so they can be taken out of action. Better human intelligence means bolstering the CIA's Directorate of Operations (DO), the main traditional espionage organization of the U.S. government. The DO has been troubled and periodically disrupted ever since the evaporation of the Cold War consensus in the late stage of the Vietnam War provoked more oversight and criticism than spies find congenial. Personnel turnover, tattered esprit, and a growing culture of risk aversion have constrained the DO's effectiveness.

Some of the constraint was a reasonable price to pay to prevent excesses, especially in a post–Cold War world in which the DO was working for the country's interests rather than its survival. After the recent attacks, however, worries about excesses have receded, and measures will be found to make it easier for the clandestine service to operate. One simple reform, for example, would be to implement a recommendation made by the National Commission on Terrorism a year and a half ago: roll back the additional layer of cumbersome procedures instituted in 1995 for gaining approval to employ agents with "unsavory" records— procedures that have had a chilling effect on recruitment of the thugs appropriate for penetrating terrorist units.

Building up human intelligence networks worldwide is a long-term project. It inevitably spawns concern about waste (many such networks will never produce anything useful), deception (human sources are widely distrusted), and complicity with murderous characters (such as the Guatemalan officer who prompted the 1995 change in recruitment guidelines). These are prices that can be borne politically in the present atmosphere of crisis. If the crisis abates, however, commitment to the long-term project could falter.

More and better spies will help, but no one should expect breakthroughs if we get them. It is close to impossible to penetrate small, disciplined, alien organizations like Osama bin Laden's Al Qaeda, and especially hard to find reliable U.S. citizens who have even a remote chance of trying. Thus we usually rely on foreign agents of uncertain reliability. Despite our huge and educated population, the base of Americans on which to draw is small: there are very few genuinely bilingual, bicultural Americans capable of operating like natives in exotic reaches of the Middle East, Central and South Asia, or other places that shelter the bin Ladens of the world.

For similar reasons there have been limitations on our capacity to translate information that does get collected. The need is not just for people who have studied Arabic, Pashto, Urdu, or Farsi, but for those who are truly fluent in those languages, and fluent in obscure dialects of them. Should U.S. intelligence trust recent, poorly educated immigrants for these jobs if they involve highly sensitive intercepts? How much will it matter if there are errors in translation, or willful mistranslations, that cannot be caught because there are no resources to cross-check the translators?

Money can certainly help here, by paying more for better translators and, over the long term, promoting educational programs to broaden the base of recruits. For certain critical regions of the world, however, there are simply not enough potential recruits waiting in the wings to respond to a crash program.

SHARPENED ANALYSIS

Money can buy additional competent people to analyze collected information more readily than it can buy spies who can pass for members of the Taliban—especially if multiplying job slots is accompanied by enhanced opportunities for career development within intelligence agencies to make long service attractive for analysts. Pumping up the ranks of analysts can make a difference within the relatively short time span of a few years. The U.S. intelligence community has hundreds of analysts, but also hundreds of countries and issues to cover. On many subjects the coverage is now only one analyst deep—and when that one goes on vacation, or quits, the account may be handled out of the back pocket of a specialist on something else. We usually do not know in advance which of the numerous low-priority accounts might turn into the highest priority overnight (for example, Korea before June 1950, or Afghanistan before the Soviet invasion).

Hiring more analysts will be a good use of resources, but there could turn out to be a low payoff, and perhaps none at all, for much of what they do. Having half a dozen analysts on hand for some small country might be a good thing if that country turns out to be central to the campaign against terrorists, but those analysts need to be in place before we know we need them if they are to hit the ground running in a crisis. In most such cases, moreover, those analysts would serve their whole careers without producing anything that the U.S. government really needs, and no good analyst wants to be buried in an inactive account with peripheral significance.

One option is to make better use of an intelligence analyst reserve corps: people with other jobs who come in to read up on their accounts a couple of days each month to maintain currency, and who can be mobilized if a crisis involving their area erupts. There have been experiments with this system, but apparently without enough satisfaction to institutionalize it more broadly.

Of course, the quantity of analysts is less important than the quality of what they produce. Postmortems of intelligence failures usually reveal that very bright analysts failed to predict the disaster in question, despite their great knowledge of the situation, or that they had warned that an eruption could happen but without any idea of when. In fact, expertise can get in the way of anticipating a radical departure from the norm, because the depth of expert knowledge about why and how things have gone as they have day after day for years naturally inclines the analyst to estimate that developments will continue along the same trajectory. It is always a safer bet to predict that the situation tomorrow will be like it has been for the past dozen years than to say that it will change abruptly. And of course, in the vast majority of cases predictions of continuity are absolutely correct; the trick is to figure out which case will be the exception to a powerful rule.

A standard recommendation for reform—one made regularly by people discovering these problems for the first time—is to encourage "out of the box" analyses that challenge conventional wisdom and consider scenarios that appear low in probability but high in consequence. To some, this sort of intellectual shake-up might well have led the intelligence system, rather than Tom Clancy, to anticipate the kamikaze hijacking tactic of September 11.

All well and good. The problem, however, lies in figuring out what to do with the work this great analysis produces. There are always three dozen equally plausible dangers that are possible but improbable. Why should policymakers focus on any particular one of these hypothetical warnings or pay the costs of taking preventive action against all of them? One answer is to use such analysis to identify potential high-danger scenarios for which low-cost fixes are available. If President Bill Clinton had gotten a paper two years before September 11 that outlined the scenario for what ultimately happened, he probably would not have considered its probability high enough to warrant revolutionizing airport security, given all the obstacles: vested interests, opposition to particular measures, hassles for the traveling public. He might, however, have pushed for measures to allow checking the rosters of flight schools and investigating students who seemed uninterested in takeoffs and landings.

Another problem frequently noted is that the analytical corps has become fully absorbed in current intelligence, leaving no time for long-term research projects that look beyond the horizon. This, too, is something that more resources can solve. But as good a thing as more long-range analysis is, it is uncertain how productive it will be for the war on terrorism. The comparative advantage of the intelligence community over outside analysts is in bringing together secret information with knowledge from open sources. The more far-seeing a project, the less likely secret information is to play a role in the assessment. No one can match the analysts from the CIA, the Defense Intelligence Agency (DIA), or the NSA in estimating bin Laden's next moves, but it is not clear they have a comparative advantage over Middle East experts in think tanks or universities when it comes to estimating worldwide trends in radical Islamist movements over the next decade. Such long-term research is an area where better use of outside consultants and improved exploitation of academia could help most.

THE WAR AT HOME

There is a world of difference between collecting intelligence abroad and doing so at home. Abroad, intelligence operations may break the laws of the countries in which they are undertaken. All domestic intelligence operations, however, must conform to U.S. law. The CIA can bribe foreign officials, burglarize offices of foreign political parties, bug defense ministries, tap the phones of diplomats, and do all sorts of things to gather information that the FBI could not do within the United States without getting a warrant from a court. Collection inside the United States is the area where loosened constraints would have done most to avert the September 11 attacks. But it is also the area in which great changes may make Americans fear that the costs exceed the benefits—indeed, that if civil liberties are compromised, "the terrorists will have won."

A Minnesota flight school reportedly alerted authorities a month before September 11 that one of its students, Zacarias Moussaoui, was learning to fly large jets but did not care about learning to take off or land. Moussaoui was arrested on immigration charges, and French intelligence warned U.S. officials that he was an extremist. FBI headquarters nevertheless decided against seeking a warrant for a wiretap or a search, reportedly because of complaints by the chief judge of the Foreign Intelligence Surveillance Court about other applications for wiretaps. After September 11, a search of Moussaoui's computer revealed that he had collected information about crop-dusting aircraft—a potential delivery system for chemical or biological weapons. U.S. officials came to suspect that Moussaoui was supposed to have been the missing fifth hijacker on United Airlines flight 93, which went down in Pennsylvania.

In hindsight, the hesitation to mount aggressive surveillance and searches in this case—hesitation linked to a highly developed set of legal safeguards rooted in the traditional American reverence for privacy—is exactly the sort of constraint that should have been loosened. High standards for protecting privacy are like strictures against risking collateral damage in combat operations: those norms take precedence more easily when the security interests at stake are not matters of your country's survival, but become harder to justify when they are.

There have already been moves to facilitate more extensive clandestine surveillance, as well as reactions against going too far. There will be substantial loosening of restraint on domestic intelligence collection, but how far it goes depends on the frequency and intensity of future terror attacks inside the United States. If there are no more that seem as serious as those of September 11, compromises of privacy will be limited. If there are two or three more dramatic attacks, all constraint may be swept away.

It is important to distinguish between two types of constraints on civil liberties. One is political censorship, such as the suppression of dissent in World War I. There is no need or justification for this; counterterrorism does not benefit from suppression of free speech. The other type involves compromises of individual privacy, through secret surveillance, monitoring of communications, and searches. This is where pressing up to the constitutional limits offers the biggest payoff for counterterrorist intelligence. It also need not threaten individuals unnecessarily, so long as careful measures are institutionalized to keep secret the irrelevant but embarrassing information that may inadvertently be acquired as a by-product of monitoring. Similarly, popular but unpersuasive arguments have been advanced against the sort of national identification card common in other democratic countries. The U.S. Constitution does not confer the right to be unidentified to the government.

Even slightly more intrusive information-gathering will be controversial, but if it helps to avert future attacks, it will head off far more draconian blows against civil liberties. Moreover, Americans should remember that many solid, humane democracies—the United Kingdom, France, and others—have far more permissive rules for gathering information on people than Americans have had, and their citizens seem to live with these rules without great unease.

RED TAPE AND REORGANIZATION

In a bureaucracy, reform means reorganization; reorganization means changing relationships of authority; and that means altering checks and balances. Five days after September 11, Tenet issued a directive that subsequently leaked to the press. In it he proclaimed the wartime imperative to end business as usual, to cut through red tape and "give people the authority to do things they might not ordinarily be allowed to do. . . . If there is some bureaucratic hurdle, leap it. . . . We don't have time to have meetings about how to fix problems, just fix them." That refreshing activism will help push through needed changes. Some major reorganization of the intelligence community is inevitable. That was the response to Pearl Harbor, and even before the recent attacks many thought a major shake-up was overdue.

The current crisis presents the opportunity to override entrenched and outdated interests, to crack heads and force the sorts of consolidation and cooperation that have been inhibited by bureaucratic constipation. On balance, reorganization will help—but at a price: mistakes will increase, too. As Herbert Kaufman revealed in his classic 1977 book *Red Tape*, most administrative obstacles to efficiency do not come from mindless obstructionism. The sluggish procedures that frustrate one set of purposes have usually been instituted to safeguard other valid purposes. Red tape is the warp and woof of checks and balances. More muscular management will help some objectives and hurt others.

The crying need for intelligence reorganization is no recent discovery. It is a perennial lament, amplified every time intelligence stumbles. The community has undergone several major reorganizations and innumerable lesser ones over the past half-century. No one ever stays satisfied with reorganization because it never seems to do the trick—if the trick is to prevent intelligence failure. There is little reason to believe, therefore, that the next reform will do much better than previous ones.

Reorganizations usually prove to be three steps forward and two back, because the intelligence establishment is so vast and complex that the net impact of reshuffling may be indiscernible. After September 11, some observers complained that the intelligence community is too regionally oriented and should be organized more in terms of functional issues. Yet back in the 1980s, when William Casey became President Ronald Reagan's DCI and encountered the functional organization of the CIA's analytical directorate, he experienced the reverse frustration. Rather than deal with functional offices of economic, political, and strategic research, each with regional subunits, he shifted the structure to one of regional units with functional subunits. Perhaps it helped, but there is little evidence that it produced consistent improvement in analytical products. There is just as little evidence that moving back in the other direction will help any more.

What about a better fusion center for intelligence on counterterrorism, now touted by many as a vital reform? For years the DCI has had a Counter-Terrorism Center (CTC) that brings together assets from the CIA's directorates of operations and intelligence, the FBI, the DIA, the State Department, and other parts of the community. It has been widely criticized, but many believe its deficiencies came from insufficient resources—something reorganization alone will not cure. If the CTC's deficiencies were truly organizational, moreover, there is little reason to believe that a new fusion center would not simply replace those problems with different ones.

Some believe, finally, that the problem is the sheer complexity and bulk of the intelligence community; they call for it to be streamlined, turned into a leaner and meaner corps. Few such proposals specify what functions can be dispensed with in order to thin out the ranks, however. In truth, bureaucratization is both the U.S. intelligence community's great weakness and its great strength. The weakness is obvious, as in any large bureaucracy: various forms of sclerosis, inertia, pettiness, and paralysis drive out many vibrant people and deaden many who remain. The strength, however, is taken for granted: a coverage of issues that is impressively broad and sometimes deep. Bureaucratization makes it hard to extract the right information efficiently from the gobs of it lying around in the system, but in a leaner and meaner system there will never be much lying around.

Some areas can certainly benefit from reorganization. One is the integration of information technologies, management systems, and information sharing. Much has been done within the intelligence community to exploit the potential of information technology in recent years, but it has been such a fast-developing sector of society and the economy in general that constant adaptation may be necessary for some time.

Another area of potential reorganization involves making the DCI's authority commensurate with his or her responsibility. This is a long-standing source of tension, because roughly 80 percent of the intelligence establishment (in terms of functions and resources) has always been located in the Defense Department, where primary lines of authority and loyalty run to the military services and to the secretary of defense. The latest manifestation of this problem was the increased priority given during the 1990s to the mission of support for military operations (SMO)—a priority levied not only on Pentagon intelligence agencies but on the CIA and others as well. Such a move was odd, given that military threats to the United States after the Cold War were lower than at any other time in the existence of the modern intelligence community, while a raft of new foreign policy involvements in various parts of the world were coming to the fore. But the SMO priority was the legacy of the Persian Gulf War and the problems in intelligence support felt by military commanders, combined with the Clinton administration's unwillingness to override strong military preferences.

Matching authority and responsibility is where the test of the most immediate reform initiative—or evidence of its confusion—will come. Early reports on the formation of the Office of Homeland Security indicated that the new director, Tom Ridge, will be responsible for coordinating all of the agencies in the intelligence community. This is odd, because that was precisely the function for which the office of Director of Central Intelligence was created in the National Security Act of 1947. The position of DCI was meant to centralize oversight of the dispersed intelligence activities of the military services, the State Department, and the new Central Intelligence Agency, and to coordinate planning and resource allocation among them.

As the community burgeoned over the years, adding huge organizations such as the NSA, the DIA, NIMA, and others, the DCI remained the official responsible for knitting their functions together. The DCI's ability to do so increased at times, but it was always limited by the authority of the secretary of defense over the Pentagon's intelligence agencies. Indeed, hardly anyone but professionals within the intelligence community understand that there is such a thing as a DCI. Not only the press, but presidents and government officials as well never refer to the DCI by that title; they always speak instead of the "Director of the CIA," as if the person were simply an agency head, forgetting the importance of the larger coordination responsibility.

Is Ridge to become the central coordinating official in practice that the DCI is supposed to be in principle? If so, why will he be better positioned to do the job than the DCI has been in the past? The DCI has always had an office in the White House complex as well as at the CIA, and Ridge will have to spend most of his time on matters other than intelligence. The real problem of DCIs in doing their jobs has generally been that presidents have not cared enough about intelligence to make the DCI one of their top advisers. Assigning coordination responsibility to Ridge may work if the president pays more attention to him than has been paid to the DCI, but otherwise this is the sort of reform that could easily prove to be ephemeral or unworkable—yet advertised as necessary in the short term to proclaim that something significant is being done.

FROM AGE-OLD TO NEW AGE SURPRISE

The issue for reform is whether any fixes at all can break a depressing historical pattern. After September 11, intelligence officials realized that fragmentary indicators of impending action by bin Laden's network had been recognized by the intelligence system but had not been sufficient to show what or where the action would be. A vague warning was reportedly issued, but not one that was a ringing alarm. This is, sadly, a very common occurrence.

What we know of intelligence in conventional warfare helps explain why powerful intelligence systems are often caught by surprise. The good news from history is that attackers often fail to win the wars that they start with stunning surprises: Germany was defeated after invading the Soviet Union, Japan after Pearl Harbor, North Korea after 1950, Argentina after taking the Falkland Islands, Iraq after swallowing Kuwait. The bad news is that those initial attacks almost always succeed in blindsiding the victims and inflicting terrible losses.

Once a war is underway, it becomes much harder to surprise the victim. The original surprise puts the victim on unambiguous notice. It shears away the many strong reasons that exist in peacetime to estimate that an adversary will not take the risk of attacking. It was easier for Japan to surprise the United States at Pearl Harbor than at Midway. But even in the midst of war, surprise attacks often succeed in doing real damage: recall the Battle of the Bulge or the Tet offensive. For Americans, September 11 was the Pearl Harbor of terrorism. The challenge now is to make the next attacks more like Midway than like Tet.

Surprise attacks often succeed despite the availability of warning indicators. This pattern leads many observers to blame derelict intelligence officials or irresponsible policymakers. The sad truth is that the fault lies more in natural organizational forces, and in the pure intractability of the problem, than in the skills of spies or statesmen.

After surprise attacks, intelligence postmortems usually discover indicators that existed in advance but were obscured or contradicted by other evidence. Roberta Wohlstetter's classic study of Pearl Harbor identified this as the problem of signals (information hinting at the possibility of enemy attack) getting lost in a crescendo of "noise" (the voluminous clutter of irrelevant information that floods in, or other matters competing for attention). Other causes abound. Some have been partially overcome, such as technical limitations on timely communication, or organizational obstacles to sharing information. Others are deeply rooted in the complexity of threats, the ambiguity of partial warnings, and the ability of plotters to overcome obstacles, manipulate information, and deceive victims.

One reason surprise attacks can succeed is the "boy who cried wolf" problem, in which the very excellence of intelligence collection works against its success. There are often numerous false alarms before an attack, and they dull sensitivity to warnings of the attack that does occur. Sometimes the supposed false alarms were not false at all, but accurate warnings that prompted timely responses by the victim that in turn caused the attacker to cancel and reschedule the assault—thus generating a self-negating prophecy.

Attacks can also come as a surprise because of an overload of incomplete warnings, a particular problem for a superpower with world-spanning involvements. In the spring of 1950, for example, the CIA warned President Harry Truman that the North Koreans could attack at any time, but without indications of whether the attack was certain or when it would happen. "But this did not apply alone to Korea," Truman noted in his memoirs. The same reports also continually warned him of many other places in the world where communist forces had the capability to attack.

Intelligence may correctly warn of an enemy's intention to strike, and even anticipate the timing, but guess wrong about where or how the attack will occur. U.S. intelligence was warning in late November 1941 that a Japanese strike could be imminent but expected it in Southeast Asia. Pearl Harbor seemed an impractical target because it was too shallow for torpedo attacks. That had indeed been true, but shortly before December the Japanese had adjusted their torpedoes so they could run in the shallows. Before September 11, similarly, attacks by Al Qaeda were expected, but elsewhere in the world, and not by the technical means of kamikaze hijacking.

The list of common reasons why attacks often come as a surprise goes on and on. The point is that intelligence can rarely be perfect and unambiguous, and there are always good reasons to misinterpret it. Some problems of the past have been fixed by the technically sophisticated system we have now, and some may be reduced by adjustments to the system. But some can never be eliminated, with the result being that future unpleasant surprises are a certainty.

Reorganization may be the proper response to failure, if only because the masters of intelligence do not know how else to improve performance. The underlying cause of mistakes in performance, however, does not lie in the structure and process of the intelligence system. It is intrinsic to the issues and targets with which intelligence has to cope: the crafty opponents who strategize against it and the alien cultures that are not transparent to American minds.

Reform will happen and, on balance, should help. But for too many policymakers and pundits, reorganization is an alluring but illusory quick fix. Long-term improvements are vaguer and less certain, and they reek of the lamp. But if the United States is going to have markedly better intelligence in parts of the world where few Americans have lived, studied, or understood local mores and aspirations, it is going to have to overcome a cultural disease: thinking that American primacy makes it unnecessary for American education to foster broad and deep expertise on foreign, especially non-Western, societies. The United States is perhaps the only major country in the world where one can be considered well educated yet speak only the native tongue.

The disease has even infected the academic world, which should know better. American political science, for example, has driven area studies out of fashion. Some "good" departments have not a single Middle East specialist on their rosters, and hardly any at all have a specialist on South Asia—a region of more than a billion people, two nuclear-armed countries, and swarms of terrorists. Yet these same departments can afford a plethora of professors who conjure up spare models naively assumed to be of global application.

Reforms that can be undertaken now will make the intelligence community a little better. Making it much better, however, will ultimately require revising educational norms and restoring the prestige of public service. Both are lofty goals and tall orders, involving general changes in society and professions outside government. Even if achieved, moreover, such fundamental reform would not bear fruit until far in the future.

But this is not a counsel of despair. To say that there is a limit to how high the intelligence batting average will get is not to say that it cannot get significantly better. It does mean, however, that no strategy for a war against terror can bank on prevention. Better intelligence may give us several more big successes like those of the 1990s, but even a .900 average will eventually yield another big failure. That means that equal emphasis must go to measures for civil defense, medical readiness, and "consequence management," in order to blunt the effects of the attacks that do manage to get through. Efforts at prevention and preparation for their failure must go hand in hand.

THE ALL-TOO-FRIENDLY SKIES

SECURITY AS AN AFTERTHOUGHT

■

GREGG EASTERBROOK

Just a few months before the September 11 terrorist attacks, the Transportation Committee of the U.S. House of Representatives held a hearing on a grave threat to airline travel. As CNN cameras looked on, Transportation Secretary Norman Mineta, the star witness, was interrogated by committee members who chastised him about the lack of federal action regarding delays experienced by passengers at the nation's airport gates. Passenger inconvenience was reaching "crisis proportions," the committee declared. One out of every four flights in the United States was being delayed for twenty minutes or longer! Constituents were complaining! Members of Congress demanded that the government get more people into the air faster. Didn't the Department of Transportation understand that even the slightest airline delay was a crisis?

Since September 11, petty complaints about the small inconveniences of air travel have come to seem ridiculous in retrospect, and all Americans have renewed awareness of what the word "crisis" really means. But to understand how the attacks happened, it is necessary to understand the culture of air travel in the United States until that horrible morning: how airlines set priorities, how flight crews were taught to respond to hijackings, how jetliners were built, what was regulated and what wasn't.

Prior to September 11, every element of the U.S. airline industry was designed to maximize passenger-miles and minimize costs. More passengers, lower prices, more luggage, more speed, and getting planes off the runway as fast as physically possible: these had been the imperatives of the U.S. airline industry for the preceding two decades, which had started off with the deregulation of the industry at the end of the 1970s. Flight safety—the technology of aircraft, plus their maintenance and operation—was taken very seriously, resulting in few accidents and ever-declining numbers of accident fatalities per passenger-mile traveled. Security was an afterthought; it did not mesh with the goal of zillions of cheap flights.

Meanwhile, numerous studies, blue-ribbon panels, and presidential commissions warned that the U.S. airline industry was dangerously vulnerable to terrorism. "Red team" inspectors, who staged tests of airport security, found it distressingly easy to smuggle weapons onto planes or to enter tarmac areas without identification. Airlines and airport authorities were warned but took little action. Security costs money and creates hassles and delays, elements unwelcome in an industry whose twin gods were lower prices and more people in the sky. As Robert Iverson, the former chief executive officer of Kiwi Airlines, noted, "Airlines are commercial enterprises that will always make poor public-policy decisions when they affect profits and losses." Congress and federal regulators hemmed and hawed, but no one forced the issue.

THE WILD WEST OF AIR TRAVEL

In the twenty years since airline deregulation, the contemporary American airport had become a scene of organized chaos. The number of trips taken by air more than doubled between 1980 and 2000. In 2000 alone, 628 million trips were taken on U.S. carriers, which equals more than two air trips annually per capita, far more than the rate at which people fly in the European Union. Putting so many people into the air was an astonishing feat of technical and economic prowess on the part of the United States. This high level of air travel contributed to American prosperity by facilitating business, it made possible a hugely successful leisure and vacation industry, and it improved living standards by enabling citizens to "feel free to move about the country," in the advertising phrase of Southwest Airlines. And because the cost of tickets had fallen significantly since 1980 (as measured in real dollars), air transportation ceased to be the preserve of the well-to-do. Middle-class and working-class people now fly to visit relatives or to vacation at Walt Disney World. Entire families fly; the toddler with a toy has become as common a sight on jetliners as the corporate executive with a briefcase. Students, secretaries, and day laborers fly. Illegal immigrants fly. Flying is cheap and convenient, so why shouldn't they? By the end of the twentieth century, America had made itself the first society in the world where everybody flies.

But the mass confusion created when everybody flies made the system an inviting target for terrorists. Before September 11, U.S. airports were mobbed with humanity. Cars, taxis, and buses clogged the lanes in front of airports; ticket counters, gate areas, and lounges teemed with people. So many people worked at airports to serve these throngs that it became impossible for security personnel to know faces; if a stranger dressed as an airline pilot or as a member of the ramp crew wandered into a restricted area, who would challenge him? Security checkpoints were staffed by minimum-wage workers. Metal-detector screenings and X-ray inspections of baggage were cursory, with an emphasis on keeping the lines moving. Pundits and politicians thundered about airport delays, a subject all three national newsmagazines featured on their covers—as if arriving at your destination 45 minutes late was a national outrage. And the conversion of the traveling fashion code from business wear to grunge-a-rama, although a triumph of equality, also meant that the suspicious no longer stood out.

In the weeks leading up to September 11, the airline industry's attention was focused, as it had been for two decades, on more price cutting and more haste. Airlines were pushing electronic tickets, which cut costs but reduce the paper trail. Airlines were pushing curbside baggage check-in and even check-in at off-site hotels, steps that reduce backups at ticket counters but are hard to police. Airlines were adding to their fleets "regional jets" that seat 50 to 100 passengers, short-range aircraft that were expected to lead to the next big increase in passenger volume by encouraging people to fly the sort of 200- or 300-mile distances that most now drive. Some airlines were experimenting with boarding those seated in window seats first, then those in middle seats, and last those in aisle seats, in an attempt to shave a few more minutes from each "turn around" of a plane. Some airlines were experimenting with "self check-in kiosks" that allowed passengers to obtain boarding passes without ever having another human being look them in the eye. United Airlines' kiosk even had a ridiculous step in which the computer would flash the message "Has anyone unknown to you given you anything to carry onto the plane?" to which the flyer would have to press a button labeled "No"—as if a terrorist would ever answer "Yes" to an automated security question.

As air travel was being steeped in mass confusion, complacency also set in. No U.S. plane had been bombed in 13 years, and none had been successfully hijacked in 14 years. Why had such incidents stopped, despite the increasingly Wild West nature of our freedom-based air travel system? Technology certainly played a role in reducing the opportunities for terrorists to target airplanes. Advanced scanners, similar to the CT (computerized tomography) machines used in medical diagnostics, were installed in baggage-handling areas, making it much harder to smuggle a bomb into the hold of a plane. Baggage-matching computers, which ensured that the person who had checked a piece of luggage actually boarded the plane, also reduced the bombing threat, although American carriers usually match baggage only on international flights—which, until September 11, had always been seen as terrorists' preferred targets.

More generally, according to an informed U.S. intelligence official, a theory had arisen that terrorist organizations had lost interest in attacking airliners. Airborne terror had backfired on some terrorists. For instance, it was believed that the Sikh terrorist faction that blew up an Air India jumbo jet over the Atlantic Ocean in 1985 had sworn off jetliner attacks after discovering that a large percentage of the passengers on that plane had been Sikhs. And with the general increase in affluence, representatives of terror-linked groups were beginning to fly more often themselves. Once the Palestinian Authority was created, for example, its leaders found themselves with expense accounts and had begun to travel all around the world attending conferences, giving interviews, or just taking vacations. Palestinian leaders, this intelligence source said, were believed to have told operatives that blowing up airplanes was no longer such a fantastic idea.

Given this changed environment, U.S. airlines could tell themselves that their planes were less threatened than before—an expedient belief at a time when maximizing revenues and passenger-miles was every U.S. airline's focus. But seen through the eyes of the fanatic who wants to die—and who so longs to become a mass murderer that he doesn't care if he kills others like himself (since many Muslims died at the World Trade Center)—the U.S. airline system on the morning of September 11 was a vast, undefended target.

(IN)SECURITY

Go through a security check in almost any European airport, and well-trained personnel will carefully inspect your belongings. Everything to be carried onto an aircraft is either X-rayed slowly, as the examiner stops the machine at each item, or else inspected by hand. Examiners feel the sides of soft baggage for hidden items, they open containers to see what's inside, they insist that laptop computers be turned on to prove that they are really laptops. Once, in Paris, I was asked to turn on my bullet-shaped pocket flashlight to demonstrate that it was actually a flashlight. Within sight of the security checkpoints in most European airports are police with assault rifles, wearing armored vests.

Pass through security at an American airport before September 11, in contrast, and you would be inspected by phlegmatic, poorly paid workers with little job motivation, many of whom are recently arrived immigrants who may have limited English skills. Security screening is usually contracted out by the airlines; contracts go to the lowest bidders, and the emphasis is on cost-cutting. Screening personnel receive a day of training, if that, and job turnover is quite high. At Boston's Logan Airport, from which two of the September 11 planes took off, the typical employee of the screening contractor lasted three months. At Washington's Dulles Airport, from which another of the hijacked planes took off, 80 percent of security screening personnel were not U.S. citizens. Rarely was any bag opened for hand inspection. Inspectors watching the X-ray machines are not required to stop at each item and examine it individually, as European inspectors are. Instead, bag after bag after bag goes by in a blur, and since rarely is anything amiss, the inspectors come to expect that nothing is amiss. It is believed that the September 11 terrorists got their knives through the X-ray machines by lying them on their edges between two books, so that to the inspector the blades would appear as nothing more than a dark line. Turning or shaking each bag exposes this trick. But U.S. X-ray inspectors were not required to make such individual examinations.

Indeed, airport screening inspectors weren't required to do anything specific, as no federal regulations governed their actions. The Federal Aviation Administration (FAA) conducts periodic tests of airport security counters, and for public consumption the agency says that about 90 percent of the security checkpoints get passing grades. Airline industry insiders believe the true figure is far lower. One of the unsettling aspects of the September attack was that the hijackers did not "slip past" some incompetent individual. They passed through checkpoints in four different airports (Boston; Newark, N.J.; Dulles, in northern Virginia outside of Washington, D.C.; and Portland, Maine), and no inspector noticed what they were carrying.

The report of the presidential commission on airline security, chaired by Vice President Al Gore, and presented to President Bill Clinton in February 1997, strongly recommended that the federal government begin certifying the contractors who run airport screening stations. Rather than simply do this, the FAA began a cumbersome screener-certification "rulemaking procedure" that was still chugging along, no action taken, when the attackers struck four and a half years later.

Furthermore, prior to September 11, police or armed guards

were rarely on hand in security areas of airports. If something seemed wrong, the overworked employees at the inspection stations were supposed to use walkie-talkies to summon aid. The officers who would respond usually required many minutes to arrive and would be armed only with pistols. Officers simply strolling through the airport, keeping watch, a common sight in Europe, were almost unheard of in the United States.

EASY IDENTIFICATION

Even the meager U.S. airport security precautions would present little barrier for those dressed like a police officer or a member of an airline's staff. In 1979, the *Chicago Sun-Times* columnist Roger Simon memorably put on a blue suit and a pair of child's plastic airline-captain wings, clipped his driver's license to his suit pocket as if it were an identification badge, and waltzed past security at O'Hare International Airport without being searched. In the years since, other reporters have done the same, as have congressional investigators. A thief named Edward Forrest Ingram repeatedly walked unchallenged through security at Los Angeles International Airport (LAX) in the late 1990s by dressing in a phony pilot's uniform and flashing fake pilot ID badges. Several suspects taken into custody by the Federal Bureau of Investigation after the September 11 attacks had costume-shop pilot's uniforms and phony IDs.

Airline maintenance workers also received minimal scrutiny. In December 1987, a recently fired employee of Pacific Southwest Airlines put a gun into his pocket, flashed an airline ID to circumvent the metal detectors at LAX, boarded a plane, and then murdered both pilots before committing suicide, causing a crash that killed 42 others. After that, the FAA said that airline personnel had to pass through metal detectors like everyone else, but that rule is not well enforced.

Regulations about direct access to planes from the runway are also lax. In most airports, ground personnel must swipe a valid ID over a card reader each time they enter runway areas, but they are not searched for weapons; once on the tarmac, they are essentially unsupervised. Box cutters like those used during the September 11 attacks were found hidden in the seat-back pockets or waste bins of two jetliners that were about to fly that day but that had been stopped on the ground when the horror began. Whether they had anything to do with the terrorists was not immediately known, but it was certain that someone placed these weapons onto the aircraft without being detected.

An airport ground worker in league with terrorists might also get them onto the runway with relative ease. In 1999, "red team" testers from the Department of Transportation found that they could wander unchallenged into many supposedly secure airport areas, drive unchallenged onto the tarmac, or get onto the field by "piggybacking"—waiting for a worker to open a secure door and then slipping through before the door closed. Testers with no ID badges passed 229 airport agents during the investigation and were challenged only 53 times. "Our successful penetration of secure areas almost always resulted in our boarding an aircraft," Alexis Stefani, a Transportation Department official, said.

A terrorist could also pose as a law enforcement agent. In 2000, testers from the General Accounting Office passed through security at Ronald Reagan National Airport (just outside of Washington, D.C.) and at Orlando International Airport in Florida by downloading phony police credentials from Web sites or by using movie-prop police badges. Flashing these IDs, they boarded aircraft carrying briefcases that had not been X-rayed. Agents testing National Airport even found that, by flashing phony identification, they could obtain official permits to take firearms through airport checkpoints legally. Perhaps the House Judiciary Committee, which asked for this investigation, was wrong to publicize it, as the details might have given someone an idea. But a study finding that it was incredibly easy to take guns through security at the airport of the nation's capital ought to have inspired a decisive response. Instead, the airlines and the FAA did nothing, while Congress fumed about gate delays.

SECURITY ON BOARD

After the security deficits of U.S. airports come questions about the security of airplanes themselves. For instance, why do U.S. jetliners have transponders that can be turned off? Transponders report a plane's location, altitude, and airspeed to air-traffic controllers; with the transponder off, an airliner appears on radar as a weak echo, its altitude and airspeed hard to determine. After the September 11 terrorists reached the flight decks of the four commandeered aircraft, one of the first things they did was to disengage the transponders. When air-traffic controllers lose transponder data and radio contact—as happened in all four hijackings—they assume that a plane has blown up or nosedived into the ground. Had the transponders remained running, controllers would have known right away that the planes were still flying and were bearing down on Washington and New York. Knowing that the jetliners had not crashed but had been commandeered might have cut precious minutes off the time it took the FAA to decide to contact the military. As it was, Air Force fighter jets arrived above New York City about 10 minutes after the second plane hit the south tower of the World Trade Center; fighters arrived above Washington about five minutes after the Pentagon was struck.

Transponders have "off" switches (technically a "standby" mode) because if the machines were on while airliners taxied on the ground, confusing readings could overload the air controllers' screens. Typically, a pilot turns on the transponder during the climb after takeoff and switches it off on the final approach for landing. An additional reason for the "off" switch is that it allows a pilot to silence a malfunctioning transponder and engage the backup. But both these tasks could occur automatically. Indeed, some corporate jets already have automatic transponders. As a plane with one of these accelerates after takeoff, the device comes on; when the plane reaches final landing speed, the transponder switches off. If the primary transponder fails, the secondary unit turns itself on. Automatic transponders could be made mandatory on all new jetliners and most existing planes could be retrofitted for them for a relatively modest cost. Then there would no longer be a switch for a hijacker to turn off.

Next is the cockpit door. For years, aviation safety experts have complained that U.S. jetliners have flimsy cockpit doors, less like barriers than like the lightweight "privacy panels" used for airliner bathrooms. Doors to the cockpits of U.S. airliners can easily be kicked in, which may be what some of the hijackers did. In fact the doors are designed to be kicked in, on the theory that pilots might need to break them down to escape the cockpit after a crash landing. What's more, locks on the doors are a polite fiction. Federal regulations require that cockpit doors be locked during flight, supposedly as a barrier to hostile entry. But keys can be seized from flight attendants, and cockpit door keys are not unique like car keys: every aircraft of a given model has the same cockpit door key. There are literally thousands of keys in circulation that unlock the cockpit door of any American Airlines or United Airlines 757 or 767, the two types of planes seized in the attack.

The solution is a reinforced door. "By far the most important design change for U.S. commercial aircraft is to turn the front end into a vault," says Vern Raburn, a pilot and president of Eclipse Aviation, which builds private jets. Israel's El Al, the most threatened and yet most secure of airlines, long ago took this approach. Its airliners have dead-bolted, steel cockpit doors with plated hinges that cannot be pried open or shot out. Flight attendants do not carry keys because there is no keyhole; the doors open only from the inside. For crash escape, one cockpit window is designed to pop out so that a rope ladder can be lowered. (American jetliners also have the pop-out window, which makes the flimsy U.S. cockpit door all the more questionable.) Despite being repeatedly targeted by terrorists, El Al has not suffered a successful hijacking since 1968, about the time it adopted the "vault" door.

U.S. airlines resisted the steel cockpit door out of complacency, to hold down costs (anything that makes an airplane heavier increases fuel consumption), and because the open cockpit—into which the captain can invite kids to gawk at the instruments—has been one of the symbols of America's people-oriented flying industry. But in the aftermath of the September 11 attacks, the Department of Transportation mandated that all cockpit doors be reinforced. Boeing, the largest airplane manufacturer, said its engineers had been working around the clock since September 11 to resolve technical details (namely, pressure differentials between the cockpit and the cabin) so that installation of the new doors could be expedited. The question remains, however: Why did it take more than 5,000 American deaths to convince the aviation system to add something basic that security advocates had been demanding for decades?

Next on the list of questions is whether there should be weapons aboard airliners. Currently the closest thing to a weapon on the flight deck is a fire ax. Many airlines bar their pilots from carrying pocket knives, although small pocket knives were an acceptable carry-on item for passengers until September 11 Absurdly, passengers were allowed to bear weapons that pilots were forbidden.

After September 11, the Air Line Pilots Association, the leading aviators' union, said it wanted nonlethal weapons such as stun guns or Mace stored in cockpits to give pilots some means of defending themselves. It also said that pilots who pass an FBI firearms handling course should be allowed to carry handguns loaded with special bullets that cannot rupture an airliner's hull. Although approximately 50 percent of commercial pilots are retired military officers and presumably are well versed in gun safety, the proposal gave even the Bush administration pause.

The alternative to armed pilots is armed sky marshals. Another reason El Al has no hijackings is that every flight carries at least one marshal disguised as a passenger, so potential troublemakers have no idea who has the Uzi. The United States has a sky marshal corps, but its numbers are so small that fewer than one percent of commercial flights before September 11 had an armed marshal on board. In the aftermath of the attack, President Bush proposed the creation of an extensive flying-police organization. Putting marshals on each of the 25,000 flights that take off each day within the United States would be expensive. (El Al's

comparatively tiny number of departures lessens its staffing task.)
Recruiting top people would be essential, because sky marshals
would have to be skilled enough not to become a threat themselves, as they would be carrying onto planes a gun that a hijacker
might seize. Endless retraining of sky marshals will be important,
since if all goes well the typical sky marshal will spend months or
years flying around but taking no action at all.

A U.S. sky marshal hierarchy could cost several billion dollars
annually. But that's still only a few dollars per ticket, and at this
point the flying public is not likely to object. For years airports
and airlines have cut every corner on security to get the price of
flying as low as possible. Maybe consumers bear part of the
blame, for demanding lowest-price travel. The cost of this approach has now been shown to exceed the benefits by an unfath-
omable margin.

Next on the aircraft redesign list is an emergency system that
locks the controls so that even if a hijacker does end up in the
captain's seat, the plane will not obey. The controls might have a
"panic button" that would transfer control to the autopilot,
which would land the plane at the closest airfield. Alternatively, a
panic button might broadcast a "mayday" code and then allow
the airplane to be remotely sent a landing code by FAA officials
on the ground. Once such a system were activated, it would become impossible to fly a jetliner to Cuba, or into a building.

How practical would such a system be? Most of today's jetliners can land themselves at a "Category III" airfield that maintains
special guidance beacons. The United States, however, boasts only
a few Category III fields—in cities such as Boston, Portland, and
Seattle, and where low clouds are common. But the majority of
jetliners built in the last decade have advanced autopilots that can
land automatically on almost any field, including the "Category
I" airports found all over the country. About ten years ago, two
Airbus test pilots sat glumly watching the sky go by and worrying
about the flying profession's job security as the newest model
took off, completed a standard climb and cruise cycle, and then
landed without a person ever touching the yoke.

The FAA does not certify use of auto-landing systems under

normal circumstances, and no one thinks computers should replace pilots. But, says Eclipse Aviation's Raburn, "there is no big technical barrier" to flight computers that take command in an emergency. If aircraft sported panic buttons that transferred control to computers for an immediate landing, the incentive to hijack would decline precipitously.

Additionally, between advanced autopilots with high data-storage ability and global positioning satellite receivers that tell many new aircraft precisely where they are, it should also be possible to design a system that refuses any attempt to fly a plane into a building or similar target. In 1995, an American Airlines jetliner bound for Cali, Colombia, slammed into a mountain, killing everyone aboard, after the pilot entered into the flight-management computer an erroneous heading that instructed the plane to fly straight at the hillside. Since then, software engineers have been working on a digital topography system that would allow aircraft computers to know where all the world's mountains, skyscrapers, bridges, and, for that matter, military installations and nuclear power plants are located and to simply refuse any command to fly into them.

Whereas the welding of reinforced cockpit doors has already begun, panic-button autopilots and "refuse to collide" software require development time. Such systems would have to be tested extensively, particularly the protocols governing when the computer can countermand the pilot. And, of course, no electronic system is foolproof; hijackers could grab the captain before the emergency devices can be turned on. There would have to be a deactivation code, and butchers like the ones who struck in September might torture the pilots to force them to reveal the code. The only defense against such outcomes would be to make sure pilots never open the cockpit during emergencies. And that leads to a final area in which the American approach to aviation proved so vulnerable to September's horrors: the training of flight crews.

THE HUMAN FACTOR

Why did four sets of pilots, including several fit, strong, former military officers, hand over their aircraft to hijackers armed only with short knives and box cutters? The terrorists may have leaped out of their seats and stabbed flight attendants or passengers to create panic, causing pilots to come out to see what was happening; sketchy cell-phone reports suggest that this happened on at least one plane. Or the terrorists may have kicked down the cockpit door and immediately slashed or killed the pilots, who, strapped in and facing forward in a cramped area, would have been at a disadvantage in the face of surprise attackers wielding knives from above and behind. But terrorists may also have simply pounded on the cockpit door and said, "This is a hijacking"—for U.S. commercial pilots are trained to give in to hijackers.

Since hijacking began in the early 1970s, a few aerial crimes have been staged by deranged individuals oblivious to personal safety. But most hijackers have had some goal that requires their own survival—wanting to extort money, to receive concessions from governments, or to win political attention. U.S. airlines tell their pilots calmly to follow hijackers' instructions and get the plane on the ground, where law enforcement can take over. U.S. pilots are reminded over and over again that their first obligation is the welfare of their passengers; yielding to hijackers is seen as the best way to prevent passengers from dying. It is assumed that, eventually, any hijacker will want to land somewhere. Essentially, airlines presume hijackings are hostage situations, and criminologists unanimously agree that the way to handle hostage-takers is to avoid provoking them and wait them out.

Additionally, some U.S. airlines have viewed acquiescence to hijackers as a legal strategy. If a hijacker takes control of a plane and something horrible happens, this line of reasoning goes, the airline's liability may be limited; but if the pilots resist and their struggle causes a crash, the airline may be found negligent.

Thus an ethos of passivity regarding hijackers has been cultivated. According to one captain for a major U.S. carrier, his airline forbade flight crews from resisting hijackers. On one of the doomed flights, the captain "keyed" his microphone so air traffic controllers could for a moment hear what was going on, and a hijacker said something to the effect of "Don't do anything foolish and you won't get hurt." This is exactly what U.S. pilots are trained to expect "rational" hijackers to say—and the terrorists seemed to know this.

Could anyone have guessed the horror that the September 11 terrorists had in mind? In 1993, the Pentagon's Office of Special Operations and Low-Intensity Conflict funded a study that included discussion of how airliners might be used as guided missiles by terrorists. But according to *The Washington Post,* officials decided not to publish the study, believing it would be too frightening for the public. In 1994, Algerian Islamic terrorists hijacked an Air France jetliner, landed in southern France, and told authorities they wanted to fly the short distance to Paris to surrender—but demanded first that the plane be fully loaded with fuel. A full fuel load was unnecessary for the distance involved, but it could have turned the airliner into a bomb. (September 11's terrorists similarly chose large planes bound on transcontinental flights in order to get aircraft with maximum fuel loads.) French commandos stormed the plane and killed the hijackers. Twenty sticks of dynamite were discovered on board, along with notes indicating that their plan had been a suicide crash into the Eiffel Tower, where the combination of fuel and dynamite would have caused a fireball to massacre civilians.

Because this disaster was foiled before it could happen, the fact that suicidal fanatics were beginning to think of jetliners as weapons did not register with U.S. airlines. They continued to train pilots to give in to hijackers; as of this writing, it is believed that the crews of the three planes that struck the World Trade Center and the Pentagon gave up the controls. Aboard the fourth plane, United Airlines flight 93, which crashed in rural Pennsylvania, there might have been some warning to the pilots of the horror that had begun, and some resistance. Several passengers learned via their cell phones what had happened in New York, and it is believed that at least four passengers charged the hijackers, unarmed, in an attempt to take back the plane and prevent it from being smashed into a Washington target and killing hundreds or even thousands of people. Had passivity not been inculcated into U.S. air crews, more of September's horrors might have been avoided.

Police tactics changed after the 1999 massacre at Columbine High School, where hundreds of law enforcement officers stood outside while victims bled to death, because the officers had been taught to assume a hostage-taking rather than a murder rampage; their training told them not to provoke. Now, police officers are trained when encountering a similar situation to assume a rampage, to charge in and kill the perpetrators as quickly as possible. American flight crews must have a similar transformation in their training.

U.S. pilots must be taught—as El Al pilots have been for decades—never to open cockpit doors during emergencies, even if they hear a flight attendant on the other side begging for her life. (Video cameras and microphones can be installed in jetliner cabins to enable the pilots to figure out what's going on without having to open the cockpit door.) The new training assumption must be that hijackers are butchers and not "rational" criminals, and that it is better to let a few passengers die than to let all of them die.

Pilots should also be trained to conduct defensive flight maneuvers, such as violently shaking the plane, partially depressurizing the cabin to make everyone gasp for breath, or staging the fearsome "negative G" dive that hurls anyone standing up against the ceiling. Innocent passengers, of course, could be harmed by such maneuvers. Violent shaking can injure those not wearing seatbelts; partial depressurization could kill a baby, a senior citizen, or a person with a respiratory problem; the "negative G" pitch forward may throw a standing person against the ceiling hard enough to snap his or her neck. Yet if the alternative is destruction of the plane, such measures may be justified.

In advance of new training, flight crews are already taking steps. Many captains are instructing flight attendants to strap a beverage cart across the cockpit door during flight, in order to slow any intruder. Some are establishing code words that will let the cockpit and flight attendants communicate in emergencies. Some are taking the fire ax out during flight and laying it where it can be reached quickly. That these ideas seem slapdash, compared to the gruesome preparations of the September 11 murderers, shows how wide-open to attack the U.S. air-travel system has left itself.

Pilots are also campaigning for increased authority. Although aviation law says that pilots of airplanes, like captains of ships, have command "without limitation," profit-minded airline managers have tried to erode that rule. American and United, the two airlines whose planes were commandeered on September 11, were insisting prior to the attacks that the pilot's authority does not begin until the airplane's brakes are released; until then, the chief gate agent has command. Pilots want command from the moment they sign in for the flight. The pilots argue that, if the gate agent is in control until the doors close, he or she will allow aboard the maximum number of passengers, for maximum revenue; if the pilot has authority at the gate, he or she would be legally able to deny boarding to anyone suspicious.

Determining who is suspicious is another issue on which assumptions must change. The 1997 presidential commission chaired by Gore recommended a system of computerized "prescreening" of passengers for security risk—a form of profiling. But the Gore commission also insisted that "no profile should contain or be based on . . . race, religion, [or] national origin." A prototype system called CAPPS, for Computer-Assisted Passenger Prescreening, was put into effect and was running on September 11. The system flags for extra inspection passengers who trip statistical indicators, such as buying tickets with large amounts of cash. But CAPPS has been scrupulously constructed to ask nothing about race, religion, or national origin (the Justice Department reviewed CAPPS to ensure that the system has zero racial or ethnic component), which may have contributed to its failure to flag any of the 19 hijackers. For reasons of national security, it is worth considering whether new passenger-profiling systems should scrutinize Arab travelers as well as those holding passports from Middle Eastern countries.

THE FUTURE OF U.S. AIR TRAVEL

In the aftermath of September 11, many things have changed about U.S. aviation. Security screening is now slower and more cautious. More carry-on bags are inspected by hand. National Guard units wander airport corridors and guard security checkpoints, mainly to reassure flyers. Reinforced cockpit doors are being installed. Sky marshals are being hired. Security screening companies are subject to tighter regulation, although at this writing it is still unclear whether the job of airport screening will be federalized. Research into panic-button autopilots and similar computer advances is being conducted on a priority basis. Pilots are practicing defensive flight maneuvers. And even though the era of running to the airport at the last moment to scoot onto a cheap flight might have been good for the economy and for living standards, it seems unlikely to return any time soon.

But although every change mentioned here must be made, these suggestions and the measures now being taken by U.S. airlines are, in essence, preparing for yesterday's battle. No one thought that an event like September 11 was possible: the 1997 Gore commission report, 50 pages long, makes no forecast resembling what actually happened. Now that we know that this particular type of horror is possible, we are on guard, and a similar event may never again occur. What other aviation horror might occur instead?

None of the current reforms focus on private aviation, everything from privately owned Cessnas to corporate jets. In private aviation there are no metal detectors, no X-rays for baggage, and, most important, no need to stage a hijacking because a suicidal terrorist with financial backing might simply buy a small plane and stuff it with explosives. Small planes themselves are not much threat to skyscrapers, owing to small fuel loads, but many "general aviation" aircraft are capable of carrying between one and two tons of high explosives, which would have similar blast power to the big, fuel-gorged planes that struck the World Trade Center. Small planes are also much harder to see on radar than are jetliners, and for daylight flying their pilots are not required to file flight plans. They cannot suddenly veer in an unexpected direction if air-traffic controllers have no idea where they are going in the first place.

Security experts have long worried about small private planes stuffed with explosives, and indeed, many presumed in the initial minutes after the first explosion that it was a small plane that had struck the World Trade Center. As we go to great lengths to prevent September 11 from happening again, we would be wise to bear in mind that the country remains vulnerable to a form of airborne terror attack about which nothing has been done—and about which there is great complacency, since everyone likes the unrestricted freedom of American private aviation, just as everyone liked the low cost and convenience of the old commercial airline system.

THE UNGUARDED HOMELAND

A STUDY IN MALIGN NEGLECT

■

STEPHEN E. FLYNN

It is painful to recall that prior to September 11, the singular preoccupation in Washington on the issue of protecting the U.S. homeland was national missile defense. The sense of urgency to construct the means to guard the United States from a potential missile attack stood in stark contrast to the complacency with which the government approached the policing of its transportation networks and the nation's land and sea borders. On September 10, just over 300 agents of the U.S. Border Patrol, supported by a single analyst, were assigned the task of detecting and intercepting illegal border crossings along the vast open spaces of the 4,000-mile land and water border with Canada. After a decade of budgetary neglect, the U.S. Coast Guard—whose job it is to maintain port security and patrol 95,000 miles of shoreline—had been forced to reduce its ranks to their lowest level since 1964 and to routinely cannibalize its decades-old cutters and aircraft for spare parts to keep the rest operational. While debates over the merits of missile-intercept technologies made headlines, the fact that America's terrestrial and maritime front doors were wide open did not rate even a brief mention.

Not everyone was asleep at the wheel. Over the past few years, a string of reports from blue-ribbon commissions and think tanks have warned of the growing risk to the United States of lethal terrorist attacks. Most notably, the Hart-Rudman Commission on National Security in the 21st Century found that "mass-casualty terrorism directed against the U.S. homeland [is] of serious and growing concern" and recommended a strategy that "prioritizes deterring, defending against, and responding effectively to such dangers." The commission concluded that the U.S. government was unprepared and possessed no adequate organizational structure to prevent or respond to such attacks. Yet these sobering findings were received with a collective yawn.

Until the World Trade Center towers were reduced to rubble and the Pentagon was slashed open on September 11, most Americans, along with their government, were clearly in denial about the growing homeland security imperative. Oceans to the east and west and friendly continental neighbors to the north and south had offered the United States a healthy measure of protection from its enemies. And Americans have generally disapproved of extensive efforts at domestic security. They were willing to staff and bankroll the defense and intelligence communities to contain the Soviet Union and to deal with conflicts "over there," but the quid pro quo was supposed to be that civilians could enjoy the full extent of the freedoms they had grown accustomed to at home.

Now Americans are trying to come to grips with their new sense of insecurity and vulnerability. As they contemplate the road ahead, the U.S. public needs to accept three unpleasant facts. First, there will continue to be anti-American terrorists with global reach for the foreseeable future. Second, these terrorists will have access to the means—including chemical and biological weapons—to carry out catastrophic attacks on U.S. soil. And third, the economic and societal disruption created by the September 11 attacks and the subsequent anthrax mailings has opened a Pandora's box: future terrorists bent on challenging U.S. power will draw inspiration from the seeming ease with which the United States could be attacked, and they will be encouraged by the mounting costs to the U.S. economy and the public psyche associated with hasty, ham-handed efforts to restore security. In light of these realities, getting homeland security right should be Washington's top priority.

AMERICA THE VULNERABLE

The world was understandably shocked by the carnage and the audacity of the September 11 attacks. But the measures embraced immediately following the strikes made clear that public-safety officials were aware of just how vulnerable the United States actually was. The attacks were carried out by hijacking four domestic airliners. Nonetheless, federal authorities immediately ordered the closing of U.S. airspace to international as well as domestic flights, the shutting down of the nation's major seaports, and the slowing to a trickle of truck, car, and pedestrian traffic across the land borders with Canada and Mexico. This draconian response reflected an appropriate lack of confidence in the routine measures used for policing the cross-border flows of people, goods, and conveyances.

Queasiness over U.S. border control and transportation-security measures quickly spread to include many of the systems that underpin the U.S. economy and daily life. Suddenly guards were being posted at water reservoirs, outside power plants, and at bridges and tunnels. Maps of oil and gas lines were removed from the Internet. In Boston, a ship carrying liquefied natural gas, an important source of fuel for heating New England homes, was forbidden from entering the harbor because local fire officials feared that if it were targeted by a terrorist the resulting explosion could lay low much of the city's densely populated waterfront. An attack by a knife-wielding lunatic on the driver of a Florida-bound Greyhound bus led to the immediate cessation of that national bus service and the closing of the Port Authority Bus Terminal in New York City. Agricultural crop-dusting planes were grounded out of a concern that they could be used to spread chemical or biological agents.

As Americans continue their ad hoc domestic security survey in the aftermath of the terrorist attacks, they may be mortified by what they find. The competitiveness of the U.S. economy and the quality of life of the American people rest on critical infrastructure that has become increasingly more concentrated, more interconnected, and more sophisticated. Almost entirely privately owned and operated, there is very little redundancy in this system. Most of the physical plant, telecommunications, power, water supply, and transportation infrastructure on U.S. territory lies unprotected or is equipped with security sufficient to deter only amateur vandals, thieves, or hackers. As a result, these vulnerable networks present extremely attractive targets for mass disruption. Consider Long Beach, California, one of the most important maritime transportation hubs in the country. The city government provides no full-time police presence within the port and instead assigns responsibility for security to the companies who lease terminal space there. This means that a private contractor provides the guards who oversee the protection of facilities such as the one where roughly 25 percent of all the crude oil consumed by the entire state of California (408,000 barrels per day) is off-loaded. Since California gasoline refineries operate at full capacity, at any given time there is only enough oil stored in the region to supply them for two days. If the kind of terrorist attack that was conducted in Yemen in October 2000 against the U.S.S. *Cole* took place against a tanker docked at the main terminal in Long Beach, the economy of southern California would grind to a halt within a matter of days.

Things are not much better on the East Coast. In south Florida, 4 billion gallons of gasoline, diesel and aviation fuel, and industrial fuel oil are imported by tankers or barges into just one port—Port Everglades—and stored in 257 aboveground oil tanks. They are then either shipped by pipeline to the region's three major airports or transshipped by 1,500 tank trucks daily to local gas stations. The commercial logic behind the construction of the Port Everglades complex is basic: by concentrating operations in a single location, oil companies can reduce overhead by eliminating the need for redundant systems. But as in the case of Long Beach, if the port were shut down, the 4 million residents of south Florida would have as little as a two-day supply of gasoline and diesel fuel. And acquiring sufficient new supplies to meet the region's energy needs would not be possible, because there are no other oil-importation ports in the vicinity with the necessary storage capacity or transshipment infrastructure.

Although the U.S. Coast Guard has the statutory responsibility to provide for seaport security, it lacks the personnel and the patrol craft to perform this mission on a sustainable basis. Until now, local civilian port authorities generally have been content with this state of affairs, viewing "less as better," since more security is widely perceived as undermining efforts to improve port efficiency and competitiveness. In the 1990s, the Coast Guard did assemble six specially trained port security units, but these are manned by reservists and funded by the Department of Defense to serve overseas to protect military forces operating in foreign ports, not domestic ones.

TERRORIST NEEDLES IN A TRANSPORTATION HAYSTACK

Of course, instead of going after targets within U.S. seaports, terrorists may choose to simply enter the country through air, land, or marine ports. Few meaningful barriers exist to thwart this aim. For one thing, the haystack within which to hide is enormous. In 2000 alone, 489 million people, 127 million passenger vehicles, 11.6 million maritime containers, 11.5 million trucks, 2.2 million railcars, 829,000 planes, and 211,000 vessels passed through U.S. border inspection systems. The majority of this traffic, furthermore, is concentrated into just a handful of ports. For example, just four international bridges between the province of Ontario and the states of Michigan and New York are traversed by 3.75 million trucks annually, accounting for one-third of all the trucks that enter the United States.

The rule of thumb in the border-inspection business is that it requires, on average, five inspectors working for three hours to conduct a thorough physical inspection of a loaded 40-foot container or an 18-wheel truck. Even with new high-tech sensors, inspectors have nowhere near the time, space, or staff to inspect all the cargo arriving. A case in point is the Ambassador Bridge between Detroit, Michigan, and Windsor, Ontario, the world's busiest commercial land-border crossing, where nearly 5,000 trucks entered the United States each day in 2000. With only 8 primary inspection lanes and a parking lot that can hold just 90 tractor-trailers at a time for secondary or tertiary inspections, U.S. Customs Service officers must average no more than 2 minutes for each truck. If they fall behind, the parking lot fills, trucks back up onto the bridge and the resulting pileup virtually closes the border, generating roadway chaos throughout the metropolitan areas on both sides.

The loads carried by these trucks are mostly low-risk shipments for the automotive industry, but a substantial amount of the cross-border cargo with Canada originates from overseas. For instance, half of the one million containers arriving in the Port of Montreal are ultimately destined for the northeastern or midwestern United States. In trying to figure out whether these containers might pose a risk, Canadian inspectors have little to go by. The cargo manifest paperwork provides only the sketchiest of details about a shipment's contents and in many cases includes no information at all about the original sender or the ultimate recipient. To get more information, these inspectors must engage in the labor-intensive and time-consuming act of tracking down shipping intermediaries, who are often difficult to reach.

Whether a container arrives in the United States directly from Europe or Asia or through Canada, it is unlikely to be examined at the point where it arrives on U.S. soil, because the U.S. Customs Service inspection system is built around clearing cargo at the final destination port rather than at the arrival port. Chicago, for example, is the nation's fourth-largest "port of entry." An importer operating there can count on customs officers' never reviewing his cargo manifest until after it reaches the city itself, even though the shipment may have entered the United States through Los Angeles, Miami, or the St. Lawrence Seaway. Furthermore, the importer has up to 30 days' transit time to make the intra-U.S. trip. What this means is that, at any given time, U.S. authorities are virtually clueless about the contents or senders of thousands of multiton containers traveling on trucks, trains, or barges on U.S. roads, rails, and waterways, destined for America's heartland.

SHIPPING NEWS

As at U.S. seaports, the neglect of security at the border has not been altogether benign. The pervasive view among many in the private sector has been, "If there are more inspectors, there will be more inspections," something seen as bad for the bottom line. More inspections mean slower shipments. As the volume and velocity of cross-border trade has grown, therefore, those responsible for providing security have been starved of personnel, forced to work with obsolete data-management systems, and, in reaction to congressional pressure, even subjected to performance sanctions if they disrupt the flow of commerce by making anything more than token random spot-checks.

For example, although the amount of U.S. trade with Canada climbed from $116.3 billion worth of goods in 1985 to $409.8 billion worth in 2000, only 700 customs inspectors are currently assigned to that border—200 fewer than worked the border 20 years ago. And at the border crossings in the states of Washington, Montana, North Dakota, Minnesota, Michigan, New York, Vermont, and Maine, routinely half of the existing primary inspection booths remain closed solely because there is no one to staff them. Those inspectors who work at the booths that are open are evaluated in part by how well they meet "facilitation" performance standards designed to reduce waiting times.

The world may be well into the electronic age, but the U.S. Customs Service is still struggling with paper-based systems. For years its proposed Automated Commercial Environment and International Trade Data System projects have run aground on the twin shoals of flat federal budgets and industry affinity for the status quo. It was only in April 2001 that the Customs Service was provided the seed money to get started on what it projects to be a seven-year development and implementation cycle. In the interim, it will have only the bluntest of data-management tools to support the work of customs inspectors.

If the data-management situation for customs is grim, it is grimmer still for other front-line organizations such as the Coast

Guard, the Immigration and Naturalization Service (INS), and
the Department of Agriculture, all of whose officers and inspectors desperately need communication and decision-support tools
to carry out their jobs. But even if these agencies could join the information age, they would still be hindered by bureaucratic and
legal barriers that currently preclude them from talking with one
another.

For example, consider the case of a ship with a shadowy
record of serving in the darker corners of the maritime trade. Its
shipping agent sends notice that it will be importing a type of
cargo that does not square with its home port or its recent ports
of call. Some of its crew are on an intelligence watch list because
they are suspected of having links with radical Islamist organizations. The ship is scheduled to arrive on the same day that a
tanker carrying highly volatile fuel is also arriving in port. It
would be reasonable for the American public to expect that, with
a shady past, suspect cargo, and a questionable crew, such a ship
would be identified, stopped, and examined before it could enter
U.S. waters. Under the current border-management architecture,
however, this interdiction would be unlikely to happen because
none of these red flags would be viewed simultaneously.

The Coast Guard would be likely to know something about
the ship itself and would also know about the scheduled arrival of
a tanker carrying hazardous cargo. The Customs Service might
have some advance cargo manifest information (although if the
ship is carrying bulk materials, this information is typically not
collected until after its arrival in the port). The INS might or
might not know much about the crew, depending on the kinds of
visas the sailors are holding and the timeliness with which the
shipping agent faxed the crew list. None of the front-line inspectors in these agencies, meanwhile, are likely to have access to national security intelligence from the Federal Bureau of
Investigation or the Central Intelligence Agency. And all of the
agencies will have more people, cargo, and ships that spark their
interest and concern than they can ever manage to inspect.

THE PRICE OF HOMELAND INSECURITY

Given the unprotected state of America's critical infrastructure and the inexcusable state of neglect of front-line regulatory and law-enforcement agencies, what is most surprising is that the United States had managed to dodge the catastrophic terrorism bullet for so long. Now that this sad precedent has been set, however, reducing America's vulnerability through appropriate protective measures has become all the more critical, for three reasons.

First, if U.S. policymakers believe that the chances of detecting and intercepting a terrorist attack are low and the consequences are high, they will be under enormous pressure to track down, arrest, or eliminate the potential perpetrators. The price tag on cooperation by others in these efforts—often some form of diplomatic concession or averted eyes—could prove very high in the long run. So restoring a sense that terrorist threats to the United States can be managed, and thus giving policymakers the breathing room to make considered choices about counterterrorism policy, is important.

Second, a sense of defeatism about the possibility of stopping terrorism or its means once in transit places a heavy burden on domestic policing and civil defense. If the assumption is that terrorists will always be able to slip through and set up shop on American soil, then the argument for allowing law enforcement and intelligence agencies permission for more intrusive domestic surveillance becomes compelling. It could also lead to the imposition of an extremely costly "security tax" on significant areas of national life.

Finally, the absence of a credible capacity to filter out illicit cross-border activity places U.S. commerce at frequent risk of disruption. This risk stems not so much from acts of terror as it does from the U.S. response to it. In the hours following the September 11 terrorist attacks, the combined result of grounding the commercial aviation fleet, stopping all inbound ships arriving in the nation's major seaports, and moving from alert condition 4 to alert condition 1 at the land border was to place a tourniquet around the transportation arteries that feed the national economy. This blunt response was prudent given the initial uncertainty surrounding the attacks. Any plane, train, ship, or truck could have been a bomb. But there is some risk that taking such drastic measures may become standard procedure, not just in the wake of a future attack but whenever policymakers receive credible information about the potential for one.

For example, imagine that a covert human intelligence operation has successfully penetrated a terrorist cell and discovered that a container has been loaded with a chemical weapon and is destined for an importer in the United States. As discussed above, right now the U.S. government has virtually no means to identify the location of such a container until it reaches its intended port of entry. Once it has left an Asian port it could be placed on a coastal freighter and then mixed among the more than a million containers handled each month by Hong Kong or Singapore. There it could be loaded aboard a container ship destined for Vancouver, Seattle, Tacoma, Oakland, Los Angeles, Long Beach, or even the Panama Canal, from which it could enter the United States through any of the seaports on the Gulf of Mexico or the Atlantic coast. Given this situation, the president would face the unhappy choice of praying that the weapon is not activated or diverted while in transit or effectively creating maritime transportation gridlock to allow each container to be examined at its port of entry.

In the future not only will the risk of another attack be higher, but the number of threats and warnings that must be taken seriously will increase dramatically. In both instances, policymakers will find themselves routinely compelled to order up a transportation quarantine as a preventive measure to protect the homeland. Over time, this cure has the potential to be worse than the disease.

Most Americans have little appreciation for the scale and sophistication of the transportation and logistical backbone that underpins the U.S. economy. Take the automotive industry, for example. General Motors, Ford, and DaimlerChrysler buy between 15 and 20 percent of the parts to build their cars and trucks from suppliers in Ontario. Some of their contracts require these Canadian suppliers to make their deliveries to the assembly plants in the United States within as little as six hours from the receipt of an order. Delivery trucks are loaded so that parts meant for specific vehicles can be unloaded and placed directly on the appropriate chassis as it moves down the assembly line. This "just-in-time" delivery system has given the "Big Three" automakers a more cost-effective and efficient production process. But the resulting savings can evaporate with even a minor delay at the border. Just 36 hours after the September 11 attacks, DaimlerChrysler announced that it would have to close one of its assembly plants on the following day because its Canadian supplies were caught in an 18-hour traffic jam on the border. This news was followed by an announcement by Ford that five of its assembly plants would have to be idled the following week. The price tag for this loss in productivity? Each assembly plant on average produces $1 million worth of cars per hour.

The automotive industry's dependence on cross-border trade and its adoption of just-in-time delivery systems, moreover, are by no means exceptional. Few U.S. manufacturing firms are not engaged in some form of outsourcing as a means of boosting their competitiveness. And most U.S. companies have also worked hard to reduce the amount of inventory they hold in reserve as a way of improving the bottom line. Maintaining inventory guarantees that supply will be available to meet demand, but hanging on to large stockpiles of goods consumes capital and may be wasteful. According to Commerce Department reports on sales and inventory, the total value of retail sales in 2000 reached approximately $3.2 trillion. To support these sales, retailers, merchant wholesalers, and manufacturers, respectively, held $372 billion, $307 billion, and $472 billion in inventory—a total of $1.1 trillion. The competitive imperative to whittle away at this $1.1 trillion inventory cost has been a powerful impetus for constructing faster and more efficient shipping, aviation, rail, and trucking fleets; constructing seamless supply chains; consolidating distribution networks; upgrading warehouse management systems; and incorporating state-of-the-art tracking, communications, and database technologies. The goal has been to leach as much uncertainty and friction as possible from the logistics and transportation networks. Now, however, companies that have made massive capital outlays in technology and infrastructure to construct just-in-time delivery systems may see their expected savings and efficiencies go up in smoke. Outsourcing contracts will have to be revisited and inventories will have to be rebuilt. The costs are difficult to calculate, but they are sure to take a toll on international trade and U.S. competitiveness.

GETTING HOMELAND SECURITY RIGHT

Any strategy for protecting the United States from the threat of terrorism must balance the imperatives of adequate control with sustaining economic and societal openness. If U.S. policymakers come down too hard on the side of control, they risk helping the terrorists achieve their aim: weakening U.S. power, resolve, and global reach by sparking internal societal and economic chaos. If it was dysfunctional for Americans to overlook their vulnerability before September 11, it is equally dysfunctional for them to strive for complete invulnerability afterward. The system of preventing catastrophic attacks on U.S. soil will never be fail-safe, but much more can be done to reduce the risk of such attacks, and more can be done to reduce policymakers' need for blunt and potentially counterproductive measures in the fight against terrorism.

To start with, the United States must embrace a risk-management approach to the homeland security mission. This means acknowledging that security always comes at a price and that every incremental measure of additional security carries a higher cost. At one end of the spectrum is the open, unpoliced, and unpoliceable commercial space within which we operated prior to September 11. At the other end is the lockdown we experienced that afternoon, when practically all people, cargo, and conveyances were stopped and examined. The pre–September 11 approach was irresponsible because there are real terrorists and criminals who have the means to exploit an open transportation network to cause catastrophic harm. But the post–September 11 approach overlooks the fact that the overwhelming majority of international carriers, cargo, and travelers are indeed legitimate and their freedom of movement should not and must not be unduly restricted. The way out of this dilemma is to focus attention on building a regime that can reliably identify the people, goods, and conveyances that are legitimate, so their movements can be facilitated. Then regulators and inspectors could focus their energies on the smaller number of participants attempting to enter their jurisdiction about which they know little or have specific concerns.

Validating users and operators as legitimate requires a layered private-public approach. For people, it is essential to move away from easily forgeable paper-based documents such as traditional visas or passports, and toward universal biometric travel identification cards that include electronic scanning of fingerprints, eye retina information, or a facial profile. These credit-card-like credentials would be issued by consulates and passport offices and presented at the originating and connecting points of an individual's international travel itinerary. This electronic identity information would then be forwarded in real time to the jurisdiction of the final destination. The objective would be to provide authorities with the opportunity to check the identity information against current watch lists. If no red flags are present, then it should not be necessary to conduct a time-consuming and intrusive search. For noncitizens, the presentation of these cards would be required when renting cars, flying on domestic flights, or using passenger rail service.

Although more complicated, a similar approach can be taken for cargo. Within each commercial sector, a common set of standard security practices must be developed to reduce the opportunities for criminals or terrorists to exploit legitimate commerce to gain entry to another national jurisdiction. Loading docks should be secured from unauthorized entry and the loading process should be monitored by video cameras. In high-risk areas, the use of cargo and vehicle scanners might be required, with the images stored so that they can be cross-checked with images taken by inspectors at a transshipment or arrival destination. As is common with safety or universal quality-control standards, harmonized security measures can be established and monitored by private trade associations. As a condition of joining and maintaining membership in such an association, a company would be subjected to a preliminary review of its security measures, would have to agree to submit to periodic and random spot-checks for compliance, and would acknowledge that failure to abide by the established standards will lead to the loss of its membership status for repeat or serious violations.

Legitimate private-sector participants involved in international trade should also agree to maintain a system of in-transit accountability and visibility. In the case of a container, this would begin with the use of a theft-resistant mechanical seal. A global positioning system transponder and an electronic tag would be placed on each container so that it could be tracked. A light or temperature sensor would be installed in the interior of the container and would set off an alarm if the container were opened illegally at some point. Importers and shippers would make available this tracking information on request to regulatory or enforcement authorities within the jurisdictions through which their cargo moves or is destined.

Finally, manufacturers, importers, shipping companies, and commercial carriers would have to agree to provide to the appropriate authorities advance notice of shipments, operators, and conveyances. As with passengers, this would allow authorities the time to assess the validity of the data, check it against any watch lists they may be maintaining, and provide timely support to a field inspector who must decide which shipments and personnel are to be targeted for examination.

Enlisting private-sector cooperation, focusing on point-of-origin security measures, and embracing the use of new technologies would all support the homeland security mission by enhancing the ability of border-control agencies to detect and intercept global terrorist activity before it can arrive on U.S. soil. This approach precludes the need to harden U.S. borders, something that has the effect of imposing an economic embargo on ourselves. It will require offering meaningful incentives to companies and travelers to win over their support. It will require a serious infusion of resources to train and equip front-line agencies, such as the Customs Service, the INS, and the Coast Guard, to operate and collaborate in this complex trade and security environment. And it will involve mobilizing U.S. allies and trade partners to harmonize these processes throughout the global transportation and logistics networks.

At some point down the road, the massive post–September 11 outpouring of public and international support for combating terrorism will wane. This prospect makes beginning the painful and vital process of reforming border-management practices all the more urgent, so that a credible system can be put in place to filter the bad from the good in the cascading flows of global trade and travel. Some of the political capital being expended to pursue the terrorists of the moment should be husbanded and applied toward managing the threat of terrorism over the long run. Getting homeland security right cannot be about constructing barricades to fend off terrorists. Its aim must be to identify and take the steps necessary to preserve an open, prosperous, free, and globally engaged society.

GOVERNMENT'S CHALLENGE

GETTING SERIOUS ABOUT TERRORISM

■

JOSEPH S. NYE, JR.

In 1999, the bipartisan Hart-Rudman Commission on National Security in the 21st Century accurately warned that "Americans will likely die on American soil, possibly in large numbers," and that the U.S. government was not organized to meet the threat. Yet when the commission's final report was issued in March 2001, *The New York Times* did not cover it, nor did the White House embrace it.

The Hart-Rudman Commission was not alone in being ignored. A June 2000 report of the National Commission on Terrorism urged that "number one priority" be given to the loose affiliations of transnational terrorists seeking to inflict mass casualties on American soil. In February 2001, the director of central intelligence, George Tenet, was even more specific when he told the Senate Intelligence Committee in open testimony that Osama bin Laden's global network was the most immediate and serious threat to the United States.

In 1994, while I was chairman of the National Intelligence Council, I supervised an internal government study that pointed out that the rise of a new type of messianic terrorist was coinciding with technological trends that put into the hands of individuals destructive powers that were once the province solely of governments. Two years later, a former director of central intelligence, James Woolsey, and I chaired a government study that warned of the lack of U.S. preparedness in the face of catastrophic terrorism and suggested a number of organizational changes. When we gave briefings on our report to officials in several agencies, we received polite responses. But as one skeptic remarked, "If it is so likely, why hasn't it happened?" As Woolsey and I wrote a year later in the *Los Angeles Times*, "the very nature of U.S. society makes it difficult to prepare for this problem. We are unlikely to mount an adequate defense until we suffer an attack."

One reason the warnings of these and many similar groups went unheeded was widespread national complacency in the 1990s about the rest of the world. With the end of the Cold War and the collapse of the Soviet Union, no country could balance American military power. The United States appeared to be both invincible and invulnerable. According to State Department reports, the number of international terrorist incidents had been falling since the late 1980s. Commentators wrote about a "unipolar system" and the "benign hegemony." Some even urged a "new unilateralism" in which the United States no longer had to play the role of "docile international citizen." At the beginning of the 1990s, the Gulf War was an easy victory, and at the end of the decade, the members of the North Atlantic Treaty Organization bombed Serbia into compliance without suffering a single casualty themselves.

Even though public-opinion polls showed a rising concern about terrorism after truck bombs killed six people in the World Trade Center in 1993 and 168 people in Oklahoma City two years later, the attention paid by the public to the outside world diminished. Between 1989 and 2000, the major television networks closed many of their foreign bureaus and cut their foreign news content by two-thirds. A January 2000 Gallup poll asking people to rank the importance of issues for the presidential campaign relegated world affairs to twentieth place. In the face of such public opinion, it was hard to mobilize enthusiasm for painful organizational change or dramatic increases in spending. For example, it is hard to imagine Congress having appropriated tens of billions of dollars for the war on terrorism before September 11, no matter what the president asked for or how many reports recommended it. Richard Clarke, the antiterrorism official handling terrorism at the National Security Council for both the Clinton and George W. Bush administrations, supposedly had the power to break down bureaucratic walls, but as he observed in a 1999 interview, "there is a problem convincing people that there is a threat. There is disbelief and resistance. Most people don't understand."

HALF-MEASURES

To be fair, some significant improvements were made in antiterrorism preparations in the later half of the 1990s—though obviously not enough to prevent the tragedy that occurred. The 1996 Antiterrorism Act made racketeering and money-laundering statutes applicable to terrorist offenses, and the Nunn-Lugar-Domenici legislation enhanced our preparations for dealing with weapons of mass destruction. In his address to the U.S. Naval Academy on May 22, 1998, President Bill Clinton announced that the United States must approach terrorist challenges in the twenty-first century "with the same rigor and determination we applied to the toughest security challenges of [the twentieth] century." He signed Presidential Decision Directive 62 to outline procedures for handling such matters; appointed a national coordinator for security, infrastructure protection, and counterterrorism to the National Security Council staff; and identified "lead agencies" to create plans and goals with specific milestones. The attorney general published a "Five-Year Interagency Counterterrorism and Technology Crime Plan." Federal spending to combat terrorism rose by more than 50 percent from its 1996 level, to approximately $10 billion by 2001. The budget of programs to improve federal preparedness for attacks using weapons of mass destruction grew from effectively zero in 1995 to approximately $1.5 billion in fiscal year 2000, making it one of the fastest-growing federal programs of the late 1990s. The Federal Emergency Management Agency (FEMA), which coordinates disaster relief, was rejuvenated and improved its relations with state and local agencies. The Counter-Terrorism Center at the Central Intelligence Agency (CIA) was strengthened, and coordination between that agency and the Federal Bureau of Investigation (FBI) improved. In 1998, FBI director Louis Freeh made terrorism a top priority, and his counterterrorism budget grew to $423 million by 2001. The CIA, the FBI, and the Customs Service successfully foiled a plot to create havoc at the time of the millennium celebrations. A covert operation was undertaken to catch or kill bin Laden.

But in the absence of a sense of urgency, none of this was enough. *The New York Times* reported two weeks after the September 11 attacks that U.S. intelligence and law-enforcement officials "failed by their own admission to share information adequately or coordinate their efforts, and were caught by surprise [by the attacks]. Washington did not build a strong international coalition to focus on defeating Al Qaeda, which was seen by other nations as an American problem." Since 1996, the FBI had had evidence of terrorists using U.S. flight schools to learn to fly jumbo jets. Two of the September 11 hijackers had been flagged by the CIA as potential terrorists, but their names were not placed on an Immigration and Naturalization Service (INS) watch list until after they had already entered the country; they also escaped placement on the larger Interagency Border Inspection System. Fighter planes were scrambled too late to have any effect on September 11. The North American Aerospace Defense Command (NORAD) lacked a direct telephone line to the Federal Aviation Administration. As NORAD's commanding officer later lamented, "if somebody had called us and said, 'We have a hijacking 100 miles out coming from Europe or South America, there are terrorists on board and they've taken over the airplane,' that's a scenario we've practiced. We did not practice—and I wish to God we had—a scenario where this takes off out of Boston, and minutes later crashes into New York City. This is a whole new ballgame."

When new programs were created, they were often poorly coordinated and underfunded. The $10 billion antiterrorism budget was largely a collection of separate agency priorities. For example, the four different bio-sensor programs funded by the government were not coordinated. The fast-growing preparedness program for terrorism using weapons of mass destruction was, in the words of Richard Falkenrath and Robyn Pangi of Harvard's Kennedy School of Government, "the result of a series of unco-ordinated legislative earmarks, which permitted a succession of relatively minor programmatic initiatives in individual federal agencies. Once established, these programs became the object of uneasy collaboration between individual legislators and executive branch agencies." There was "no guiding strategy, concept or program architecture." The General Accounting Office (GAO) re-ported that the government's bioterrorism planning was "so dis-jointed that the agencies involved could not even agree on which biological agents posed the biggest threat. Officials at the Centers for Disease Control and Prevention, for instance, consider small-pox a major risk." But the FBI did not even put smallpox on its list.

The Department of Justice created a Center for Domestic Pre-paredness to train first responders—police officers, firefighters, and emergency workers—but in three years it trained only about 6,000 of the nation's 11 million first responders. Its $15 million budget was not even enough to keep it running at full capacity. Moreover, according to the GAO, there was little coordination with similar programs run by FEMA and the Defense Depart-ment. The National League of Cities has reported that nearly half of all communities have no plans to defend against or respond to terrorist attacks. The General Services Administration, which manages more than 8,000 federal buildings or offices, spent more than $1.2 billion to safeguard federal workplaces after the Okla-homa City bombing in 1995, but in 2000 undercover agents from the GAO were able to pass security checkpoints at each of the 19 federal buildings they tried to infiltrate, including the Pentagon, the CIA, and the Department of Justice. According to Thomas In-glesby of Johns Hopkins University, the Department of Defense "spent $264 billion to deter regional conflicts, $28 billion to pro-tect against a 'peer' nuclear attack, and $3 billion on all other bi-ological, chemical, cyber and nuclear assaults." Congress provided $9.7 billion in fiscal year 2000–2001 to fight terrorism, but in the words of a Stimson Center report, this funding was sprinkled across "a convoluted maze of agencies, offices, bureaus, task forces and working groups." More than 46 federal bureaus and offices in 20 agencies are involved in antiterrorism.

BUREAUCRATIC HURDLES

There were three main causes of the inertia that accounts for our lack of preparedness: complacency, an unwillingness to spend money, and the fragmented bureaucratic structure and procedures of our government. The first two were blown away on September 11, but the third remains a problem despite President George W. Bush's decision to name Pennsylvania governor Tom Ridge to head the new Office of Homeland Security. The list of vulnerabilities that Ridge faces is daunting: 1.3 million people, well over 300,000 vehicles, and 58,000 shipments worth $8.8 billion crossing our borders each day. Thousands of reservoirs, stadiums, malls, stations, airports, and buildings are vulnerable, not to mention nuclear reactors, electric power grids, the banking system, and communications. And no single organization is in charge.

By using the rhetoric of war to frame our response to the September 11 attacks, President Bush successfully called on the public resource of patriotism and persuaded Congress to provide funds. But the danger in using war rhetoric is that counterterrorism may be conceived as a military task requiring military organization. The military role, although important, is only a small part of the solution. There are many types of terrorism and many types of terrorist weapon. Even if we succeed in eliminating bin Laden, we have to remember that Timothy McVeigh was a purely homegrown product. And as we succeed in battening down the cockpits to prevent civil aircraft from being used again as giant cruise missiles, terrorists will be exploring other vulnerabilities in our open society and investigating even more devastating weapons. Fortunately, nuclear and biological weapons are not as easy to make as popular fiction suggests. But there have been reports of terrorists trying to purchase stolen nuclear weapons from the former Soviet inventory. We also know that in the 1990s, the Japanese cult Aum Shinrikyo used sarin to kill people in the

Tokyo subway system, and now anthrax has been delivered through the U.S. mail.

Suppressing terrorism is very different from a military campaign. It requires continuous, patient, undramatic civilian work, including close cooperation with other countries. It will also require coordination within our government for a systematic approach that addresses what to do before, during, and after a potential terrorist attack. The CIA and the FBI must improve their ability to work together on detection, and they must reconcile their different authorities and programs in intelligence and law enforcement. The FBI, the INS, the Customs Service, and the Defense Department must improve their cooperation on prevention and protection. FEMA has to work with local governments on domestic responses. The CIA and the State, Defense, and Treasury departments must coordinate international responses, including diplomatic, financial, and military retaliation. New research-and-development programs are needed for each of the phases of a crisis, as are accelerated acquisitions of new technologies and special training and exercises that test both parts and the system as a whole.

When Americans think of reorganization at the federal level, they often think of creating a new department with new powers. The Hart-Rudman Commission suggested this approach: the creation of an independent, cabinet-level National Homeland Security Agency with responsibility for planning, coordinating, and integrating various U.S. government activities involved in homeland security. Such an agency would oversee FEMA, the Coast Guard, the Customs Service, and the Border Patrol. Elaine Kamarck has suggested a better plan that has FEMA handle responses while the other three agencies plus a new airport-security force and responsibility for visas are combined in a department focused on prevention. Many members of Congress are attracted to this approach, *The Washington Post* has reported, not only because it would give congressional committees more control over the office, but because "many Republican and Democratic lawmakers fear that without statutory authority over the budgets and operations of agencies related to anti-terrorism, Ridge will lack the clout essential to mount an effective nationwide effort to quash further terrorist threats and put in place improved security and emergency response measures." Senator Joseph I. Lieberman commented, "My feeling is the best way we should assure the job gets done is to put [Ridge] in a new Cabinet department, giving him both budget and direct line authority. The president's announcement was a significant step forward, but we need to make sure the job of homeland defense gets done."

Realigning and combining similar agencies in a new department may improve some operations (after the dust of bureaucratic disruption finally settles), but it will not solve the problem of coordination. It is impossible to put the whole government into one department. The 46 agencies frequently mentioned have other legitimate work to do in addition to combating and preempting terrorism. And even a new cabinet department of homeland security that combines five prevention functions would still need to be coordinated with 40 or so other bureaucracies.

A second common American approach to government reorganization is to talk of a "czar" to lead a "war on poverty" or a "war on drugs." The use of this term is particularly ironic because American government was created to ensure that there would never be any czars. The nation's founders were more concerned with ensuring liberty than with maximizing efficiency. As one wag put it, the Constitution was designed to ensure that King George could never rule over us again—nor could anyone else. The very call for a czar represents a sense of frustration about the difficulty of overcoming our fragmented governmental structures. On the other hand, there are two officials elected by all the people who stand above all agencies: the president and the vice president. An effective coordinator will have to borrow that power. "Drug czars" and "poverty czars" in the past have failed because they have not really had the ability to borrow presidential power. As former drug "czar" Barry McCaffrey observed, "If all [Ridge] has are five people and a black sedan, he'll be a speakers' bureau for U.S. counter-terrorism efforts and nothing more." As Ernest May points out, James Byrne's Office of War Mobilization had this power during World War II, and national security advisers have had significant power since the days of the Cold War. The Bush administration has chosen the National Security Council (NSC) model of empowerment through proximity to the president rather than using a congressional grant of budget and legal authority to establish the power of the new Office of Homeland Defense.

If Ridge is known to speak for the president, chairs a committee of secretaries from the relevant agencies where budgets and operational programs reside, and has the power to approve their antiterrorism budgets, he may have a workable model. But the Office of Homeland Security will have a more difficult task than that of the National Security Council. The latter deals primarily with policy rather than operations, words rather than dollars and organizations. The NSC has never had much leverage over the defense budget, or the budgets of other departments, for that matter. The key for Ridge will be budgetary authority. A new account could be created in the federal budget that includes parts of agency budgets relating to the homeland security functions (just as the federal budget's 050 "defense" account now includes parts of budgets from several agencies) and gives Ridge some funds of his own. If agencies need Ridge's agreement to get their budgets approved, they will be sure to return his phone calls. Ridge's small staff of 100 or so (about the same size as the NSC) should work closely with the Office of Management and Budget to develop and monitor a long-term strategy and consistent multiyear plans that will be executed through established agency programs. In addition, the White House should encourage the congressional leadership to establish a new Joint Committee on Terrorism and Homeland Security and allow Ridge to testify before it on a regular basis, rather than following the NSC model, which is deliberately isolated from Congress.

In addition, the White House will have to work out the relationship between the Office of Homeland Security and the National Security Council. Since much of terrorism is transnational, it does not clearly fall into the existing division of jurisdiction along domestic/foreign lines. The same is true of international economic policy, where the solution has been to have some overlapping staff members reporting to two bosses. President Bush has named retired general Wayne Downing to join the NSC as a counterterrorism coordinator. Presumably, he will focus on overseas operations and coordination of foreign intelligence. But since effective action against terrorism not only will require maintaining diplomatic coalitions, but will also involve many domestic agencies working beyond the borders of other countries and inside our own, the lines will be blurred. Knitting together this policy seam inside the White House will be crucial to the success of the endeavor.

Another set of organizational divisions that Ridge will have to manage is between the federal government and state and local authorities. The American federal system comprises some 87,000 local governments, including counties, municipalities, townships, school districts, and numerous kinds of special districts. They vary enormously in budgets and capacities, but many play a crucial role in preparedness. As mentioned earlier, there are some 11 million first responders (police officers, firefighters, and emergency personnel) in the country. Ridge will have to use the bully pulpit of his office as well as federal grants and subsidies to try to establish priorities and bring about some degree of coordination among these disparate entities.

A SPECIALIZED PLAN

Rather than build up excessive staff in the White House, Ridge's office should be supported by one or more specially created, federally funded research-and-development corporations, analogous to the RAND Corporation, which was created to deal with the nuclear threat early in the Cold War. Such a structure would avoid the rigidities and inadequate salaries that plague the federal bureaucracy yet be responsive to Ridge's priorities. It should be organized to think systematically and comprehensively about terrorism, starting with intelligence and warning, then moving through deterrence and prevention, crisis and consequence management, and postevent retaliation and system repair. As Ashton Carter, a professor at the Kennedy School of Government at Harvard University, has pointed out, warning will require measures ranging from better spies to chemical- and biological-agent "sniffers" to be installed in subway tunnels, water supplies, and government buildings. Protection will require bomb-resistant building codes, vaccines against anthrax, and firewalls to keep computer viruses out of critical information networks. Deterrence and retaliation will require coalitions of friends and supporters worldwide. Each stage of the process needs careful attention.

This staff would have the responsibility of helping to plan the system as a whole, looking for gaps and overlaps in agency budgets and programs, examining weaknesses in private systems such as computer networks and building codes, and planning ahead to anticipate how different types of terrorists would look for chinks in our armor. It would conduct regular exercises between specially created "blue teams" and "red teams" to war game and test the vulnerability of various systems in our society. Had we done this for our airport security system, for example, we might have realized that it was designed to detect guns and bombs of the type that destroyed Pan Am flight 103 over Lockerbie, Scotland, rather than to stop suicide pilots armed with knives and box cutters.

The campaign against terrorism will likely last a long time. After all, it took Europe and Japan more than a generation to overcome the transnational terrorism of the 1960s and 1970s. It takes only a fraction of a percent of any population to create the physical damage and disruptive psychological effects that terrorists seek. There will be others to follow in bin Laden's footsteps. The defeat of Al Qaeda will not end the terrorism problem. Our government organization will undoubtedly evolve as well. We will need flexibility in organization, imagination in considering future challenges, and an attention to the antiterror system as a whole. The Bush administration has made a reasonable start, but we will need effective organization long after Ridge and Bush leave office. The tragedy of September 11 has banished forever the complacency that made the earlier efforts at reorganization so difficult. But sustainability is the important issue in our democracy. The key to our future will be maintaining our newfound focus.

GERM WARS

THE BIOLOGICAL THREAT FROM ABROAD

■

RICHARD BUTLER

The delivery of anthrax through the U.S. Postal Service in the weeks subsequent to September 11 has brought the specter of biological terrorism into our daily lives. Where once it had been a subject of only the most far-fetched theories, the threat of bioterrorism has become credible practically overnight. The unthinkable has not only become thinkable; it has become real.

For the countries that have pursued biological weapons programs during the past three to four decades, anthrax has been the most popular agent. It can be grown relatively easily from just a few spores, through a simple process of fermentation. Anthrax becomes a more potent weapon, however, when the spores are reduced in size through a process of drying and milling. When that particle size makes it possible for anthrax to be aerosolized—delivered through the air—it is able to infect human beings through the lungs, a far more deadly form of the disease than the more common cutaneous anthrax, contracted through the skin.

On the overall scale of things, the recent terrorism of anthrax-by-mail has not been large. If it is the object of terrorists to cause massive death, as was clearly the case on September 11, then the anthrax letter campaign has failed, unless it expands considerably from its scattered beginnings. But if the objective is to cause terror, then the anthrax mailings have been outstandingly successful. The run at pharmacies on the antibiotic Cipro, among other things, demonstrates this.

Considerable speculation exists, however, that the anthrax mailing campaign has been a blind—a diversion designed to distract authorities (and the public) from far more substantial terrorist attacks on the United States that are planned for the weeks and months to come. There is no way to answer such speculation or even to tell, at the time of this writing, who was responsible for the mailings and whether they were connected to the September 11 attacks. Sadly, we are compelled to wait and see. But characterizing the anthrax mailings as a mere sideshow misses the point entirely. The story of Saddam Hussein's biological weapons program illustrates the depths of the danger we face.

A CLOUD OVER BAGHDAD

In 1972, agreement was reached on the text of the Biological Weapons Convention, an international treaty outlawing the manufacture and use of such weapons. Iraq signed that treaty and thus accepted the obligations set forth in it. A number of years later, however—it is not known exactly how many—Saddam Hussein directed that a clandestine program to manufacture and deploy biological weapons begin. Iraq then proceeded to develop a range of such agents—including anthrax, botulinum toxin, gas gangrene, aflatoxin, and ricin—and worked vigorously on ways to weaponize and deliver them. Evidence suggests that Saddam has, at times, also been interested in plague, smallpox, and other infectious agents. Some of these agents are considerably more useful in military situations than others, but all are insidious. Aflatoxin, for example, shows no immediate effects, but does cause liver cancer five to ten years after exposure. Iraq has never explained why it had made aflatoxin, but the answer may now lie in the fact that southern Iraqi refugees who have emigrated to Europe are today showing rates of liver cancer considerably higher than the community average. It is no coincidence that these people come from a part of Iraq that has repeatedly rebelled against Saddam's rule.

From the beginning of the U.N.'s arms control efforts—spearheaded by the U.N. Special Commission (UNSCOM), created at the end of the Gulf War in 1991—Iraq pursued a policy of denial when questioned about its biological weapons program. For several years Baghdad claimed that it had no such program, but when UNSCOM's investigations demonstrated this to be palpably untrue, Saddam's government shifted its stance, claiming that its biological weapons program was tiny and merely defensive. (What a "defensive" biological weapons program might be was never adequately explained.) Even after years of extensive inspections and investigations, UNSCOM was never able to pin down the magnitude and nature of Saddam's biological weapons program. But it was clear from the severity of his resistance to UNSCOM that the program was not small and that it was one to which he attached great importance.

On one occasion, Iraq's deputy prime minister, Tariq Aziz, told me in private that "of course" Iraq had a biological weapons program. He also told me why: "to use on the Persians and the Jews." Nor did Saddam see biological weapons as a sideshow; they were an integral part of his preparations for a future war—perhaps against Iran or Israel, or perhaps against the United States.

ENFORCING THE NORM

The critical questions that still need answers with respect to the anthrax mailings in the United States are these: Who carried them out and how can the attackers be stopped? These questions are being investigated along two paths—the postal and the scientific. Tracking the passage of the mail through the postal system could identify the letters' point of origin and, possibly, the perpetrators. The scientific path—tracking the kind of anthrax enclosed in the letters—opens up wider possibilities. If, as seems the case, the anthrax is of a sophisticated grade, this would imply both the application of know-how and relatively sophisticated equipment for its production. That knowledge and equipment could theoretically be available to a criminal within the United States or a few other Western countries, but it certainly has been available in the two countries that have maintained significant biological weapons programs, Russia and Iraq. It may be possible to determine, on the basis of the intrinsic characteristics of the anthrax, where the microbes were made. Whatever emerges with respect to possible foreign involvement in the anthrax mailings, the United States must now accept that biological warfare agents have entered the terrorist arsenal. This has two major implications, one domestic and the other international.

On the domestic level, every relevant element of state and federal government from police to public health authorities must now prepare for the use of biological weapons against citizens. Such planning and action is fundamentally defensive and rests on the assumption that biological warfare agents will continue to exist and will be used. That assumption contradicts the norm established in the 1972 Biological Weapons Convention. But the implementation of the convention has been impeded by the failure to date of signatory states to agree on a means of verifying adherence to the terms of the treaty. A draft verification protocol has yet to be adopted—not least because the United States decided earlier in 2001 that the draft was unacceptable.

Verifying compliance with the convention is difficult. More so than with other weapons of mass destruction, the manufacture of biological warfare agents is nearly indistinguishable from the manufacture of benign and useful medical and pharmacological substances. This problem of "dual-use" technology is serious, and does not have a ready answer. Soft-headed though it might sound, especially when faced with a ruthless dictator like Saddam Hussein, we are in fact compelled to rely for protection mostly on "civilization"—that is, the expectation that states and their leaders will accept the practical and moral norm set forth in the Biological Weapons Convention.

There is, however, an additional remedy available—reliable enforcement of the norm and obligations set forth in the convention. If we have learned anything from our dealings with Saddam Hussein, it is that he was correct in calculating that if he were to hang tough for a very long time and accept periodic military attacks, and if he were to wage an extended propaganda campaign about the suffering of the Iraqi people under sanctions (the relief of which was tied to his compliance with arms-control requirements), he would be able to retain his weapons of mass destruction. He would not face enforcement of Security Council resolutions, the Biological Weapons Convention, or the Nuclear Nonproliferation Treaty.

In the case of biological weapons, the international community needs to leap over the problems of verification (while still working on a solution) by taking one simple step. It should be agreed among nations that the manufacture, possession, or use of biological weapons are by their very nature crimes against humanity. There is logic in this position. What possible purpose can the weaponization of germs have other than to wage an attack on humanity itself at its most fundamental level? How else, for example, could one characterize the use of smallpox for terrorism, given its wildly contagious characteristics? Like so many issues after September 11, this question is no longer strictly theoretical. After all, both the Soviet Union and Iraq considered using this disease as a biological weapon.

If the international community were to agree that action by any state or group to manufacture, acquire, or use chemical or biological weapons would be immediately considered—without qualification—a crime against humanity, then enforcement action could be taken immediately to remove the offending facilities or laboratories involved. Were this the norm, it would be unlikely that germ weapons would be made anywhere. To ensure that such a policy would work, the Security Council or an international organization established specifically for this purpose would have to be notified, on reliable evidence, that the rule had been broken. The guilty state or group would then be warned and told to desist. If it refused to do so, enforcement action could be taken immediately to remedy the situation.

The road ahead on biological weapons will be tortuous. The difficulties are immense, starting with the dual-use problem and the ubiquity and necessity of biological science and technology. But, as we have so clearly seen, biological warfare in the midst of civilian society is no longer a phantasm, and demands unique responses. We need defense at home. But above all, the community of nations must finally declare that biological weapons lie beyond the pale of humanity and civilized society—and ensure that they stay there.

COUNTERING BIOTERRORISM*

WHO'S IN CHARGE?

■

LAURIE GARRETT

The list of nations possessing biological weapons capabilities cuts across lines of ideology, politics, and geography. It is a long list, consisting of Iraq, Iran, Syria, Libya, China, North Korea, Russia, Israel, Taiwan, and possibly Sudan, India, Pakistan, and Kazakhstan. In addition, according to intelligence sources in Europe and the United States, militant political groups across the globe are now developing or seeking to purchase biological weapons for terrorist use.

Meanwhile, the sophistication of biological weaponry has improved by leaps and bounds. Until 1985, all of the world's biological-weapons makers were stuck with the same list of pathogens and toxins that could kill thousands of enemies and be delivered with missiles or large-scale aerosol systems. Each nation knew the list and stocked antidotes and vaccines. It was a stand-off.

But biology in the last decade has been what physics was in the 1940s and 1950s: a field of exponential discovery. What seemed impossible in 1980 was accomplished by 1990 and, by 2000, had become ho-hum fodder for high school biology classes. By the late 1990s, a massive pool of bioengineers, equipped with genetic blueprints to guide their efforts, had emerged. Determining the

*This essay is adapted from an article published by *Foreign Affairs* in January 2001, which was excerpted from *Betrayal of Trust: The Collapse of Global Public Health* by Laurie Garrett. Copyright © 2000 by Laurie Garrett. Reprinted by permission of Hyperion. Though the events of the fall of 2001 have led to several changes in the picture described below, the main theme and principal points are as relevant, if not more so, today.

genetic sequence of a virus, such as Ebola, was no longer much of a feat. In 1998, scientists at the Frederick Cancer Research Center in Maryland determined, at the genetic level, exactly how anthrax kills human cells.

In response to such advances, Western militaries hardened their defenses against biological warfare as they vaccinated troops, stockpiled antitoxins, stored appropriate antibiotics, purchased protective suits and masks, practiced war-game drills involving biological weapons, and supported research on potential microbe-detecting devices. But no one had a master plan for dealing with the collateral impact of biological weapons on civilians located around the combat zone—or the deliberate impact of bioterrorist damage inflicted on an unsuspecting community.

Were a terrorist to disperse the smallpox virus, for example, populations that were once universally vaccinated would now be horribly vulnerable. As of early 2001 the U.S. government stowed only about 15.4 million doses of the smallpox vaccine—enough for less than seven percent of the American population. The World Health Organization (WHO) kept another 500,000 doses in the Netherlands, and other national stockpiles totaled about 60 million more doses of varying quality and potency. If the smallpox virus were released today, therefore, the majority of the world's population would be defenseless, and given the virus' 30 percent kill rate, nearly two billion people could die.

For other diseases preventable by vaccine, such as anthrax, the lag time between inoculation and the development of powerful antibodies could be far longer—up to a year, even with boosters. And of course, immunization efforts would be useless against vaccine-resistant pathogens, such as those created by Soviet scientists working on anthrax weapons. Furthermore, a determined bioterrorist could simply try a succession of microbial weapons—or use a cocktail at the outset—defying even the best-organized vaccination programs.

Even if cities were well equipped for a bioterrorist attack, they would still have a difficult time recognizing that such an attack had occurred. If the microbe were rare, like those that cause anthrax, Q fever, Ebola, smallpox, or plague, local facilities would probably be unable to diagnose the problem. With precious time passing, people dying, and disease possibly spreading, local officials would then await word from the diagnostic labs at the Centers for Disease Control (CDC) in Atlanta. In the case of a bioterrorist attack, valuable time—and lives—might be lost during such an identification process.

In a large urban center, the true costs of a bioterrorist attack might be the consequences of panic, such as a stock market collapse in New York or a commodities market crash in Chicago.

Although before the Fall of 2001 most people remained ignorant of the issues raised by bioterrorist scenarios, handfuls of Internet-hooked extremists, right-wing militia members, psychologically imbalanced belligerents, and postmodern fascists are well versed in the fine points of bioterrorism. Recipes for producing botulinum and anthrax are posted on the Web. Books describing biological-warfare assassination techniques are readily available. Some private militia groups train to use biological weapons.

Indeed, law enforcement leaders claim that religious cults and militant political groups are likely to engage in biological terrorism. After all, they argue, members of an Oregon-based religious cult led by Bagwan Shree Rajneesh carried out the first bioterrorist attack in America in 1984. The cult members, hoping to disrupt an upcoming county election, contaminated local salad bars with salmonella, infecting hundreds of Oregonians.

RAISING THE BAR

In response to such threats, in recent years Congress has passed a number of laws aimed at making it harder for anyone—domestic or foreign—to attack America with biological weapons. In 1989, Congress passed the Biological Weapons Act, outlawing the possession, trade, sale, or manufacture of a biological substance "for use as a weapon." In 1991, it enacted an embargo, soon enforced against Iraq, barring U.S. companies from trading with countries believed to be developing biological weapons.

After the 1995 Oklahoma City bombing, Congress passed the Anti-Terrorism Act of 1996, allowing federal authorities to arrest anyone who even "threatens" to develop or use biological weapons. And the following year, by order of Congress, the CDC named 24 infectious organisms and 12 toxins as "restricted agents," the use or possession of which requires a federal permit. Although these measures now provide legal instruments for federal law enforcement officials, it is impossible to judge how effective they have been in deterring potential acts of biological terrorism.

The Clinton administration hoped to stave off the worst threats by training the National Guard and local hazardous-material defense teams to rapidly respond to bioterrorist attacks. But the teams, comprising elite local police squads and fire department personnel, handled chemical and biological threats as if they were roughly synonymous—a fatal mistake, according to biologists. Having been trained in classical techniques for limiting the spread of lethal chemicals, the defense teams assumed that a visible source of contamination could be identified, that exposed individuals could be isolated, and that a toxin could be swiftly cleared out of the environment with water or neutralizing chemicals. None of these assumptions holds true for lethal microbes, biologists argue, because their long incubation periods in potentially contagious human beings render it nearly impossible to identify and contain a source. Furthermore, "washing" an area contaminated with pathogens might only spread them.

Congress sought technological solutions as well, allocating money for Department of Defense (DOD) research on devices that might sniff out bugs and sanitize contaminated areas. First in line was the Navy's TagMan, a sophisticated gene scanner that could, in less than half an hour, determine whether a liquid sample contained any of several known pathogens. But the system had significant limitations: weighing 300 pounds, it was hardly portable. And it could not detect pathogens of high "biohazard levels"—precisely the most worrisome microbes. Most significant, the device could not analyze air samples.

In 1998, Congress also gave the DOD's Defense Advanced Research Projects Agency (DARPA) $2 billion to sponsor projects so far-out that standard civilian funding sources would not consider them. These projects included $61.6 million for bioweapons defense efforts, the foremost of which was the development of a fast, cheap, safe, and portable way to sample air for the presence of nasty pathogens. Most of the research focused on unique genetic attributes of bacteria and viruses.

Even the simplest technological defense against biological weapons has proven to be too much for defense contractors. In the spring of 2000, DOD officials revealed that the protective suits U.S. troops had relied on during the Persian Gulf War (and that still form the basis of soldiers' defense against deadly microbes) were defective. The General Accounting Office (GAO) found that the Pentagon had overcounted by more than 300,000 the number of protective suits it had in its stockpile, and that inventory control was so poorly managed that the department had issued expired and defective suits to personnel while better equipment sat unused in military warehouses. According to the GAO, 682,331 U.S. military personnel had gone unprotected due to inventory errors, faulty suits, and insufficient supplies, putting the military at what the agency termed "high risk" in a biological or chemical contingency.

It seems unlikely, then, that a technological quick fix will soon be found. The three immediate American responses to bioterrorism—military defense, hazardous-material defense teams, and high-technology sensors—appear to be seriously flawed.

WHO'S IN CHARGE?

In the event of a successful release of drug-resistant anthrax spores in a subway system, the most important responders would not be the military or law enforcement officials. They would be the doctors, epidemiologists, ambulance drivers, nurses, and bureaucrats of the public health system. It is they who would note—days after the actual attack—that large numbers of citizens appeared to be ill, suffering similar symptoms.

With further questioning they would perhaps realize that all the ailing individuals routinely took the same subway train or stopped at the same station. Whether or not anyone would ever discover that terrorists had sprayed a lethal biological mist in the station, it would be the public health workers who would track down and treat the patients, dispense appropriate drugs, determine whether the outbreak was spreading from the source, and analyze the microorganism for any special attributes.

Yet it has been military-style responses that have dominated Western government thinking. During role-playing episodes in 1998–99, the DOD claimed the right to seize command during a bioterrorist attack. And on February 1, 1999, then Defense Secretary William Cohen announced the creation of a special command within the DOD designed to coordinate responses to domestic bioterrorist attacks.

Public health was a late entrant to the bioterrorism field, and it is obvious that public health, law enforcement, and defense officials have very different priorities in the event of a bioterrorist attack. For public health workers, the paramount concerns are limiting the spread of infection, identifying the cause of the disease, and if possible, treating and vaccinating the public. Law enforcement agents, however, are in the business of stopping and solving crimes—and to them, the scene of any bioterrorist incident is therefore, first and foremost, a source of evidence. Managing a response to an outbreak thus poses a conflict of interest, since the police and the FBI would, by mandate, focus on detaining witnesses and obtaining evidence, even if those efforts ran counter to public health needs.

Even within the military itself, priorities blur when it comes to bioterrorism. The DOD's primary mission is to protect the United States against military foes. A secondary concern is to defend the health of American troops. How those priorities square with intervening—and indeed, commanding—responses to domestic bioterrorist attacks is not at all clear.

What is even less clear is how a public health system can respond to bioterrorism without destroying the basis of its credibility. When a public health system needs to intrude on individuals' lives to protect the larger community, it does so in limited ways and usually under the hard-and-fast promise of confidentiality. During an epidemic, for example, individuals may be asked to submit to blood tests and medical exams, and their medical charts may be scrutinized—but all under the promise of confidentiality. In the long term, a public health system protects the community by monitoring disease trends, which requires tracking who has which diseases. Again, this information is generally stored under confidential or anonymous terms. On a global level, the WHO and a variety of other groups keep count of nations' diseases, monitoring for the emergence of new epidemics. After the 1995 Ebola outbreak in Zaire, for example, the WHO sought to create a more rigorous surveillance system and pushed countries to be more open about epidemics in their populations.

All of these functions, in all tiers of public health systems, require the maintenance of a crucial social contract: the individual or country agrees to openly disclose information for the sake of the larger community's health. In return, public health authorities promise never to abuse this trust, maintaining discretion and protecting patient privacy.

But the fear of bioterrorism threatens to destroy that vital social contract, which is not shared by law enforcement and defense officials. The closer a public health system draws to the other two systems, the greater the danger that it will lose credibility in the eyes of the public. Indeed, suspicions already run high in many American minority communities, prompting widespread belief that such microbes as the AIDS virus were created by the U.S. Public Health Service, the National Institutes of Health, or the CIA with the intention of obliterating key minority populations.

Many advocates argue that the public health system's role in the fight against bioterrorism can be comfortable only if it is an equal partner of the law enforcement and defense communities. Only then will it have the authority and wherewithal to enhance the readiness and capacities of local, state, and federal health departments for responding to both natural and deliberately created epidemics. After all, it is impossible to tell at an epidemic's outset whether it is a natural or ghoulishly unnatural event.

The Bush administration must work out these tensions among public health, law enforcement, and military authorities. The Clinton administration offered a broader definition of national security, bringing emerging infectious diseases and the AIDS pandemic under the security umbrella. That allowed agencies more traditionally concerned with terrorism, such as the National Security Council, the CIA, and the FBI, into the public health arena. The future balance of authority and influence in the fight against bioterrorism will undoubtedly hinge on whether a larger view of national security is adopted.

Public health's role in the bioterrorism issue will also be better defined when its leaders come up with a clear consensus on what exactly they want. Before September the issue was so new to most public health officials and raised so many uncomfortable questions that the profession was unable to speak with a clear, united voice. In contrast, the law enforcement and military communities appear comparatively determined and direct in their views of the bioterrorism threat and their desired responses to it.

Public health officials have been urged to jump on board a train already in motion, conducted by the law enforcement and defense communities. In fiscal year 2000, the train was fueled by an $8.4 billion budget of which a mere 3.7 percent was allotted to public health. With such comparatively paltry funding, it is no wonder that public health found itself sitting at the back of the train, watching the scenery race by as other government players steered the locomotive's course. In the wake of the recent anthrax mailings, national priorities are likely to change. If they don't, the train is going to crash.

THE NEW SECURITY MANTRA

PREVENTION, DETERRENCE, DEFENSE

■

WILLIAM J. PERRY

In the wake of the attacks on the World Trade Center and the Pentagon, America has been mourning its dead and tending to its wounded. But the country also has been building up an angry resolve to respond to this outrage against humanity, and a pragmatic resolve to reduce its vulnerability to future attacks. The world has seen just how terrible the consequences can be when terrorists have the hatred to murder innocent civilians, the resources to coordinate and conduct systematic operations, and the fanaticism to sacrifice their own lives. The evil genius who conceived of using a passenger airplane in kamikaze mode calculated that its 200,000 pounds of jet fuel would make it a weapon of mass destruction. And so it was, with almost 5,000 deaths resulting from the planes used against the World Trade Center, more than ten times the fatality rate caused by past attacks with truck bombs.

The United States can take many actions to make this sort of attack more difficult to carry out, and it will do so, despite the inconvenience and expense. But as Washington moves to reduce the vulnerabilities exposed by the last strike, it should also try to anticipate the next one. As deadly as the World Trade Center disaster was, it could have produced a hundredfold more victims if the terrorists had possessed nuclear or biological weapons. And the future threat could come from hostile nations as well as from terrorists.

Nuclear or biological weapons in the hands of terrorists or rogue states constitute the greatest single danger to American security—indeed, to world security—and a threat that is becoming increasingly less remote, as the recent anthrax mailings demonstrate all too clearly. Several nations hostile to the United States are already engaged in covert programs to develop nuclear weapons, and multinational terrorist groups have demonstrated both by word and by deed that their goal is to kill Americans and destroy symbols of American power. Such terrorists have escalated their methods from truck bombs to the near equivalent of a tactical nuclear weapon, and they clearly have the motivation to go further up the ladder of destruction. Indeed, Osama bin Laden has told his followers that the acquisition of weapons of mass destruction is a "religious duty." The only question is whether they will succeed.

Since the end of the Cold War, the barriers to that success have been lowered. The know-how for making nuclear weapons is increasingly available over the Internet. Security controls on the world's huge supply of nuclear weapons (which number in the tens of thousands) and fissile material (amounting to hundreds of tons) are becoming increasingly uncertain. And the thriving black market in fissile material suggests that demand is high. In the next few years this combination of forces could result in a nuclear incident with results more catastrophic than the destruction wrought by the Hiroshima and Nagasaki bombs, which together killed an estimated 200,000 people.

A nuclear attack's capacity for destruction is familiar by now, but recent simulations indicate that an attack with smallpox germs could cause just as many deaths. Furthermore, as the anthrax mailings show, there are good reasons to fear that terrorists will find biological weapons increasingly attractive. They can be produced without the massive infrastructure required for their nuclear counterparts, and developments in biotechnology and the pharmaceutical industry are proliferating these production techniques. Hostile groups that cannot develop their own weapons, meanwhile, may be able to buy them through illicit channels. The Soviet Union produced a large supply of biological weapons during the Cold War, some of which may still be available. China, North Korea, and Iraq have all had biological weapons programs, as did the Aum Shinrikyo cult in Japan, which in 1995 released a chemical weapon, sarin, in a deadly attack on Tokyo's subways.

Finally, the threat posed by long-range missiles has received much attention. But a long-range missile in the hands of a hostile force does not pose a significant new danger unless the missile has a nuclear or biological warhead. Nuclear and biological weapons, in contrast, are dangerous even in the absence of missiles, since they can be delivered by a range of methods, including trucks, cargo ships, boats, and airplanes—or even through the mail. Indeed, given its attractions, covert rather than overt delivery is not only feasible, it is the more likely method of attack as recent events establish.

Considering the level of catastrophe that could occur in a nuclear or biological attack, mitigating such threats should be an overriding security priority today, just as heading off a nuclear attack was an overriding priority during the Cold War. In that era the United States essentially depended on a single strategy: deterrence. Now it can add two other strategies to the mix: prevention (curbing emergent threats before they can spread) and defense. Rather than relying exclusively on any one strategy, the sensible approach is to deploy a balanced mix of all three. Missile defense should be one element of national policy, but if the single-minded pursuit of it conflicts with programs designed to curb proliferation and strengthen deterrence, it could decrease America's security rather than increase it.

PREVENTION

Prevention is the first line of defense against the proliferation of weapons of mass destruction, but it requires cooperation from other powers. Any actions that the United States takes to stop the spread of weapons can easily be nullified if Russia, for example, decides to sell its technology, weapons, or fissile material. Russian leaders know that it is in their national interest to fight proliferation, but they may at some point be torn between their security interests and the need to earn hard currency. This financial incentive might delude them into thinking that the sale of commercial nuclear technology to Iran, for instance, would not facilitate Iran's development of nuclear weapons.

The cooperation necessary to prevent proliferation is manifested through treaties already in force, such as the nuclear Nonproliferation Treaty, the Strategic Arms Reduction Treaty (START), and the Biological Weapons Convention; through treaties not yet implemented, such as the Comprehensive Test Ban Treaty, START II, and START III; through bilateral and multilateral agreements, such as the Trilateral Agreement (among the United States, Russia, and Ukraine), the Agreed Framework (between the United States and North Korea), and the missile agreement under discussion with North Korea; and through cooperative programs to reduce nuclear risks and manage Cold War–era nuclear arsenals, such as the Nunn-Lugar program with Russia and other former Soviet states.

Many of these programs have been quite successful. The Nunn-Lugar initiative, for example, in concert with START and the Trilateral Agreement, has already been responsible for the dismantling of more than 5,000 nuclear warheads and the complete elimination of nuclear weapons in Ukraine, Kazakhstan, and Belarus. And as a result of programs designed to immobilize or commercialize leftover Soviet plutonium and weapons-grade uranium, material that was once intended for Soviet bombs will soon meet half the supply needs of American nuclear power reactors.

To prevent future proliferation, the United States should sustain and build on these programs, by extending the Nunn-Lugar efforts to tactical nuclear weapons, for example, and by funding proposed efforts to immobilize plutonium. But some weapons materials have already spread, and future prevention efforts will not always be effective (as evidenced by the expelling of United Nations weapons inspectors from Iraq). So the second line of defense must remain deterrence.

DETERRENCE

Even if START II and START III were fully implemented, the United States would still be left with a nuclear force capable of destroying any nation reckless enough to use nuclear weapons against it. In particular, a nuclear attack using ballistic missiles would be instantly tracked to its place of origin and thus invite immediate retaliation by U.S. nuclear forces—a fact known by all. Some worry that a nation with nuclear weapons might attack a U.S. ally with conventional weapons, believing that Washington would not honor its defense commitment for fear of provoking a nuclear attack on U.S. cities. But any such move would be a serious mistake, since the United States would respond in kind—with its own conventional military forces—to a conventional attack on an ally. The aggressor might then threaten a nuclear strike but would have to contemplate, once again, the certain knowledge of immediate and catastrophic retaliation. So long as the United States maintains strong conventional forces, therefore, the threat of nuclear extortion reverts to the classic deterrence scenario. Moreover, if threatened, the United States has the capability to destroy a hostile nation's launch sites, storage sites, and production facilities with its long-range, precision-guided, conventionally armed weapons—and others know it. Whatever Washington's stated policy, therefore, no hostile nation could rule out that possibility.

In short, the United States has a powerful and credible deterrent involving both nuclear and conventional weapons, which should make a direct nuclear attack or nuclear extortion by a nation very unlikely. The chance still exists, however, that a hostile nation armed with nuclear or biological weapons could end up under a leader who is mentally unbalanced or who miscalculates the consequences of his or her actions. And a terrorist group is probably less deterrable; its members might believe that an attack could not be traced back to them, or they might even be seeking to die for their cause. Both prevention and deterrence, in other words, could fail in the face of terrorism, and there is always the possibility, however remote, of an accidental or unauthorized launch from another nuclear power. Any of these contingencies would create a catastrophe, so it is reasonable for the United States to seek "catastrophe insurance," much as individuals buy earthquake insurance to cover the possibility that their house might be destroyed by such an event.

DEFENSE

The most immediate grave danger is of a terrorist group delivering a nuclear bomb or biological weapon with a truck, airplane, or boat. Such an attack could be tactically similar to what the United States has already experienced—in the 1993 World Trade Center bombing, the 1996 explosions at the Khobar Towers in Saudi Arabia, the attacks on the U.S. embassies in Kenya and Tanzania in 1998, and the bombing of the U.S.S. *Cole* in 2000— and the ultimately responsible parties would be equally difficult to identify. The probable culprit would be a well-organized multinational group, acting with direct or indirect support from one or more hostile nations. Regular military defense tactics by the United States would be largely irrelevant, since the attackers would conceal the place and time of the strike, and Washington cannot maintain terrorist alerts continuously for the entire nation. The first line of defense against this threat, accordingly, is to develop an intelligence network able to give the government advance warning of an attack so that it can be stopped before it is launched.

As Washington tries to step up its intelligence activities, however, it will face two barriers: the restrictions imposed on U.S. intelligence agencies' investigations of domestic suspects, and the disconnect between intelligence and law enforcement. Resolving these problems without unduly infringing on Americans' civil liberties will take judicious new legislation, as well as a restructuring of the executive branch. President George W. Bush's creation of an Office of Homeland Security provides a useful basis for the necessary changes.

At the same time, Washington should pursue an aggressive campaign against the bases of terrorist groups and their possible state sponsors. Terrorist groups often have activities and support scattered in several countries, so the United States needs joint intelligence collection and analysis efforts with other nations, particularly those where terrorist cells are located. It will be perhaps most important (and most difficult, even after September 11) to get this type of cooperation from Russia and China. But just as future success in preventing nuclear proliferation will require joint programs with Russia and China, so will success in collecting intelligence on multinational terrorist groups.

Hostile nations can also pose a danger if they develop the capability to attack the United States with nuclear or biological weapons. In addition to the covert means available to terrorists, states could place their weapons in aircraft, perhaps in the guise of commercial planes, or in cruise missiles, perhaps based in freighters off the U.S. coast. Here again, intelligence is key: putting the necessary defense measures in place requires a timely warning of the time and location of a planned strike.

A hostile nation might also strike with long-range ballistic missiles, a possibility that has received a great deal of attention recently. Not wanting to depend on deterrence alone in such a situation, the Bush administration has stated its intention to deploy a national missile defense (NMD) for added protection. NMD is, in a sense, an insurance policy that becomes relevant if both prevention and deterrence fail and the aggressor nation chooses to deliver its weapons using ballistic missiles instead of aircraft, cruise missiles, or covert means. The controversy surrounding missile defense may be thought of as a debate about how likely the United States is to need such insurance, how much the policy will cost, and whether the nation can collect on it if needed (i.e., whether the defenses will work). These are all reasonable questions to ask before committing to the purchase.

The ground-based missile-defense system now well advanced in its development is designed to intercept incoming warheads in midflight—essentially trying to "hit a bullet with a bullet." Much controversy has arisen about this system, particularly after the failure of several tests of system components. But even though success will demand quite advanced technology, I believe that the United States will demonstrate a convincing mastery of the system before long, perhaps after another five to ten tests. In a few years, therefore, NMD could demonstrate on the test range a technical effectiveness of 80 to 90 percent.

Assessing the likely operational effectiveness of such a system is a different matter, and it involves taking a realistic view of various possible degrading effects. An NMD system could sit unchallenged for years, for example, and then have to operate perfectly the first time it is needed, probably without any advance warning. Such a scenario is exactly the opposite of the situation on the test range, where the crew is primed and ready (and the firing is postponed if they are not). Experience with other military systems, moreover, suggests that they achieve their best performance only after significant use in combat conditions. Tactical air defenses are fine-tuned after operating against repeated waves of bombing attacks. A missile-defense system operating against a nuclear attack would have to perform well during its first and only mission.

In a real attack, finally, one must expect the aggressors to employ technical or tactical countermeasures, such as decoys, chaff, radar jamming, or nuclear-induced radar blackout, to evade the NMD system. Washington is not likely to know which countermeasures might actually be used against its system, but it is prudent to expect them to be tailored to the specifics of the U.S. NMD program as it is described in the public record. Countermeasures are not simple to develop, but the incentive for the missile designer to acquire them is quite high. This inherent vulnerability of an air-defense or missile-defense system is a problem that can be addressed but never fully resolved.

Susceptibility to countermeasures is not new; indeed, it is a classic weakness common to all air-defense systems. Missile-defense systems have no significant operational history yet, but the United States and other countries have a history of air-defense operations that extends over 60 years. Historically, these activities have demonstrated an ability in combat to shoot down between 3 and 30 percent of an attacking force; under some operational conditions they have done even less well. This record did not stop the United States from building and deploying air-defense systems to defend its military forces from repeated attacks by conventionally armed bombers, because a shoot-down rate even as low as 10 percent would eventually exhaust an enemy's bomber force. But this low success rate is one reason the country had no comparable air-defense system capable of defending its cities against a strike from nuclear-armed bombers, for which a shoot-down rate of even 30 percent would be insufficient and unacceptable.

Early in the Cold War, the United States considered deploying an air-defense system to protect its population from the growing Soviet bomber fleet. The plans called for large radars, a nationwide command-and-control system, F-106 interceptor planes, and substantial complexes of antiaircraft missiles around each major urban area. Anti-aircraft missiles were actually deployed at a few sites, but in the end Washington concluded that even if the system could achieve historically high shoot-down rates, it could not provide meaningful national protection against a nuclear attack from the air.

Moscow, meanwhile, made the opposite decision. At the time, U.S. intelligence estimated that to protect their cities against our B-47 and B-52 bombers, the Soviets spent more than $100 billion (in 1970 dollars) building and deploying their air-defense system, which included thousands of surface-to-air missiles. In response, the U.S. Strategic Air Command developed technical and tactical countermeasures that they judged would enable a high percentage of American bombers to penetrate the Soviet defenses and devastate the Soviet Union. This judgment was never put to a test, but its assessment of the Soviet system's vulnerability achieved credibility in the 1980s when a light civilian plane flew from West Germany and landed in Red Square without being intercepted.

The comparison between air defense and ballistic-missile defense is imperfect, and one cannot simply apply the track records of the former to the latter. But it is hard to make a persuasive argument that shooting down a ballistic missile is easier than shooting down an airplane, or that a nation capable of deploying a force of intercontinental ballistic missiles could not build relatively challenging countermeasures. Even if the current NMD system eventually demonstrated a 90 percent rate of technical effectiveness on the test range, therefore, it is reasonable to question whether it could ever come close to that under operational conditions.

Today's U.S. policymakers must understand the fundamental limitations of missile-defense systems against nuclear-armed missiles (just as their predecessors came to understand the limitations of air-defense systems against nuclear-armed bombers) and recognize that even if successful in that arena they would provide virtually no protection against a cruise missile or bomber attack, not to mention covert delivery by other means. Failure to recognize these limitations could create a false sense of security and lead to inappropriate defense priorities. In the 1930s, the Maginot line, erected to protect France against a German invasion, had just this effect on French leaders, with terrible consequences for their nation. The Maginot line failed not because it was poorly designed or implemented but because the Germans recognized precisely how formidable a defense it was and devised a strategy for going around it. Committing the bulk of U.S. homeland defense resources and energies to NMD tempts a similar fate: hostile nations have not only countermeasure options but also the options of carrying their weapons on aircraft or cruise missiles, thus going around our defenses.

THE COST OF A LAYERED CUT

Several different NMD systems for protecting American military forces are in advanced stages of development. Theater defenses, which operate against medium-range missiles, will likely be deployed in the next few years at a cost that is reasonably well known. Coming up with a credible estimate of what a national missile defense would cost, on the other hand, is more difficult.

The Bush administration has not yet decided on a final design for such a system, but it has testified that it wants to move to a "layered" approach, in which different components could operate in sequence against a ballistic missile in its boost phase, in midcourse, and in its terminal phase. The Congressional Budget

Office has estimated that a full-scale version of the midcourse system now under development would cost $50 billion (for production and deployment of the sites and ten years of operation), plus an additional $10 billion for the space-based sensors. A system aimed solely at a missile's terminal stage probably would not require a new development program, since it could be based on the theater missile-defense systems that will be deployed in a few years. But because terminal defenses can protect only relatively limited areas, a national network of them would have to include not only a global command-and-control system but separate and complex packages of missiles and radars for each urban area to be covered.

The boost-phase component of the project has not yet been designed. An air-based version of it, if alerted and deployed in a crisis, might provide an emergency defense against a missile launched from North Korea or Iraq, but not against one from northern Iran. Complete coverage would require either a constellation of spacecraft or bases on the territories of Russia and several of the Central Asian republics. Because of their access to the missile during its boost phase, space-based systems have inherent advantages over those based on the ground, in the air, or at sea. But at the same time, they entail considerably more complex technical problems, raising difficult questions about cost, schedule, and feasibility.

It is hard to imagine either a space-based boost-phase system or a nationwide complex of terminal systems costing less than the ground-based midcourse defense system now under development. In the end, the cost of a layered approach to NMD could be several times higher than the $60 billion estimate for the midcourse system alone—enough to drain significant resources from other military needs. Even if the Defense Department were to save the money it hopes to by reforming the defense acquisition system and closing unnecessary bases, and even with the new willingness since September 11 to commit additional resources to national defense, the administration will have to make difficult choices about how to distribute its spending among force structure, readiness, and new investments, including missile defense.

During my tenure as secretary of defense, I found that setting funding priorities for defense programs and then defending those priorities to the president, Congress, and the public was a very demanding task. I judged then—and continue to believe now—that although the NMD program is important, it should have a lower priority than those programs that are key to maintaining military readiness. I would also accord NMD a lower priority than critical programs designed to upgrade American conventional forces. In particular, I believe there is an urgent need to replace U.S. fighter-bombers with the new generation of aircraft that have been developed over the last ten years, the technology of which (especially stealth capabilities and precise weapon delivery) will give the United States air supremacy in any military conflict for several decades to come. Operation Desert Storm demonstrated how air supremacy enhances all aspects of military operations; it allowed the United States to win the Persian Gulf War quickly, decisively, and with minimal casualties. The Persian Gulf War also illustrated to the rest of the world the futility of directly confronting the U.S. military. The current crisis has once again shown the unique role played by aircraft carriers in rapidly projecting American military power. Washington must support the programs under way to modernize its carrier battle groups. U.S. forces must be transformed with modern information technology, which the Bush administration has rightly made a priority.

All these programs will be expensive, and they will compete with NMD for funding. Unlike NMD, however, these other investments serve more than one purpose. They allow the country to prevail in likely conflicts, they help sustain U.S. global leadership, they help deter conventional war, and they are a vital complement to nuclear forces in deterring the use of nuclear and biological weapons against the United States or its allies. Sacrificing the maintenance of U.S. conventional military supremacy to carry out an extensive NMD program would decrease rather than increase the nation's ability to deter nuclear as well as conventional war.

THE REST OF THE STORY

Responding to the dangers of proliferation and terrorism involves more than defense programs. The United States must also assign a higher priority and devote more funding to intelligence and law-enforcement programs that could help the authorities penetrate those terrorist groups planning attacks, as well as to intelligence efforts that illuminate the nature of the proliferation threat more generally.

Because even the best intelligence efforts can never offer perfect protection, the country also needs to increase its investments in programs designed to cope with an attack once it has occurred. In the case of a biological weapon, for example, quick and effective "consequence management" could reduce prospective fatalities as much as tenfold. Local and state governments, especially firefighters and police, will necessarily be on the front line, but National Guard and Reserve units can and should be strengthened to provide more effective support. None of these forces, however, has the special equipment, medicine, and training needed to deal fully with a biological attack—only the Centers for Disease Control can direct an effective response. To prepare itself to deal with the wide variety of microbes that might be used in a future attack, Washington must begin immediately to mobilize the medical and pharmaceutical industries so that they will be ready to respond with the needed vaccines, medicines, and health-care facilities. All these steps and more, presumably, will be the responsibility of the new Office of Homeland Security, but overcoming bureaucratic divisions and programmatic inertia will be more difficult than some might expect.

Increased efforts to stop or slow proliferation, meanwhile, hold more promise than many critics seem to think. Since the end of the Cold War, four nations (Ukraine, Kazakhstan, Belarus, and South Africa) have given up their sizable nuclear arsenals and two others (Argentina and Brazil) have terminated their nuclear weapons programs short of success, a trend partially offset by the decisions of India and Pakistan to come out of the nuclear closet.

Continuing the existing nonproliferation efforts is important, as is aggressively pursuing opportunities to reduce new threats before they emerge—for example, by negotiating an agreement whereby North Korea abandons its long-range missiles.

Serious nonproliferation efforts must involve Russia and China. Sustained dialogue with both is crucial, but the most important subject for such dialogue is proliferation, not missile defense or even reductions in strategic forces. Moscow and Beijing must take serious actions, in cooperation with the United States, to curb the unconventional weapons programs in Iraq, Iran, Libya, and North Korea. To get Moscow and Beijing on board, Washington should be prepared to make some compromises on other issues. Both governments appear to care less about proliferation than about preserving their ultimate nuclear deterrent. The United States should take the opposite approach, thus opening space for mutually beneficial discussions.

If effective agreements to curb proliferation cannot be reached, the threat will continue to grow. Indeed, if the present impasse in the consultations on missile defense continues, it could lead China to dramatically increase the long-range missile modernization program it now has under way and could lead both Russia and China to provide missile and counterdefense technology to nations hostile to the United States. If the attempt to deploy a missile defense resulted in an increase in proliferation, it would represent a net decrease in U.S. security. If discussions with Russia and China could succeed in reaching meaningful proliferation curbs, on the other hand, the Bush administration would seize a unique and historic opportunity to prevent new nuclear and biological threats from emerging. It is of course possible that the needed cooperation will not be forthcoming from Russia or China. But the stakes are too high to not make every effort.

If the Bush administration works to maintain U.S. conventional military supremacy, boosts efforts at intelligence gathering and consequence management, and pursues international cooperation on the pivotal nonproliferation issue, it is unlikely to have enough funds or diplomatic leverage for the near-term deployment of a full-scale, layered NMD system. It should still be possible, however, to support an accelerated program to produce and deploy theater missile defenses. Once the new systems have been developed, they could be deployed rapidly during crises to defend against ballistic-missile threats in those (relatively few) cases where the missile's boost phase would fall within range of the system. Deploying a naval-based missile-defense system or an airborne laser to South Korea, for example—much as the Clinton administration deployed Patriot missiles during the 1994 crisis caused by the breakdown in nonproliferation talks with North Korea—would be one way to respond to an attempt at nuclear extortion.

It should also be possible to maintain a robust missile-defense research and development program, the results of which might change the calculus on such issues down the road. A central objective of this effort should be to gain a sophisticated understanding of missile defenses' vulnerability to countermeasures and develop appropriate means to defeat those countermeasures. In particular, the Defense Department should have a much more aggressive program to test the performance of American NMD systems against all realistic countermeasures. Testing can play an important role in validating the design of mechanisms to thwart countermeasures. But only very detailed and extensive simulations, monitored by an objective "red team" of outside observers, can allow officials to evaluate how well the system would work against the diverse countermeasures that it might have to face.

STEP BY STEP

The United States has suffered the most devastating terrorist attack in world history. It can and will respond. But the attack demonstrates that there are large, well-organized groups whose primary objective is to kill large numbers of Americans. These groups understand all too well that nuclear or biological weapons can fulfill that mission even better than truck bombs or kamikaze aircraft can and the recent anthrax mailings have shown just how ill-prepared the country is for such an unconventional attack. The

United States also faces a small number of nations that believe they can advance their own interests by mounting unconventional threats. Future U.S. security therefore depends on actions taken today to prevent the further proliferation of nuclear and biological weapons tomorrow. Nonproliferation efforts, in turn, depend on effective cooperation with the other nuclear powers. Achieving such cooperation is therefore a critical national security objective.

Even if the United States fails to prevent proliferation, it still has a powerful and credible deterrent of both nuclear and conventional weapons. But it is reasonable to take out insurance against the contingency that both prevention and deterrence fail. National missile defense is such an insurance policy. As the government considers the priority to give to missile defense relative to other national security efforts, both within the defense budget and without, it should recognize that NMD would not provide any protection against the most likely forms of terrorist attack, nor would it be effective against a strike by cruise missiles or bombers. The insurance policy would thus cover a possible but not the most likely contingency, would come at a high price, and could stimulate an increase in the level and sophistication of the threats the country faces.

Theater missile defenses, in contrast, address a clear and direct threat to deployed American forces from short-range missiles, and the military should move to deploy the next generation of these defenses as expeditiously as possible. It makes sense to continue a robust research and development program for defenses against ballistic missiles, but it would be a mistake to let deployment plans interfere with attempts to prevent proliferation or hamper achieving the joint international programs necessary to respond effectively to the immediate terrorist challenge. In any event, informed judgments about the wisdom of deploying an NMD system can be made only after officials can get realistic estimates of its effectiveness in the face of probable countermeasures and credible estimates of its financial and diplomatic costs. That day is still several years away.

WAGING THE NEW WAR

WHAT'S NEXT FOR THE U.S. ARMED FORCES

■

WESLEY K. CLARK

Since the end of the Cold War commentators have called for the transformation of the U.S. military, but the purpose, scope, and essential nature of this transformation have never been clear. The events of September 11 have given a new impetus to calls for a transformation, and they have also helped set some parameters for the changes required. Although no military leaders believe that military action alone can resolve the problem of terrorism, the military clearly has a role to play in winning the fight.

At the conclusion of the Persian Gulf War in 1991, the U.S. military consisted of just over 2 million active personnel and some 1.2 million reserves. These troops were organized along the traditional lines of U.S. forces, built on the experience of World War II and modified after the Korean and Vietnam wars. With its more than 700,000 men and women in uniform, the Army was the largest force, designed to fight and win a sustained land battle with support from the Air Force. The Army's combat capabilities were vested in 14 divisions, each comprising between 10,000 and 17,000 soldiers, with additional support tucked into higher-echelon commands that commanded and supported several divisions simultaneously.

The Air Force was organized into squadrons and wings, each distinguished by the type of aircraft flown and by function. Squadrons usually consisted of 18 aircraft with the necessary crews and support, and wings were composed of two or more squadrons, with some dedicated to tactical fighters and others to bombers or reconnaissance. Wings, in turn, were grouped into "numbered" air forces, roughly the equivalent of an Army division or corps. At the end of the Gulf War, the Air Force comprised some 24 tactical fighter wings, 231 heavy bombers, several intercontinental ballistic missile wings, hundreds of tanker aircraft, and other support organizations, with a total of 510,000 men and women in uniform.

The Navy was organized by ships, squadrons, and fleets, with its actual operations grouped into task forces—collections of ships of various types formed for a specific mission. At the end of the Gulf War, the Navy encompassed 527 ships of various types (including more than 100 attack submarines), 15 aircraft carriers, and 570,000 sailors.

The Marine Corps, with 194,000 personnel, was the smallest of the services, composed of three divisions. It usually operated in marine expeditionary units, built around a reinforced marine battalion augmented with aircraft and support and launched on a handful of ships capable of supporting amphibious landings or helicopter operations.

And by 1991 there was a new command, created by the Defense Authorization Act of 1987, that had its own, independent congressional funding: the Special Operations Command, which comprised a collection of Army, Navy, and Air Force units and was located at MacDill Air Force Base in Florida. Commands from within the other military services, such as the Army Special Operations Command, managed the unique special operations forces. In addition, a special hostage-rescue and counterterrorist strike force known as the Joint Special Operations Command was created at Fort Bragg, North Carolina. There were also five special forces groups, small organizations of under 1,000 people who are regionally oriented in culture and languages, which provided training and assistance to foreign military forces. And finally, there was the 75th Ranger Regiment, consisting of three 600-person battalions of specially skilled airborne troops who conducted the most demanding combat tasks.

The fundamental military problem the United States faced in the early 1990s was to prevent the exhilaration of having won the Cold War and the resulting cry for a "peace dividend" from causing the collapse of the American military. Spending cuts were mandatory; the only question was how large they would be.

TRANSFORMING THE MILITARY

Commentators and critics argued that in addition to spending cuts, some kind of fundamental transformation was required, sometimes citing the lessons of the Gulf War, and at other times arguing for some new kind of approach. The idea of transformation seemed to be connected as much with saving resources as with new missions and requirements, although some continued to use the Soviet term, "revolution in military affairs" (RMA), to highlight the opportunities for transformation. Proponents of an RMA could argue that high technology, particularly the so-called precision strike weapons, had made large ground forces obsolete and enabled sizable reductions in force structures. Some spoke of the need to skip a generation of weaponry to pursue even more advanced (though never fully defined) weapons technologies, a step that would also, it was argued, reduce the enormous personnel costs of maintaining the Cold War–era force.

Struggling to cope with these continuing pressures to reduce the defense budget, General Colin Powell, then Chairman of the Joint Chiefs of Staff and the nation's seniormost military leader, expounded the idea of the "Base Force." This was to be an irreducible minimum size for the military, which was justified in only the most general ways as having been derived from the worldwide interests and security responsibilities of the United States. Under Powell's leadership the military significantly reduced its assets overseas, cutting the European-based force, for example, from around 300,000 troops to a little more than 100,000 by 1996. The congressionally mandated Base Realignment and Closure Commission was created in 1988 to solve the political puzzle of how to distribute impending military reductions around the United States, and four rounds of cuts were undertaken, resulting in the closure of some 97 installations.

In the early years of the Clinton administration, it was recognized that the defense budget simply could not be sustained at existing levels unless a more specific case was made for why the military required the forces and assets it had. Moving from "illustrative planning scenarios" through a series of internal studies known as the "Bottom-Up Review," the administration eventually decided on requirements sufficient to fight and win two nearly simultaneous "major regional contingencies," or MRCs, such as new wars in Iraq or Korea.

Although this two-MRC standard provided a benchmark that generally halted the shrinkage of the size and structure of the armed forces, it failed to answer fully the fundamental questions about military requirements: What exactly do we need and why? To guide thinking in this area, in 1996 the Pentagon published the first of a series of new documents titled "Joint Vision 2010." This vision was heavily influenced by the technological successes of precision weaponry and modern communications in the Gulf War, but it also tried to project requirements for forces and capabilities across the "full spectrum of conflict" that could be imagined, ranging from peacekeeping to major war.

Despite all this overarching policy thinking, by and large the military services were going their own ways. The Army clung to its division-based force, making gradual and largely marginal changes in the size and composition of its divisions to accommodate personnel reductions down to an active strength of 491,000 men and women. The Army also found itself trying to emulate the Air Force's tighter integration of active and reserve forces. The Navy, for its part, moved dramatically to cut its fleet to 359 vessels by 1996 and explored new, more efficient designs for surface ships and submarines. The Air Force reorganized itself twice during the 1990s, first forming "composite wings" composed of a tailored mix of aircraft aligned more closely with the needs of Army units, and then creating the air expeditionary forces, which were packaged for rapid overseas deployments. In the process the Air Force shrank by some 20 fighter squadrons, by more than 100 heavy bombers, and by 121,000 uniformed troops. Finally the Marine Corps—protected by legislation that ensured that its minimum strength would not fall below 172,500 personnel—worked to enlarge the scope of its activities and the range of its capabilities. No reduction was made in the strength or capabilities of the Special Operations Command.

In all of the services, the powerful lure of publicity and high technology drove intense interest in "precision" weaponry, which uses lasers or video technology to help it pinpoint targets. The Army improved the accuracy and range of its large, tactical ballistic-missile system; the Navy modernized its stable of existing aircraft to enable precision strikes in a ground attack; and the Air Force, already the leader in this field, developed enhanced munitions with longer ranges and, using the global positioning system, the capability to strike in any weather conditions. The Air Force also fielded its new "stealth" bomber, the B-2, to augment the squadrons of F-117 stealth fighters that had been used in the Gulf War. Other technologies began to appear as well, including very high-powered, long-range electro-optical systems mounted on aircraft, as well as increasingly sophisticated pilotless "drones" to be used for reconnaissance. Even some Army attack helicopters, tanks, and armored fighting vehicles were enhanced with new optics, computer communications, and, in some cases, radar systems to pinpoint targets. This entire process came to be known as "platform modernization" (as opposed to platform replacement), meaning that older airframes, vehicles, and ships could be enhanced with new technology and capabilities for a fraction of the cost of procuring new high-tech airframes, tanks, or other complete systems.

Nevertheless, the services also scrambled to acquire new platforms. The chief contenders were three different tactical fighters: the supersonic-cruise, stealthy, and very expensive F-22 for the Air Force; the robust, lower-cost, joint strike fighter, which could be used in multiple roles; and the Navy's enhanced F-18E/F plane. Additional demands were made for the V-22 aircraft, capable of taking off and landing vertically, which would potentially extend the Marines' reach much farther inland, as well as provide enhanced capabilities for the Special Operations Command's forces. Other claimants on the defense procurement budget were Army helicopter modernization, a new self-propelled Army artillery piece known as the Crusader, a new amphibious assault vehicle for the Marines, a new submarine, a new class of destroyers, and even additional C-17 transport aircraft. And after 1999, embarrassed by its painful failure to meet public expectations in its slow deployment to Kosovo, the Army began a broad effort to transform its heavy forces into a lighter, more readily deployable organization that could reach far-flung theaters beyond the reach of forward-positioned heavy forces. Adding to the budgetary pressures were the plans for development of theater and national missile defenses, which in turn involved the development of new radars, missile systems, and communications systems; as well as the increasing demands for defenses against chemical and biological warfare.

There simply wasn't enough money in the defense budgets to buy all that was sought, even with the enlargements of the defense budget that began during the second Clinton administration. Small wonder that the Joint Chiefs of Staff were seeking an additional $50 billion per year or so from the incoming Bush administration, even before the full scope of an enhanced missile-defense program was laid out. Despite all the efforts that had been made to rationalize military requirements, it appeared once more that some sort of transformation was going to be driven as much by budgetary constraints as by changes of mission.

FIGHTING A NEW KIND OF WAR

The events of September 11, 2001, have dramatically altered the resources available to the Department of Defense, while at the same time clarifying how the U.S. military itself must be transformed. For the most part, the military operations of this war must be fought using the tools we already have: the Army divisions, the B-2 bomber, the ships, and the special operations forces that have been carefully built up over the past fifteen years. The challenge will be to adapt the existing organizations, procedures, and capabilities to meet the somewhat different requirements of this new kind of war.

The requirements, of course, will be driven by the mission, our adversaries, and the environment within which any military operations must be conducted. Some missions may appear familiar, evoking memories of the air campaigns over Iraq or Yugoslavia, and intended to gain freedom of the skies or, as it is usually termed by the military, "air superiority." Missions may even require amphibious assaults or some conventional land battles. But much of what will occur will require that forces and capabilities be tailored to a specific need, a kind of "mix and match" to fit the objectives and constraints of the various missions at hand. Some of these arrangements may appear innovative; others may simply seem bizarre.

The war against terrorism is not a war that can be won from the skies; it will require troops on the ground in many different roles. The first steps in this war have, of course, involved airpower. In taking the war first to the Taliban regime in Afghanistan, for example, the United States relied on its formidable air forces to destroy the limited air-defense capabilities in that country. In a now-familiar orchestration, cruise missiles and stealth bombers swept in at night to attack early-warning radars, antiaircraft missile sites, and airfields. The attack force was tailored, of course, with Air Force B-1 and B-52 bombers taking off from Diego Garcia in the Indian Ocean, B-2 bombers beginning their missions from the United States itself, and Navy aircraft based on carriers at sea.

But from this point onward, the forces will have to be adapted more specifically for the kind of war they are fighting. As the Air Force learned in its operations over Kosovo, it is difficult to spot dispersed and hidden enemy forces from the air. By augmenting manned air patrols with unmanned drones, which are able to loiter and revisit suspected areas for several hours while transmitting to their controllers pictures of the landscape below for detailed examination by specialists in rear areas, the Air Force can facilitate the detection of enemy forces on the ground. During the Kosovo campaign, both the Predator and the Hunter drones were used in this way with some success.

Once these measures have been taken from the sky, the next step may be to deploy forward reconnaissance elements, small teams made up of special forces or long-range surveillance units able to hide among enemy positions and then call in strike aircraft to attack enemy forces. These small groups can infiltrate on foot or by vehicle, or they can be inserted by helicopters or parachute drops far beyond friendly positions. These techniques, though little discussed publicly, were pioneered during the Cold War. With satellite radios and laser designators, these special groups can provide critical directions for air attack on a continuing basis. Another technique will be to use attack helicopters, either the small special operations type with highly experienced crews, or the larger, more heavily armed Apache helicopters.

These techniques were quietly explored, though never fully implemented, in Kosovo. In that conflict in the spring of 1999, highly experienced special forces teams maintained liaison with the Albanian forces looking into Serbia, and in some cases positioned themselves so that they could directly observe enemy forces. Intelligence was the critical ingredient for their success, and every effort was made to exploit the knowledge of the host country and of those fighting on the ground. Counterbattery radars, capable of detecting artillery and mortar fire and calculating firing positions, were also deployed and put into action in Kosovo. And, of course, the Apache helicopters were organized, trained, and rehearsed for the mission of flying over the mountains into Kosovo to detect and strike Serb forces. The conflict in Afghanistan is likely to make use of the kind of tailored forces created during the bombing campaign against Yugoslavia.

Another strategy that is being used in the conflict in Afghanistan, and one whose use was under active consideration when Yugoslav president Slobodan Milosevic surrendered in the summer of 1999, would involve dispatching into the theater special teams of commando forces or even reinforced Ranger companies to conduct raids and to strike at enemy forces using heavy firepower from the air.

And, as was the case in Kosovo, standard ground forces will also be required in Afghanistan to secure bases and provide reaction forces in the case of trouble. It appears that these bases will be located initially in the states surrounding Afghanistan, such as Uzbekistan, but eventually it will be possible to move some small forward-operating bases into the areas of Afghanistan that are under the control of the Northern Alliance. These bases will use specially organized forces consisting of reinforced infantry units augmented with mortars, radars, and perhaps a few armored vehicles.

Organizing such forces is challenging because typically the situation calls for conflicting strategies: keeping the force small helps to minimize the logistical burden, and yet there is also a requirement for robust and versatile capabilities. These trade-offs will demand deploying the most modern technologies in support of the force, including more modern communications systems, wheel-mounted rocket artillery, and perhaps even new infantry weapons capable of firing exploding projectiles. Forces must be capable of delivering direct fire at extended ranges using sniper rifles and automatic grenade-launchers to accommodate the rough terrain and long-range fields of fire that are characteristic of arid Afghanistan. And because of the need for a small "forward footprint," much of the parent division-sized force stationed in the United States is apt to be left behind.

With these small and variable forces, the combat in Afghanistan is likely to be of unpredictable duration. A collapse of the Taliban forces is a distinct possibility, but the terrain and ethnic composition of the country also encourage persistent factional fighting that could, under the right circumstances, continue for some time. In the meantime, a pattern of raids, strikes, and offensive maneuvers is likely to provide episodic glimpses of a remote theater of war. Still, if the United States succeeds in isolating the Taliban from all significant outside assistance while retaining the support of the majority of the Afghan people, builds on its air dominance, and moves ahead patiently with the insertion of airborne and ground-based reconnaissance and small numbers of other special ground forces, the ultimate outcome cannot be in doubt.

Less visible will be some of the activities in friendly states seeking assistance in dealing with terrorists inside their own borders. In these states—in Southeast Asia or perhaps North Africa—U.S. forces will function as trainers and will take direct action only in exceptional circumstances. But again, the forces for such direct action would chiefly be those already organized and trained: elite special operations forces. Operating from the sea or from friendly forward bases, such forces can launch strikes hundreds of miles inland against terrorist-training camps and facilities, or, with the consent of the host government, can call in air strikes that can simply wipe out terrorist-training camps. In these locations the most important requirement for success will be surprise. Not only will the plans for such activities be extremely closely held—so will be the results.

In Afghanistan and in those states seeking assistance, the real key to effective operations will be information about the terrorists: details about their identities, locations, habits, logistics, and aims. The most valuable information is predictive in nature; it enables security forces to determine where the terrorists will be, not just where they have been. But information of this nature is also the most difficult to acquire. In theory, it may be gained through electronic means, pilfered plans, or personal contact. In practice, it is best gained by well-positioned observers, including informants and infiltrators of terrorist cells—so-called "human intelligence." Often working from the inside, human intelligence is the best way to track an enemy's intentions and to provide critical assistance in targeting individuals and small groups. Human intelligence may come from national sources or from allied states, and it will often be last-minute, quickly perishable information. This means that the special forces involved in operations must have exquisite linkages to intelligence agencies, enabling them to receive pertinent information with virtually no delay. It also implies a rapid-response capability that argues for greater decentralization in decision-making during counterterrorist operations.

These operations will also run counter to the conventional conservatism of the post-Vietnam military, which has proved time and again that it is risk- and casualty-averse. If the targeting of forces in Afghanistan is done from the air by unmanned vehicles or helicopters, there will always be the risks of engagement by antiaircraft fire and missiles. Special forces teams will also face risks; the battle of October 3, 1993, in Mogadishu (when 18 U.S. soldiers were killed in the streets of that city) remains a stark reminder that even superb troops with overwhelming firepower can still get themselves in trouble. More risks will be imposed by the need to identify, detain, and interrogate terrorists, than by operations to simply strike and kill them. Accepting such risks will prove challenging for U.S. high-level commanders on three counts: first, because any tactical failures will give the enemy a moral advantage that can be exploited by an adroit information campaign; second, because highly trained, experienced troops are difficult to replace; and finally, because the strong bonds between military commanders and their soldiers favor the exploration of lower-risk alternatives. Still, there should be no doubt as to the readiness of the military at all levels ultimately to accept the potential sacrifices required in these operations.

CONFRONTING ROGUE STATES

The force and operations described above will most likely be used against terrorist organizations and within failed states like Afghanistan that lack the developed infrastructure and military organizations of functioning states. But in some instances the United States may confront functioning states that themselves sponsor terrorism. Particularly difficult cases will be those states believed to possess nuclear, chemical, or biological weapons. No doubt all alternative means will be considered to remove the possibility of terrorism before considering the use of force, which would in these cases be a last resort. The influence of an aroused, determined America should not be underestimated in these circumstances.

But should such states persist in harboring terrorists, U.S. counterterrorist operations will look much more like conventional military operations, and they will draw heavily on all the existing force structures, doctrines, and procedures developed during the Cold War and modified slightly over the past decade. Experience with Iraq has indicated that limited strikes from the air are of little value against a regime determined to acquire and maintain weapons of mass destruction. Hence, more complete combat operations, starting with a campaign to gain air superiority and followed by overland, amphibious, and air-delivered ground incursions, could be expected. In the worst case, another Desert Storm–like operation might be mounted but aimed this time at regime change. Lesser operations could be aimed at defeating the enemy's ground forces, eliminating terrorist infrastructure and networks, and destroying facilities for the production and storage of weapons of mass destruction.

In any operations in such states, as well as in Afghanistan, there must be an endgame, a strategy involving some sort of international administration or support, substantial demilitarization, and long-term arrangements for security likely to be assured by an international force. Such missions will be familiar to all North Atlantic Treaty Organization member armies, including that of the United States, that have participated in missions of a similar nature in Bosnia or Kosovo. These missions require land forces in significant numbers, equipped with substantial heavy weaponry, helicopters, military police, engineers, logistics, and robust communications. Such missions also pose special requirements for interacting with civilian populations and supporting deployed international law-enforcement organizations, and the work after entry could continue for years. Surely, the most important lesson to have emerged from the fiasco that is Afghanistan is that theaters of past military operations must not be quickly abandoned, as the United States did in that country after the pull-out of the Soviet troops in 1989.

Throughout the counterterrorist campaigns, which may well stretch on for months and even years, the U.S. armed forces will gradually transform themselves into lighter, more deployable structures. They will implement new technologies to complement precision strike weaponry: theater missile-defense capabilities from high-speed interceptor missiles and airborne lasers; more capable drones and ground vehicles for reconnaissance, fighting, and engineering tasks; more capable, more lethal, and lighter-weight infantry weaponry with longer ranges; more sophisticated automated scanning, identification, and targeting systems that rely on multispectral, seismic, and perhaps even biometric technologies; new logistics featuring electric propulsion, automated prefailure diagnostics, and significantly reduced forward logistics footprints.

Thus the events of September 11 mark a crucial turning point in the debate about defense transformation. There is a practical answer now to the cry for the RMA. The "readiness debate" is over: the point at which forces must be ready is now, or within a few months, not at some indefinite time in the future. We will fight largely with what we have, inserting as much new technology as we can, tailoring organizations to emphasize more teamwork among the armed services, and reducing the numbers of troops deployed overseas. The armed forces are likely to leave some equipment and elements behind as they "skinny-down" for actual operations. And at the margins they will seek to create additional capabilities like those of the special forces. Ultimately, however, the United States will be grateful for the relatively robust structures left over from the Army's stubborn reluctance to depart from its traditional divisional structure. The two-MRC strategy has served its purpose: it led U.S. forces through an ambiguous post–Cold War period with substantial capabilities and largely ready to fight.

Looking ahead, defense analysts will find no easy answer in the next, postwar round of defense cutbacks. Fundamental questions about the ultimate structure of the international system and potential competitors will likely remain; new technologies will be required, either to take advantage of new opportunities or to offset emerging vulnerabilities; and sizable numbers of ground forces are likely to be engaged in numerous postwar activities abroad. As a global power, the United States will need to retain the capacities to respond simultaneously to more than one crisis or in more than one region. And defense analysts will have to create the strategic formulations to justify this need to the public.

DIPLOMACY IN WARTIME

NEW PRIORITIES AND ALIGNMENTS

■

MICHAEL MANDELBAUM

In the wake of the attacks on the World Trade Center and the Pentagon on September 11, the word most often used to characterize the consequences for American foreign policy was "war." The terrorist assault, it was said, had inaugurated World War III, or if not that, then at least, as President George W. Bush called it, "the first war of the twenty-first century."

In important ways, however, the term war is misleading in this context. The campaign against terrorism does not involve rival organized military forces fielded by recognizable political entities for the purpose of controlling territory—the traditional definition of war. In the current conflict, the Central Intelligence Agency, the Federal Bureau of Investigation, the Immigration and Naturalization Service, local law-enforcement agencies and public health services, and the Departments of State, Justice, and the Treasury will assume responsibilities as important as, and perhaps considerably more important than, those of the Department of Defense.

Yet war is a useful term to describe what the events of September 11 set in motion, for these events will affect America's role in the world and its relations with other countries in the same ways that war usually affects a nation's foreign policy. The September 11 attacks will have four major effects on the conduct of American foreign policy. First, they will loosen restraints on the use of military force abroad. Second, they will serve as a focal point for American diplomacy. Third, they will move to the top of America's foreign policy agenda the goal of removing from power a certain type of government. And fourth, they will give rise to a diversion from the main business of combating terrorism, in the form of a vocal minority urging the U.S. government to address what it alleges to be the underlying causes of the acts of terror against the United States.

MILITARY PROSPECTS

As a result of September's attacks, it will now be easier for the U.S. president to commit troops to battle, with the risk of casualties, than it has been in the past. Risking American lives has always been difficult for the nation's commander-in-chief. Neither George Washington in the Revolutionary War nor Abraham Lincoln in the Civil War was able to draw on a standing federal military force of any size, and both devoted much of their time and energy to urging their countrymen to supply the manpower needed to keep armies in the field. Franklin Roosevelt had an easier time of it during World War II, but even then American officials worried that morale in the United States would flag. Indeed, during two protracted Cold War conflicts morale did flag: a substantial decline in public support for Washington's policy contributed to the stalemate in Korea and to the American defeat in Vietnam. The disinclination to support wars abroad reached its zenith during the presidency of Bill Clinton, who ordered military operations in Haiti, Bosnia, and Kosovo with the understanding that the maximum number of politically permissible American casualties was zero.

Americans' reluctance to have their fellow citizens killed or injured, even if they have voluntarily joined the armed forces, is scarcely the least attractive feature of the country's political culture. Nor does it stem from a principled opposition to all wars: the United States is not now and never has been a pacifist country. Americans have remained willing to fight for one reason above all others: self-defense. None of the Clinton administration's military ventures, however, could be credibly portrayed as having anything to do with the security of the United States or the safety of its citizens.

The deaths of more than 5,000 people in the September 11 attacks settled the question of whether international terrorism poses the kind of threat that Americans will sacrifice their lives to oppose. In this sense their impact recalls that of the event to which, in the days that followed September 11, they were often compared: the Japanese attack on the American fleet at Pearl Harbor, Hawaii, on December 7, 1941. But an earlier episode from the first half of the twentieth century, one in which the United States did not take part, offers an even more instructive precedent: the policies adopted toward Nazi Germany by the United Kingdom and France before the outbreak of World War II.

In the years following that conflict Americans became convinced that the failure to check Adolf Hitler earlier had paved the way for an avoidable and tragic war. It thus became a cardinal principle of American foreign policy during the Cold War to avoid the great mistake of the 1930s by fighting communism wherever it threatened to dominate, rather than allowing the Soviet Union and its allies to gain strength through unopposed victories. This was the rationale for the American military interventions in Korea in 1950 and in Indochina in the 1960s.

The attacks of September 11 create a similar rationale for forceful preemptive attacks against terrorists wherever they are. Henceforth, the argument that a military operation is designed to avoid a repetition of those terrible events will be a powerful one, which American commanders-in-chief will be able to employ to win public support for such operations.

In general, the enterprise of war requires a country to invest three different kinds of capital: military, economic, and political. For the United States in the post–Cold War era, the third has been the least available. But the events of September 11 have considerably expanded the supply of it.

DIPLOMATIC ALIGNMENTS

Wars reshape diplomacy. Victory becomes the supreme goal of foreign policy and diplomatic alignments are adjusted to help achieve it. This can make for strange political bedfellows.

Winston Churchill made the point most memorably after Germany attacked the Soviet Union on June 22, 1941. Seeking cordial ties with the Communist government in Moscow that he had opposed for nearly 25 years, the British prime minister said that if Hitler invaded hell he would make at least a favorable reference to the Devil in the House of Commons.

Similarly, during the Cold War the United States made common cause with regimes that neither preached nor practiced the political values in which Americans believe. The need for the broadest possible coalition against the Soviet Union justified the American affiliation with these "friendly tyrants." Among the groups to which American assistance found its way were Islamic fundamentalists fighting the Soviet army of occupation in Afghanistan in the 1980s, the best known of whom in 2001 was Osama bin Laden.

The same pattern emerged in the wake of September 11. The countries bordering Afghanistan, the initial target in the war against terrorism, suddenly acquired a new appeal in Washington. At the same time, shortcomings that the United States had not only noticed but put at the center of its disapproving policies toward these countries abruptly lost their primacy. In the wake of the attacks, Washington made a friendly gesture toward the government of Iran, a country to which the State Department had only recently awarded the distinction of being the world's leading sponsor of terrorism. The U.S. government launched a diplomatic campaign to win the active support of the government of Pakistan, lifting the economic sanctions it had imposed in response to the Pakistani decision to violate a major principle of American foreign policy, nuclear nonproliferation, by conducting nuclear weapons tests in 1998. Washington made similar overtures to governments in Central Asia that, before September 11, it had routinely criticized for their rejection of democratic practices and their violations of human rights.

The most enduring and consequential diplomatic effects of September 11, however, involved Russia. Here, the causes of American distaste for Afghanistan's neighbors were not present. Unlike Iran, Russia did not sponsor anti-American terrorism. Unlike Pakistan, Russia opposed nuclear proliferation. Unlike Tajikistan, Uzbekistan, and Turkmenistan, Russia held relatively free elections and permitted relatively free speech.

Indeed, as a victim of terrorist attacks itself, Russia was a natural ally in this war, and President Vladimir Putin was quick to express solidarity with the United States and to give his approval of the American use, for operations in Afghanistan, of military facilities in the countries of Central Asia, where Russia retained influence, bases, and troops.

Yet before September 11 the United States and Russia had been at odds over a number of issues, their bilateral relationship marked by increasing animosity. One such issue was Moscow's war against rebels in the predominantly Muslim province of Chechnya, a war that the Russians saw as a struggle against Islamist terrorism but that the U.S. government had regarded as a brutal exercise in the gross violation of human rights. (It was, in fact, both.) In the wake of September 11, official Western criticism of Russian policy toward Chechnya became all but inaudible.

The U.S.-Russian relationship before the terrorist attacks had also been strained by the Bush administration's efforts to abandon the 1972 Anti-Ballistic Missile Treaty and to offer membership in the North Atlantic Treaty Organization to Estonia, Latvia, and Lithuania, thereby bringing the Western military alliance to Russia's borders. These measures troubled the Russians, who regarded them as heedless of their interests and potentially threatening to their security. Before September 11 these two commitments were on track to be the principal—and the most controversial—American foreign policy initiatives of 2002. In the wake of the attacks, the importance of these initiatives receded but did not vanish entirely. Their fate was uncertain after September 11, as it had been before, but that fate would henceforth be bound up with the war against terrorism.

REGIME CHANGES

The United States waged World War II to achieve the unconditional surrender of Nazi Germany and Imperial Japan, which meant the destruction of the governments of those two countries, which had begun the war. During the Cold War the removal of governments played a less prominent role in official American rhetoric. In the 1950s the Eisenhower administration proclaimed its commitment to the "rollback" of communist power in Eastern Europe but never seriously tried to achieve it. In the 1980s the Reagan administration supported insurgencies against regimes sponsored by or sympathetic to the Soviet Union in Central America and Asia, but the predominant American Cold War aim was to "contain" Soviet power, not to overthrow it. Yet "regime change" was in fact central to American foreign policy in the Cold War, the initial cause of which was the forcible imposition of communist governments in Central and Eastern Europe and the end of which came when those governments collapsed.

Regime change is one of the American goals in the war against terrorism, as well. The reason is that terrorists need a base from which to operate. Any terrorist base will be located within a sovereign state, the government of which will therefore be complicit in the terrorists' activities, because its active cooperation or at least tacit approval is necessary for those activities to take place. President George W. Bush declared in his address to a joint session of Congress on September 20 that the United States "will pursue nations that provide aid or safe haven to terrorism. Every nation, in every region, now has a decision to make. Either you are with us, or you are with the terrorists."

Bush administration officials subsequently implied that the regimes that sponsor terrorism would have an unspecified period of time to change their ways. Perhaps some of the offending regimes—Iran, Iraq, Syria, Libya, the Palestinian Authority, Afghanistan—will see fit to evict or abandon the terrorists within their borders. But their disposition to do so will depend heavily on the price they calculate the United States will exact from them if they do not, and their estimates of that price will rise to the extent that the United States does in fact take steps to remove terrorist-harboring regimes.

Even if such estimates turn out to be credibly high, these regimes will find it difficult to reject terrorism altogether because it has been central to all of them. The governing philosophy of each, such as it is, includes deep and abiding hostility to Western values and institutions. And terrorism—against the people they rule—is at the heart of the governing strategy of the Iraqi and Syrian regimes. Saddam Hussein's mass killings of thousands of Kurds and other Iraqis, and Hafiz al-Assad's massacre of 25,000 people in the Syrian city of Hama in February 1982 demonstrated the lengths to which these leaders would go to remain in power. The local memory of those events, combined with active and brutal secret police forces, form the foundation on which the two regimes stand. Regime change seems, therefore, an unavoidable aim of the war against terrorism, and for American foreign policy this aim presents both opportunities and challenges.

In no case is the task of dislodging these regimes an overwhelming one. None is powerful. None enjoys anything like broad popular domestic legitimacy. In Iraq the disappearance of Saddam Hussein and his sons and in Libya the fall of Muammar al-Qaddafi would very likely put an end to the current governments in those countries. The Syrian regime represents not only the Assad family but the religious sect, the Alawis, from which it comes. But the Alawis make up only 12 percent of the Syrian population, and their rule does not command enthusiastic support among the majority Sunni Muslims, many of whom do not even consider the Alawis to be part of the Islamic faith. In Iran, the rule of the radical clergy who sponsor terrorist groups has twice been repudiated by the public with the election in 1997 and re-election in 2001 of the more moderate Muhammad Khatami as president, but the clerics have used their control of the security agencies and their own militia to retain power in the country.

The illegitimacy of these regimes provides the basis for hope that the pattern that ended the Cold War will be repeated in the war against terrorism: in 1989 and 1991 the communist governments of Eastern Europe and the Soviet Union, once thought to hold an unbreakable totalitarian grip on the societies they ruled, collapsed without direct assault by the United States or its allies. The people whom these governments ruled overthrew them.

Similarly, military pressure (rather than an actual invasion), smothering economic embargoes, and perhaps the example of at least one terrorist-harboring government brought down by direct attack could conceivably create sufficient internal resistance to topple several other of the world's terrorism-sponsoring regimes. But even in that case the goal of regime change would not be easy to accomplish. It involves, after all, two elements: removing the offending government and replacing it with one willing and able to suppress terrorist activity within its borders. The first may turn out to be more feasible than the second. There is no guarantee that successor regimes to those of Saddam Hussein and Bashar al-Assad would assure that Iraq and Syria remain free of terrorists. The problem is likely to be particularly acute in Afghanistan, the primary target of the antiterrorism campaign.

Afghanistan's centrality carried with it an irony: no Afghan was involved in the attacks on the United States, which were carried out by men from the Arab Middle East. Still, the Taliban regime, which controlled most of the country, had provided shelter and some material assistance to a number of terrorist groups, including Osama bin Laden's Al Qaeda, the one suspected of perpetrating the assaults on the World Trade Center and the Pentagon. Indeed, so generous was the Taliban's hospitality to terrorists that it seemed to have turned Afghanistan into the home base and the nerve center for international terrorism, the place where the initial U.S. military operations against terrorism would have to begin, as they did on October 7, 2001.

Narrowly based, brutal, fanatical, unpopular, and apparently uninterested in or incompetent at the ordinary tasks of government, the Taliban did not seem likely to be able to resist a determined Western effort to topple it, especially if logistical assistance from Pakistani military intelligence and financial contributions from Saudi Arabia came to an end. While displacing the Taliban might be a relatively straightforward matter, however, the same can not be said of the second part of regime change: replacing it with a government capable of keeping terrorists out of the country.

Afghanistan contains numerous ethnic and linguistic groups, religious factions, and tribes and clans—all of which have been constantly at war for more than two decades, first against the Soviet army and then against one another. The constant warfare has devastated an already poor country, leaving no functioning national institutions and precious little modern infrastructure— roads, bridges, schools, hospitals, electrical grids. Moreover, Afghanistan has borders with Pakistan to the east and south, Iran to the west, and Russia to the north (through its influence on the three Central Asian countries bordering Afghanistan). Each of these neighbors harbors large numbers of Afghan refugees; each will, for that and other reasons, demand a say in Afghanistan's political evolution; and none of them is likely to have the same vision of the country's future as the other two. Afghanistan offers, in short, unpromising material from which to construct a stable, functioning government.

The Bush administration made no secret of its disinclination to try to construct such a regime, repeating, after September 11, its previously stated distaste for what it called "nation building," which the Clinton administration had embraced enthusiastically in Somalia, Haiti, and the Balkans, with dismal results. Afghanistan appeared to be, if anything, an even worse place to try to build a viable state; but in the aftermath of September 11 the United States seemed likely to be all but compelled to make the attempt.

THE WRONG ROOTS

War, the saying goes, begins in the minds of men. Recent American wars have prompted Americans and others to advocate changing the minds and winning the hearts of those who oppose the United States by addressing the grievances that underlie their opposition. In keeping with this pattern, even before the fires in lower Manhattan and at the Pentagon had been extinguished, the American public and the American government were being advised from various quarters, both at home and abroad, that the key to ending terrorism was a concerted effort to address its root causes. Two putative causes received particular attention: poverty and Israel.

Although the outcome of the American campaign against terrorist-sponsoring regimes is uncertain, the consequences of trying to eliminate poverty in the countries that breed terrorism and of seeking a resolution of the Israeli-Palestinian conflict by pressuring Israel to make concessions to Yasir Arafat and the Palestinian Authority are entirely predictable: the first will be futile, the second, counterproductive.

Since Osama bin Laden comes from one of the wealthiest families in the world, and Mohammad Atta, the alleged mastermind of the airplane hijackings, was the son of an Egyptian lawyer, the attacks of September 11 cannot have been the result exclusively of anger induced by material deprivation. And even if widespread poverty in the Middle East did help to create the terrorist networks that have targeted the West, the United States is not going to eradicate it.

The identification of poverty as the chief cause of violence and other pathologies is often accompanied by calls for American generosity toward the afflicted peoples in the form of a "new Marshall Plan," a program of economic assistance comparable to the grants and loans that the United States provided to Western Europe beginning in 1947 to speed recovery from the devastation of World War II and thereby dissuade the people of the recipient countries from supporting local communists. As it happens, two of the countries from which the September 11 hijackers came, Saudi Arabia and Egypt, have already received the equivalent of Marshall Plans: Saudi Arabia in the form of the enormous inward flow of wealth in payment for the oil that happens to be located within its borders, and Egypt through the tens of billions of dollars in U.S. foreign aid it has received since the mid–1970s.

The results have not matched the European experience after World War II. The per capita income of Saudi Arabia actually fell by more than 40 percent between 1979 and 1999, and Egypt has remained a poor country throughout the half-century since gaining de facto independence from Great Britain, with a per capita income less than half the world's average. The fault clearly does not lie with American stinginess. Instead, the chief obstacle to economic success in Saudi Arabia and Egypt, as in other countries in the region and almost all poor countries everywhere, is their own governments. The ruling regimes are corrupt and predatory, taking much of their countries' wealth for themselves. They cannot or will not protect property rights or enforce laws fairly and evenhandedly, curb the government's appetite for society's resources, or provide the basic services that underpin productive economic activity. To address the root causes of poverty in the countries that breed or harbor terrorists would therefore require the promotion of regime change on a scale not contemplated by even the most ambitious U.S. official. Such an enterprise would include the replacement of the governments in Saudi Arabia and Egypt that it has been a decades-long goal of the United States, for sound geopolitical reasons, to keep in power.

If poverty is a massive and forbidding target for those seeking to address the "root causes" of terrorism, Israel is a smaller and thus more inviting one. The argument that Israel is a root cause of terrorism, popular in western Europe and not without proponents in the United States, has two parts. The first is that the conflict between Israel and the Palestinians, which since the autumn of 2000 has been a violent one, inflames opinion in the Arab world and thus inspires attacks on Israel's Western friends. The second is that this anger inhibits Arab governments from cooperating with the United States and its allies in the fight against terrorism, for fear of incurring the wrath of the people they rule.

Neither proposition rests on a solid empirical foundation. Before September 11, Osama bin Laden displayed no great interest in Israel. As for the Arab governments, the war against terrorism requires them simply to crack down on, rather than export to the West, the terrorist groups that they have long pursued because one of the chief goals of these groups' chief is to unseat those very regimes. No doubt a settlement of the Arab-Israeli conflict is desirable, even in the absence of any relationship to the events of September 11, but what those who deem it a root cause of terrorism prescribe will fail to settle it.

Addressing the cause of the "destructive despair" that lay behind the attacks, the French commentator Dominique Moisi wrote in the *Financial Times*, means "imposing territorial sacrifices on [the West's] allies, including Israel." But well before the September 11 attacks, Israel had shown a willingness to make such sacrifices. In the summer of 2000, Israeli Prime Minister Ehud Barak volunteered to give up more than 95 percent of the territory that Israel had captured in the 1967 Arab-Israeli war—begun by an Egyptian act of war against Israel—in order to create a Palestinian state, to compensate this state for the other few percent with territory that had been part of Israel prior to June 1967, and even to give it part of Israel's capital, Jerusalem, including control of Muslim holy places. In response, Arafat flatly rejected Barak's offer and made no counterproposal. He started, or at the very least enthusiastically joined in, a war against Israel the chief tactic of which was the murder of Israeli civilians. He finally insisted that any settlement would have to include the right to return to live in Israel of millions of people claiming descent from the Arabs who had left in 1948—because of a war begun with an unprovoked attack by the surrounding Arab countries on the Jewish state that the United Nations had created. This insistence is a formula for the destruction of Israel. There is no credible evidence that Arafat is seeking a Palestinian state alongside Israel, and all too much evidence that his goal is a Palestinian state instead of Israel.

The necessary condition for an Israeli-Palestinian settlement, therefore, is not pressure on Israel, which will only reward Arafat for his rejection of compromise and his campaign of terror. Instead, peace requires regime change in the Palestinian Authority, to replace Arafat and his associates with people who acknowledge that Jews as well as Arabs have rightful national claims in the Middle East and that Israel is a permanent, legitimate part of the region.

THE DEFINITION OF VICTORY

The American wars of the twentieth century came to decisive conclusions marked by symbolically potent events: the Japanese surrender aboard the U.S.S. *Missouri* in Tokyo Bay in 1945, the armistice in the Korean War, the helicopters lifting off from the U.S. embassy compound in Saigon in 1975, the hundred hours of the Persian Gulf War. Even the Cold War, more an era than an event, had its dramatic end point: the opening of the Berlin Wall in November 1989.

The war on terrorism, as U.S. officials emphasized repeatedly after September 11, will not end so neatly. Success in this conflict will be measured not, as in other wars, by what American military forces do, but rather by what terrorists do not do. In this new war a day when nothing happens will be a good day for the United States.

In this sense terrorism is more like a disease: a sudden, virulent outbreak has claimed thousands of lives and shocked the country into a major effort to understand, to detect, and to combat it. Few of the great killer diseases of human history have been entirely eradicated; but many have been brought under control, claiming only a few victims each year. So it will be if the war against terrorism succeeds. And the measures put in place to prevent terrorism will not be abandoned any more than vaccinations and other public health measures are discontinued even after a dread disease is brought under control. Victory will have been achieved in the war against terrorism when the issue disappears from the forefront of public attention and when the innovations of foreign policy, law enforcement, and public safety established in the wake of September 11 are absorbed into the everyday fabric of American and international life.

The definition of victory in this, the first war of the twenty-first century, comes from the aftermath of the initial conflict of the last one. President Woodrow Wilson took the United States into World War I and, when it ended, brought to the Paris Peace Conference a sweeping vision of a new and better world, which he failed to implement. He was succeeded in office by Warren Harding, a man without his predecessor's soaring ambitions either at home or abroad. Harding's presidency remains memorable for the scandals it produced and for the phrase that expressed his postwar program, which also succinctly captures the goal of the war on terrorism: a return to normalcy.

STIRRED BUT NOT SHAKEN

THE ECONOMIC REPERCUSSIONS

■

MARTIN N. BAILY

Finding the right economic response to the crisis caused by the September 11 attacks is a vital part of showing the terrorists they have not undermined the strength of the United States and its allies. Americans had believed that they were safe from foreign aggression in their own country, but today many feel understandably nervous about the future. Consumer confidence is weak. According to a CNN/*Time* poll taken shortly after the attacks, 40 percent of consumers plan to cut back on spending and 42 percent plan to cut back their travel because of the attacks. Many businesses were directly affected by the crisis, and many others are cautious about making new investments.

Prior to the attacks, indicators were mixed. Consumer spending had been higher in August and seemed to be proceeding normally in early September. Motor-vehicle sales in the first ten days of September had been running at about the same level as in August, and chain-store sales were down only slightly. There were some signs that the economy was turning the corner.

On the other hand, investment remained in a slump, having fallen 15 percent in the second quarter. The August employment report was weak and construction spending fell during the month. The stock market was soft, and consumer confidence in early September was declining. On balance the economic portents were fairly negative. Instead of seeing the hoped-for rebound in economic activity, we were already seeing signs of very weak or even negative growth for the country's gross domestic product (GDP) in the third quarter. U.S. manufacturing had lost nearly a million jobs over the course of the preceding 12 months.

The United States was not the only country experiencing economic problems. Japan was in deep trouble, its economy declining and its financial system on the edge of collapse. Europe was holding up better, but forecasts were dropping there, too, notably in Germany, which is heavily affected by the worldwide demand for capital goods. A recent report showed that industrial production in the eurozone (the 12 countries that have adopted the euro as their common currency) had declined 1.4 percent in July. The newly industrialized Asian economies that rely on exports were facing the near-collapse of demand for high-tech goods and services. U.S. imports of computer-related products had fallen by $80 billion in 2001. Latin America was struggling as well, especially Argentina, and Turkey was having a particularly difficult time, too.

There is broad agreement that the terrorist attacks will push the teetering U.S. economy into recession and the global economy into a period of slow growth. U.S. GDP will likely decline by 1 percent in both the third and fourth quarters of 2001, with a much larger decline possible in the fourth quarter if consumers remain cautious. The forecasting group Macroeconomic Advisers estimates that the attacks destroyed $13 billion worth of private and government capital and lowered economic activity in the third quarter by $24 billion, when calculated at an annual rate.

Some industries were directly affected, notably airlines, hotels, and insurance companies. U.S. airlines announced the layoff of around 90,000 employees shortly after the attacks; the cutbacks in air travel immediately spilled over into other industries, as well. Boeing announced layoffs of around 30,000, anticipating that orders for its aircraft would fall. Many meetings and conventions were canceled, and tourism was down sharply. Layoff announcements can often be misleading, but there was little doubt that many companies were in difficulty.

The short-run impact of the attacks is broader than just the suffering of the industries directly affected. There has been an increase in uncertainty, fostering a desire among businesses and consumers to wait and see before undertaking major economic commitments. It is natural for each individual consumer to react to such uncertainty by holding back on spending decisions. But the impact of such caution by all consumers becomes self-fulfilling, as a drop in total consumption brings on layoffs and rising unemployment, and thus less disposable income to spend. Businesses also react to uncertainty by holding back on capital spending, and that could slow or abort the needed recovery.

One piece of good news is that so far there has been no spike in oil prices. In fact, oil prices now have fallen because of weaker demand and the pledge by the oil-producing countries to maintain stability in the oil market. But the possibility of a disruption of the world's oil supply hangs over the global economy, and an extensive conflict could result in a sharp run-up in oil prices. If that happens, the recession will be deeper or longer than otherwise anticipated.

SHORT-TERM AND LONG-TERM CONCERNS

Sound policies are being pursued to restore confidence and bolster demand. Central banks around the world, notably the U.S. Federal Reserve Board and the European Central Bank, added liquidity to the global financial system, thus allowing banks to borrow cash and reserves more easily to tide them over shortages of cash or other liquid assets.

Fiscal policy, at least in the United States, should also serve to promote a recovery. A stimulus package is being added to the tax cut already enacted and the rebate checks already sent to taxpayers. Congress has passed a $40 billion emergency package of increased spending, available for rebuilding, for the military and for enhanced security needs. And a package of around $15 billion has been passed to help the airlines. In Europe, however, governments are bent on balancing their budgets, a serious mistake during a massive downturn. A better plan would be to temporarily set aside the targets of the European Stability Pact to allow the automatic stabilizers of fiscal policy to work.

Spending weakness will continue in the United States through at least the end of 2001 and probably into the first part of 2002.

Still, the chances are good that the economy will recover quickly. Once the inventory overhang caused by slackening demand is worked off and short-lived equipment wears out or becomes obsolete, production should resume and investment should begin again. The latest blue chip forecast suggests 3 to 4 percent growth by the second half of 2002.

Since 1945, the average length of recessions in the United States has been eleven months, a fact that suggests that recoveries come pretty quickly, unless there is some unusual drag on the economy. Beyond the natural resilience of the U.S. economy, the policy steps just described will start to take effect and will buoy the economy back into positive growth. Monetary policy always takes some time to work, but in general it does work. And over the next 12 months, a fiscal boost amounting to almost 2 percent of GDP is in the works, a combination of tax cuts already in the pipeline, additional defense and security spending, and the likely stimulus package.

There may well be some ugly economic numbers coming out in the months ahead, but the prospects for recovery are excellent. The United States will not go into a multiyear slump, so long as there is not a series of large-scale, successful terrorist attacks against the United States or a wider war. The prediction of a speedy recovery is based on the assumption that the United States and its allies find a way to contain the terrorist threat. Beyond this, there will be some lasting, moderate costs to the economy coming from increased uncertainty and what one can call a "security tax"—costs that will be built into the price of goods and services to cover new security procedures.

The fiscal stimulus package should put money in the hands of those most likely to spend. Its size should be large enough to be effective but not so large that it undermines budget discipline. President George W. Bush's suggestion of $60 to $75 billion in addition to the spending already under way seems about right for the immediate future, but it is important, for reasons of fiscal discipline, that these tax cuts and spending increases have sunset provisions or be consistent with long-term goals.

On the consumer side, further tax rebates should be targeted at moderate-income taxpayers, including those that pay payroll taxes but did not receive the rebates handed out so far. This would be seen as equitable and it would not create problems for fiscal discipline down the road. It would give money to families with low and moderate incomes, who would be likely to spend most of it. Although tax rebates are not a surefire solution to economic weakness, they would nonetheless help in stimulating consumption.

One plan, proposed by the Princeton economist Alan Blinder, would have the federal government reimburse states that give temporary sales-tax holidays to encourage immediate consumer purchasing. An added benefit of his proposal would be the relief provided states that otherwise might have to raise taxes or cut spending to meet balanced-budget rules. Some form of transfer to the states by the federal government may become necessary to prevent states' fiscal policies from worsening the recessionary cycle.

The Bush administration's push to accelerate the permanent tax-rate reductions passed earlier in 2001 would avoid the political wrangling that usually attends fresh tax proposals. But these permanent tax cuts concern some as being too big over the long run and as undermining fiscal discipline. Any acceleration of the rate cuts should therefore focus not on the top rates but on immediately reducing the middle, 28 percent rate to 25 percent, instead of having it fall gradually over five years, which is the current schedule. This rate has its biggest impact on middle-income taxpayers and would not be too expensive in lost revenue (the acceleration would cost about $54 billion over the ten-year budget window).

Another worthy policy, suggested by the economists Lori Kletzer and Robert Litan, would be to provide wage insurance to those laid-off workers who suffer substantial pay cuts in taking new jobs. Under a wage-insurance program, the federal government would, for a fixed period of time, pay workers a portion of the difference between the wages they earn on a new job and the wages they were paid on the former job from which they were laid off. Such a program would cushion the blow of layoffs that are now taking place and would encourage laid-off workers to take new jobs rather than collect unemployment insurance. Wage insurance is a controversial policy and it may be hard to introduce quickly in a short-run package, but it is a policy that has much to commend it in good times, and it would be very helpful now that more layoffs are a likely prospect.

On the business side, the current stimulus favorite is to allow more generous depreciation of capital spending to counter the massive drop in investment that has been a major cause of the weak economy. Accelerating depreciation would get an influx of cash into the hands of companies that are investing. A temporary investment stimulus could be more effective than a permanent one, based on the same logic that Blinder uses. The government would be saying to companies, Invest over the next year and get a tax break. If a company puts off the investment until later, the tax break will be gone. Under such a program, some companies may well decide to upgrade their computers or buy a new fleet of autos this year rather than waiting until next year.

Policies that would not be effective in stimulating the economy include a capital-gains tax cut or a cut in the corporate tax rate. Neither policy has been shown in econometric studies to provide much stimulus to investment. A cut in the capital-gains tax could even have the perverse effect of encouraging people to sell stocks, which would send the stock market lower—not a desired result.

Over the longer term, budget targets should not be abandoned. Both the United States and Europe face pressing budget problems in the coming years as their baby boom generations move into retirement. For the United States, it is vital to keep paying down the national debt while the opportunity is there and before facing the massive increases in pension and health-care costs that are looming on the horizon. Saving the Social Security surpluses and even the Medicare surpluses is good policy for the long run. In addition, it is important for the United States to increase its national savings in the long run, even as it increases spending in the short run, to reduce its foreign borrowing. Running budget surpluses will help achieve both these goals. Good policy, in short, means easing the constraints on budget policy this year and maybe next, but simultaneously re-examining the long-run budget prospects and looking for ways to preserve long-term fiscal discipline, which will keep long-term interest rates low and speed economic recovery. Even before the September 11 attacks, the Congressional Budget Office had issued a new set of budget projections with sharply lower estimates of the surpluses. Since that time and since the attack, the prospects for a weak economy are far greater in the short run and the uncertainty about the long-run prospects for growth has increased. In addition, sharply higher spending on defense and security are likely for years to come. The short-run stimulus package, although necessary, will also have a small adverse effect on the budget outlook even over the long term, because it raises the national debt and the interest burden.

It is clear that the budget arithmetic has changed and the pledge to preserve the Social Security surpluses has been forgotten for now. Recessions and wars are expensive and it is only to be expected that if we spend more and tax less now, there will be less money available later. There should be a realistic debate about whether it is more important to preserve the entire tax-cut package passed earlier in 2001, or whether it is more important to preserve budget surpluses.

SUSTAINING GLOBAL GROWTH

A large inflow of global capital, due to a persistent trade deficit, has been a boon to the United States, fueling the country's strong economic performance in the 1990s. The U.S. trade deficit was also a boon to the rest of the world. Other countries were happy to sell their goods to Americans and to use part of the proceeds to buy American assets. The United States indeed has been the locomotive of global growth.

This pattern of international trade and capital flows, however, has created two problems for Americans. Net foreign indebtedness has risen sharply and keeps on rising (it increased by $445 billion in 2000), threatening future economic welfare with too much foreign debt. Moreover, the strong dollar that resulted from the inflow of capital has undermined competitiveness and thereby weakened the U.S. manufacturing sector.

Over the next several years, the goal should be to rebalance the world economy by increasing the inadequate U.S. savings rate, exporting more, and importing less. In order for this rebalancing to work, other countries would have to develop their own investment opportunities, add to their domestic demand, and rely less on the United States as a market. As a result, the dollar would decline, particularly against the euro.

Since the September 11 attacks, the dollar has remained strong against the euro as the United States, so far, has retained its appeal as a safe and profitable place to put funds. And the U.S. stock market is weathering the crisis pretty well. Having fallen substantially in the period prior to the attack, it fell further immediately after the attacks. The Dow Jones Industrial Average on September 10 was down about 18 percent compared to its high, and then fell a further 14 percent after the attacks. It is striking, however, that by mid-October the market had regained much of the ground it had lost after the attacks. So far it seems there is confidence that a recovery of both the economy and profits in the United States will be as strong as or stronger than in Europe.

Clearly, other countries have to energize their economies and expand domestic demand, as there is a limit to the trade deficits the United States can run to fuel global growth. Around the world, policies that are overly reliant on manufacturing and exporting must be reconfigured to provide incentives for employment growth in the service sector. Over time the global economy will have to adjust to a lower trade deficit in the United States, and that almost certainly will involve a realignment of exchange rates and a stronger euro.

It is vital that Europe, in particular, do its best to sustain growth in the face of the new threat to stability. If the downturn worsens, further interest-rate cuts may be needed from the European Central Bank. Japan must also take forceful steps to avoid falling further into recession. Following the end of the 1980s boom, Japanese policymakers failed to take quick and decisive monetary and fiscal steps to reverse the resulting slowdown. Even today, the Japanese government is unwilling to face up to and deal with the bad-loan problems of its banks. It must address its financial crisis and not become a stone dragging the global economy under water.

THE PRICE OF SECURITY

Human behavior tends to ignore the chances of catastrophic, large-scale disasters. We underestimate the probability of earthquakes or floods. Reflecting this pattern, the insurance premiums for airlines and skyscrapers did not reflect the possibility of their being destroyed by terrorists. Once a disaster does happen, the pendulum swings the other way, and we think the chances of its happening again are very high. An obstacle to invigorating the economy is that insurance premiums have soared, especially for airlines. Insuring against terrorist attacks will pose a problem, perhaps for a long time. From now on, it will be more costly to fly and to run airports and airlines. And it will be less attractive to build tall towers and create visible attractions like Walt Disney World.

There is a solution to sky-high insurance rates, albeit a flawed one. For decades, the United Kingdom has been living with the threat of terrorism from the Irish Republican Army, and the British government runs a risk pool to provide payments in the event of large economic losses from terrorism. The U.S. government may want to consider organizing such a risk pool for the airlines and other high-profile terrorist targets. Everyone pays into the pool, and if future losses are not great there is enough money in the pool to pay all the claims. If there is a massive claim, the government steps in and supplements the payout. Having the government provide insurance of last resort is the best way to deal with the current situation, but it is not ideal to put government in the position of providing guarantees for private companies. Government insurance for banks and against floods has provided stability for the economy, but these programs have also been subject to abuse or overuse.

Another enlarged uncertainty since September is that of corporate defaults. The probability of default on high-yield debt has sharply increased in many industries, notably in aerospace, services, and nondurable consumer goods. The risk of default was already very high in the telecommunications field, and it has risen further. Blue-chip corporations also face higher borrowing costs. They are now paying 2.5 percentage points above Treasury rates, compared to the 2.15 percentage points surcharge they were paying prior to the attacks and 1.25 percentage points paid in 1999. This shows that most of the rise in the risk premium was already in the market before September 11, but the attacks made things worse.

The increased risk premium faced by business borrowers should drop sharply or even disappear once the economy recovers, but it is a problem right now. Companies are cautious about investing to begin with and the increased cost of financing adds to their reluctance, thus contributing to recessionary conditions. One bright spot in this general picture of higher risk premiums is the very low rates being charged to mortgage borrowers. Cautious consumers have been reluctant to buy new homes, but the low rates are providing a powerful lure to bring them back into the market.

Internationally, there has been an increase in the risk of borrowing, with potentially serious consequences for emerging markets that were already weak. For example, Argentina is now paying interest on its debts at a rate 18 percent above U.S. Treasury rates, and Brazil and Turkey are also in trouble. It looks as if these three emerging countries will have to go back to the International Monetary Fund (IMF) for more help. The United States is likely to reluctantly go along with further IMF allocations to these countries or easier repayment terms rather than risk a new financial crisis to rival the one that plagued emerging markets in 1997–99.

It was well known that security at U.S. airports was dreadful, but no one really believed it would matter, at least not on the scale of what happened on September 11. So both the government and the industry concentrated on cost-cutting. No one wanted to pay the cost of a top-of-the-line security system and instead there were low-paid ill-trained workers with frequent turnover operating the screening devices. Now we know that things have to change.

From an economic point of view, the cost in higher ticket prices of having an efficient but tighter security system at airports is a price worth paying. Security at El Al, commonly described as the best protected airline in the world, amounts to 7 percent of the airline's total costs, compared to 2 percent for U.S. airlines. (A percentage of El Al's security costs is paid by the Israeli government.) Maybe we do not need to pay that much, but it is time to do the calculation.

The issue of security, of course, extends well beyond the airline sector. There will be a "security tax" on economic activity for some time, perhaps indefinitely. Government spending will be higher and will have to be paid for with higher taxes. The war on terrorism will be expensive. Travel will not be as easy. Obtaining visas may take longer. Security precautions are costly and will add to prices. The security tax is already being felt in some sectors, as U.S. manufacturers have faced supply shortages as a result of trucks unable to enter the United States from Canada and Mexico.

Security measures can be expensive, but with innovation and the benefits of widespread use and production, costs will come down. When air bags were first introduced for passenger cars, the cost per air bag was high. Many people complained about having to pay for this "safety tax." Today, however, mass production has sharply lowered the cost and many consumers buy cars with multiple air bags. The world needs to develop best-practice approaches to security, practices that maximize safety while minimizing delays and disruptions. A security tax will modestly reduce productivity. Hiring 200,000 additional people to provide security at an overall cost (including salaries, benefits, support, and infrastructure) of $100,000 per employee would cost $20 billion. But even this seemingly large figure amounts to just 0.2 percent of GDP in a $10 trillion economy—not enough to cramp economic growth.

THE FUTURE OF GLOBALIZATION

The keys to the success of the U.S. economy in the 1990s were openness, mobility, and the benefits of globalization. Talented people from around the world were drawn to the United States to be part of the cutting edge of technology. Immigrants from China and India founded 30 percent of the start-up technology companies in Silicon Valley in the late 1990s. Without the skills these people brought with them, progress would have been less rapid. As well as the flow of people, the inflow of capital was essential to the investment boom that contributed heavily to the acceleration of U.S. productivity growth. And, of course, the international flow of goods and services was also essential in providing the building blocks of the new economy. In turn, technology development depended on finding global markets to justify the requisite risky investments.

Expanding globally became the accepted strategy for success among large companies during the 1990s. Improved computer and telecommunication technologies made it easier to operate a global company, and the profit potential in new markets provided a tremendous lure for companies that had reached the limits of expansion in their domestic markets. McDonald's had about 15,000 restaurants overseas in 2000, up from about 3,000 in 1990; it now has more restaurants overseas than in the United States. Taking a successful business system and applying it in new markets has been a key driver of profit growth for many U.S. companies and multinational corporations around the world.

International comparisons have suggested that an important driver of high productivity is competition against best-practice companies worldwide. U.S. auto companies changed their ways and improved efficiency as a result of the pressure of competition from Japanese automakers. Globalization also increases the intensity of competition and forces companies to change and innovate or be driven out of the market. Globalization has thus been an important driver of productivity advances.

Despite the benefits of globalization, there was a reassessment of global strategy taking place at many companies even before the September 11 attacks. Globalization faces increasing political resistance. The violent protests at economic summit meetings in Seattle and then in Genoa showed the intensity of the opposition, even if the protesters were a tiny minority. A much broader group of people, in Europe, in the United States, and around the world, has misgivings about the path of the global economy. Many workers, especially those without college degrees, believe that globalization has hurt their standard of living. Nevertheless, the case for globalization is a strong one. Most economists argue that, although expanded trade can hurt groups of workers, on balance globalization is good for the living standards of the majority as well as for profits.

The forces that have driven globalization forward so forcefully in the past will still be there in the future. Many industries, like those that manufacture computers, semiconductors, or autos, are global industries. There is no turning back for these companies. But the speed and direction of globalization may shift.

In the 1990s, many companies believed they were facing a globalization imperative. Markets around the world were growing faster than in the United States, and they had to be part of that growth. The financial crises of the late 1990s started a change in perception. For example, it is no longer taken for granted that the Asian "tigers," those Asian economies that grew with remarkable speed in the 1980s and 1990s, will keep growing rapidly. The next shift came with the realization that having a strong U.S. brand can be a mixed blessing. Most customers still love McDonald's and Coca-Cola, but these brands now carry the risk of alienating a vocal part of the population.

The terrorist attacks have not changed the fundamental economics of globalization, but they have added to the concerns that were already developing. And they have raised the costs of travel and of doing business globally. The security tax and the impact of greater uncertainty affect domestic as well as global activity, but they do fall more heavily on economic activity outside the home country.

Going forward, companies will make more careful assessments

of the risks and rewards of global expansion. They will develop trade ties with and invest in countries that offer environments friendly to multinational corporations. That will be a loss for countries whose citizens perceive multinationals as an enemy, even though their economies could benefit from expanded trade and the inflow of capital and expertise that direct foreign investment provides. Forming alliances with domestic partners has often been a key element in companies' global strategies and will become even more desirable going forward.

Emerging markets have already been hurt by slow growth in the global economy, given their heavy dependence on exports. The growth forecast for these countries for 2001 had been cut to about half of the growth they achieved in 2000. Along with declining exports, emerging markets are finding the international flow of capital to their economies is declining sharply, too.

The end of the global boom should serve as a reminder to emerging countries of the need to maintain the economic reform effort even when economic growth picks up again. The right response to current economic conditions must come primarily from within emerging economies.

The international financial institutions can play a role in easing the short-term difficulties of emerging economies. They should monitor events and stand ready to make larger loans if contagion effects of the crisis begin to spread. It would be a mistake, however, to hand out large sums of money just because world growth has slowed down. Countries need to have in place policies that are robust and that can withstand the vagaries of the business cycle.

Since the destruction and loss of life at the World Trade Center, at the Pentagon, and in western Pennsylvania, the world has changed. The terrorist attacks exacerbated economic problems that were already apparent. But the fundamentals of the U.S. economy are very strong. Economic growth and the pace of globalization may be a bit slower in the next decade than they were in the 1990s, but globalization will proceed. Economic fears will be overcome.

THE HOME FRONT

AMERICAN SOCIETY RESPONDS TO THE NEW WAR

■

ALAN WOLFE

The terrorist attacks against the United States, meant to divide Americans from one another, have united them as at no time since World War II. Immediately before the events, we were still discussing the 2000 presidential election and whether the person elected with more blue states than red ones—or was it the other way around?—held office legitimately. The issues we debated then included whether frozen embryos were human beings and whether the Boy Scouts could exclude homosexuals from their ranks. People talked seriously about a deep chasm between one America that was presumed to be devout and another that was routinely described as secular. Political speculation focused on whether President George W. Bush could cut taxes and expand the military at the same time and what the Democrats would do to ensure that he could not. And underlying the whole discussion was a debate taking place over whether Americans were losing their sense of civic participation and concern for the direction of their society.

It takes a real war to make Americans realize how insignificant our culture war has been. Twice in recent years Americans have been victims of murderous terrorist attacks at home: one took place in Oklahoma, the other in lower Manhattan and on the outskirts of Washington, D.C. Oklahoma, in many ways the most conservative state in the union, symbolizes the side in the culture war that stands for a return to the religion, values, and morality of years past. Lower Manhattan, probably the most liberal slice of America, represents modern urbane cosmopolitanism, racial and ethnic diversity, and openness to the rest of the world. And

Washington, as the nation's capital, stands in the conservative mind for big government and in the liberal mind as the embodiment of U.S. military power. Yet what the terrorists proved by their acts is that, no matter how different Americans may be from one another in their religious beliefs or political views, they are all equal before the onslaught of machinery transformed into weapons. The United States really is one nation, even if it needs other nations, or international bandits without a nation, to remind it of that fact.

America was the target of the September 11 attacks because its commitments to free speech, religious liberty, gender equality, and racial and ethnic diversity were intolerable to theocrats persuaded that only one truth exists and that it is their mission to ensure that no one thinks otherwise. The United States was made vulnerable to terrorist attack because it has open borders, a dedication to civil liberties, an aversion to discrimination on the basis of group characteristics, a free market, and a strong belief that the pursuit of the good life and the quest for zealotry are incompatible. How much will change as a result of September 11? Certainly airport security will be tightened, electronic and other forms of communication will be more closely monitored, and police will be more forthright in their use of profiling—racial and otherwise—to stop violent acts before they happen. But none of these steps will change America's commitment to liberal and democratic values. Instead, the most likely effect of the terrorist attacks will be to strengthen American liberties by grounding them in reality and underscoring why we value them in the first place.

RELIGIOUS DIFFERENCE

Illustrative of what is likely to emerge in the America shaped by the events of September 11 is a firmer sense of the proper role for religion in a society no longer shaped by a common faith tradition. Although the Constitution formally separated church and state, America was nonetheless governed throughout the nineteenth century by an unofficial Protestant morality that structured its educational system, political values, approach to child-rearing, work ethic, and even foreign policy. As Catholics and Jews increasingly made the United States their home, however, the nation's understanding of morality could no longer be based on the assumptions of one faith. Not without serious conflict, American morality did change. For a time, the term "Christian" came to replace "Protestant" in descriptions of the nation, so as to include Catholics. Then, as the country fought a war against the most anti-Semitic regime in modern history, it broadened the description once again to "Judeo-Christian," even though Jews and Christians had been fighting each other for two thousand years.

Before September 11, there were already more Muslims in the United States than Episcopalians, and it is only a matter of time before adherents of Islam replace Jews as the largest non-Christian religious group in the country. Scholars were engaged in an effort to develop a replacement term for "Judeo-Christian" that would cover this new reality, with "Abrahamic" emerging as the leading candidate, since Muslims, like Jews and Christians, trace their origins back to Abraham. Although this term has its limits—it does not encompass Hinduism, Buddhism, or many other religions now practiced by large numbers of Americans—it does continue a long-standing process of recognizing the increasing religious diversity that characterizes American society. When President Bush spoke at a Washington mosque on September 17, praising Muslims for their "incredibly valuable contribution to our country," his words could be understood as an official recognition of post-Judeo-Christian America. (And when, in the aftermath of attacks on turban-wearing Sikhs across the country he invited a group of Sikhs to the White House to reassure them, he moved beyond "Abrahamic" religion as well.) It took an act of Middle Eastern terrorists to make Americans realize that many peaceful, hard-working, and law-abiding Muslims live in their country.

Just as Americans have learned something about their religious diversity from the attacks launched on them, they have also learned something about the proper role for religion in a society committed to separation of church and state. Before September

11, the U.S. Supreme Court tended to draw a sharp wall between these two institutions. In June 2000, for example, the Court ruled that prayers before a high school football game, amplified over loudspeakers, created a coercive atmosphere and thus amounted to an unconstitutional establishment of religion. Although the Court's jurisprudence in this area has often been inconsistent (it has also ruled that student fees collected at a public university cannot be denied to a conservative Christian student publication) the trend has been in the direction of questioning an active role for faith in the American public square.

Yet in response to the terrorist attacks, the country's entire political elite assembled in the National Cathedral and was led in prayer by religious leaders of many faiths—and no one thought to object. The fact that religion and politics were so seamlessly blended, and that no danger to the Republic followed from their mixture, suggests that in an emergency the right balance will be found. One side in the debate over religion and politics can take heart from the fact that Americans, even when they assemble in public, need the healing that faith offers to overcome tragedy. And the other side can recognize that, under contemporary conditions of religious diversity, no single religious point of view will be used to coerce others. The World Trade Center and Pentagon attacks brought out common sense on one of our most contentious issues, a lesson that may be found useful as future court decisions are handed down in this area.

One American who showed no appreciation for common sense in the days following the attacks was the Rev. Jerry Falwell, and one of the more important cultural responses since September 11 has been the widespread revulsion against his hateful message blaming gays, feminists, and civil libertarians for the tragedy. In an odd way, the terrorists were more egalitarian than Falwell: they cared not a whit whether the Americans they killed were gay or straight, left-wing or right-wing, devout or secular, male or female, black or white—or even whether they were Americans. Hatred that indiscriminate reminds us why more discriminate forms of hatred are un-American. So long as Falwell was viewed as a man who might deliver votes, politicians bent over backward to appease him. Now that he is rightly seen as a man who instead delivers hate, they will avoid him. Falwell's intolerance establishes a barrier than no preacher of hate will be able to scale for the foreseeable future. Let someone start attacking people for the fact of their difference in the years ahead, and someone else will remind them that our enemies make no such distinction.

FREE TO BE

But surely, it will be said, the United States has responded by going to war, and war is harmful to the exercise of civil liberty. At one level, this is obviously true: depending on how we pursue this war, we can expect pressure on newspapers to support their government, accusations against dissenters that they are aiding and abetting our enemies, and greater suspicion of those whose appearance or language marks them as somehow "different." Those who fear a potential encroachment on civil liberties can point to the Bush administration's proposal to Congress for new legislation that would loosen restrictions on wiretapping and would allow police and the courts to rely on foreign evidence gathered by means that did not meet U.S. constitutional standards. Yet the fact is that Congress has raised serious questions about the administration's more draconian proposals, reminding everyone of why we insist on the importance of civil liberties in the first place. There is no reason to believe that a U.S.-led campaign against terrorism will make such extensive inroads into civil liberties that anything like a police state will result.

There are two additional reasons why we are unlikely to see substantial encroachments on freedom as we mobilize for a response to terror. The first is that America has become a much more tolerant society than it was throughout most of the twentieth century. It was not that long ago when, in response to World War I, we banned the teaching of German in our schools or when, during the next world war, we locked up people who shared the same heritage—Japanese—as the enemy we were fighting. Nor can it easily be forgotten that, during the McCarthy period, we practiced a politics of intolerance that stigmatized the guilty and the innocent alike. The periods of intolerance that have marked our past have raised legitimate questions about how we will respond in the future.

Yet how we have changed! In interviews I have conducted with middle-class people from every corner of the United States, I have seen that a culture of nonjudgmentalism has become widespread in this country. With the exception of homosexuality and, to a lesser degree, illegal immigration, Americans seem increasingly reluctant to insist that certain ways of life are wrong, cruel, sinful, or misguided. Such nonjudgmentalism can have its downside; as the terrorist attacks remind us, there are times when we need to insist that some kinds of acts are so evil that no excuse or justification for them is possible. But this particular variant of nonjudgmentalism has made few appearances in the aftermath of the attacks. Except for a few isolated voices on the left who found moral equivalence between the destruction of the World Trade Center and events such as the U.S. invasion of Grenada, most people in this country made the snap, and quite correct, judgment that the perpetrators of such evil acts can and ought to be punished for their deeds.

There is also a positive side to nonjudgmentalism: compared to intolerance, it allows people to find the good among the bad. That may be why we are not likely to enter a new McCarthy period in the wake of the terrorist attacks, despite the fact that most of the terrorists were entered this country surreptitiously and that their religion is one that historically has fought wars against both Christians and Jews. It is true that in the days immediately following the attacks, incidents of hatred were directed not only against Muslims but also against others, such as Sikhs, who were mistaken for Muslims. There are no excuses for such deplorable acts. Yet they were not contagious; nothing in the response of the American people suggests anything like a hysterical, panic-driven movement to find scapegoats and hold them responsible. September 11 was not Pearl Harbor and we are no longer the country of the Ku Klux Klan.

Another reason exists for concluding that a war against terror will fail to result in a serious diminution of civil liberty. Past wars, for all the restrictions on free speech they brought, also significantly expanded other kinds of liberty. Before World War II, America had no modern welfare state and individuals had few protections against corporate power. In part because war demands that all of those recruited to fight it be at the peak of physical and mental health, World War II, even more than the Great Depression, modernized the American state. Once the war was over and the troops returned home, no one could make the case that veterans did not deserve access to housing through a subsidized mortgage program, to education through the GI Bill of Rights, or to health care or death benefits. One of the effects of the war was to lift an entire generation of Americans into the ranks of the middle class and, by doing that, to expand their opportunities and those of their children. Despite the subsequent election of conservative presidents such as Dwight Eisenhower, Richard Nixon, and Ronald Reagan in the decades after the war, Republicans chose not to stop the expansion of government that the war started. It is fair to say that the old isolationist and small-government right wing never really survived World War II.

A GOVERNMENT OF ALL THE PEOPLE

In a similar way, the terrorist attacks on the Pentagon and the World Trade Center, as well as the need to mobilize the country to retaliate, will further diminish the influence of the extreme right. Americans were already prepared for this by the Oklahoma City bombing in 1995. Once it became clear that Timothy McVeigh saw himself as the enemy of government, the attack on "big government" led by Speaker of the House Newt Gingrich came to an end. Suddenly talk of black helicopters and conspiracies to deprive Americans of their liberties were revealed for the dangerous words they had always been. America's political culture matured in the aftermath of Oklahoma City. When the Republican leadership in Congress tried to shut down government later that year, Americans quickly realized why they have government in the first place.

It is true that in his campaign for president, George W. Bush echoed conservative distrust of government when he talked about how tax revenues really belonged to the people. Yet no one paid much attention. Tax-cutting remained a peripheral issue for most Americans, even after Congress, responding to Bush, cut taxes. Unlike during an earlier mania for supply-side economics, the Bush tax cut was not fueled by popular pressure from below but was passed because the president was able to persuade the Republican majorities that then existed in both houses of Congress to support his signature policy.

Situations of war and national emergency, because they require a response from government, are conducive to raising taxes, not lowering them. Already in the aftermath of the attack, one can begin to see a new centrist approach establishing itself. For one thing, the idea that we can rely on the market to solve all our problems has taken a double blow, from the recession that seems to have begun shortly before the attacks and from the failure of the airlines, concerned with cutting costs and raising profits, to provide sufficient security. Even *The Wall Street Journal*, a longtime champion of unrestrained market competition, has criticized the market failure that allowed terrorists to board planes without scrutiny. This does not necessarily mean that the federal government will assume vastly increased responsibility for airline security; once the crisis subsides, a certain amount of lobbying by groups that stand to benefit from one policy or another can be expected, and conservative Republicans in Congress have already begun to object to an expanded government role in the aftermath of the tragedy. But outside of Washington, most Americans are more likely to view the market as a means rather than as an end—to be encouraged when it works, but to be questioned when it does not.

At the same time, it is also difficult to imagine government operating blatantly in the interests of only one class of people when people from all walks of life were killed in the attacks. The idea of cutting corporate or capital gains taxes to stimulate the economy, without offering any comparable benefits to Americans on the lower rungs of the income ladder, is likely to be a political nonstarter. Even the immediate effort by Congress to give a "bailout" to the airline industry was met with skeptics who asked what well-paid airline executives have done to deserve such generosity. It is one thing to reward the richest and most powerful Americans in a time of peace, as Bush's tax cut primarily did. But such forms of class politics cannot easily be practiced in a time of war. Bush's popularity does not give him a free hand; instead, it ties his hands. If he wants to be the president of all the people—and he has rightly decided that he does—he cannot afford to appear to be the president of only some of them. In that sense, the terrorist attacks represented the end of the Bush campaign, even as they symbolized the beginning of the Bush presidency. Compared to the first six months of his administration, when his popularity was relatively low and his proposals contentious, Bush's support has broadened as his proposals have become more inclusive.

The sense of solidarity that emerged out of the terrorist attacks has altered the complexion of American politics. In good, bipartisan fashion, it is fair to say that Americans have not been blessed with great leaders in recent years. This may be because they did not want or need great leaders. Times of peace and prosperity, as beneficial as they are for our economic well-being, are not always conducive to our political well-being; times of war and crisis, however much they cause pain in our private lives, usually elevate the character of our public life. After years of not even knowing what good leadership is, Americans responded to the example of New York's mayor, Rudolph Giuliani, as if discovering for the first time what leadership can do. It was not Giuliani's controversial proposals and shoot-from-the-hip style that inspired such devotion; it was his ability to strike the right note in the right way at a traumatic time. Leadership, it turns out, is not about securing your political base and getting legislation passed by one or two votes; it is about speaking and acting from the heart. The more room there is for that kind of leadership, the less room there is for ideological posturing and finger-pointing. Mobilization will make it difficult for the Democrats to shift to the left in the next election, but it will also make it difficult for Republicans to shift to the right. We will no doubt soon begin to hear screaming talk-show hosts blaming the attack on their favorite targets. But it is increasingly unlikely that most Americans will pay much attention.

CIVIC RE-ENGAGEMENT

One of the unanswered questions stemming from the September 11 attacks is whether Americans will return to the culture of civic disengagement and lack of interest that, according to critics such as Harvard political scientist Robert Putnam, has characterized U.S. society since the passing of more civic-minded generations. In some ways, the question answers itself. If rates of participation and involvement do in fact vary with generations, then the generation that will deal with the aftermath of September 11 is also the generation that will change the most. Americans in their 20s and 30s have never experienced recession or a war that threatened their homeland. Now they are getting both at the same time. That may be enough to shift their attention from dot-com start-ups to blood donation. Who, after all, would have thought that there would be more Americans prepared to help the injured than there were injured? Yet there were, and not only because the sheer violence of the attack left so few survivors, but also because those who survived wanted to do something, anything, to help. Americans went in a flash from bowling alone to surviving together.

It is also unlikely that one aspect of the recent civic disengagement—a tendency to ignore anything that takes place outside U.S. borders—will be sustainable in the aftermath of the attacks. As the president brings more foreign leaders to the White House and travels around the world in search of new partners, Americans will inevitably find themselves learning more about other countries and how their citizens view the world. No one at this point can predict how forceful and persistent the American response to terror will be. But it is not hard to predict that America will be more engaged with the rest of the world than it has been for the past two or three decades.

War cannot cure any of the pathologies that afflict the country. If indeed Americans have lost the sense of moral wholeness that conservatives believe they once possessed, they are unlikely to recover it just because some of their fellow citizens will be called on to sacrifice their comforts, and perhaps their lives, to combat terrorism. America may give too much to rich white males and too little to women and people of color, as many on the left charge, but neither the attacks themselves nor the responses to them will eliminate inequality and privilege. Then again, perhaps America was never in quite as bad shape as many of its critics suggested. To be sure, its moral condition has changed, just as its civic life has. But such changes have always been part of American history. And they rarely go only in one direction or only at one pace. If the attacks and their aftermath have effects on American civic culture, those effects are likely to be gradual rather than dramatic. They will take the form of reminders: suggestions that there are good reasons to be concerned with public life and warnings not to turn our backs on the needs of our fellow citizens.

Public life in the aftermath of September 11 will have its frustrations and restraints. We may never be able to stop terrorists from doing what they do. Americans may never get used to the new restrictions on the freedom to travel where and when we want. Political leaders may start looking for new moral campaigns at roughly the same time that economic leaders start putting profit first. Yet some aspects of the country's public life will be better for having lived through the attacks of September 11. Before that day, the American political system, for all its faults, guaranteed a level of personal freedom and democratic stability rare anywhere in this world. That has not changed and will not change because some fanatics hate us so much for doing so many things so well. If the tragedy generates a moment to pause and to reflect on who we are as a people and how we have changed from the days when we wrongly believed that the world's problems would never affect us, we will have matured as a nation.

THE COLD WAR IS FINALLY OVER

THE TRUE SIGNIFICANCE OF THE ATTACKS

■

ANATOL LIEVEN

The United States has been the target of a very serious act of war, conducted by a formidably cruel, brave, fanatical, and well-organized enemy with a terrifying capacity for both savagery and self-sacrifice. The U.S. military response, begun on October 7, is both necessary and right in itself, although its timing may have been premature, given the situation on the ground in Afghanistan. Not to meet force with force would betray the victims and display weakness. Successful war, however, requires both a capacity for ruthlessness and an intelligent political strategy, including the attraction and conciliation of essential allies. So the United States also desperately needs to fundamentally reassess many of the attitudes that have guided its policies since the end of the Cold War. In some areas at least, this process may have already begun, for although war produces strongly emotional responses, it can also provoke clarity of thought and a radical reordering of priorities.

Such new thinking is essential, not only on the part of the United States but also by the United Kingdom and other U.S. allies. This is not just because the United States will expect the full support of its allies in hunting down and destroying the perpetrators of these atrocities. It is also because cities in allied countries are under the same threat, and the extent of this threat may be determined by what actions and policies the United States now pursues. U.S. allies therefore must work with America to shape common strategies.

The attack has underlined the irrelevance of America's dominant security priorities, which are still rooted in Cold War attitudes and structures. Indeed, it could be said that as far as dominant groups in the U.S. security establishment and politics are concerned, the Cold War did not end until September 11, 2001. This is above all true in three areas. First is the attempt to cast Russia and China as major threats to vital U.S. interests. Second is the strategy of national missile defense (NMD) and the militarization of space. And third is policy toward Israel and its occupation of the West Bank and Gaza—since this attack originated in the Muslim world and was motivated in part by hatred of Israel and of U.S. support for Israel.

A hard-line response from the United States is appropriate in the short term. Moreover, it would be wrong to execute any significant policy shifts that could be construed as a victory for the terrorists. But if the U.S. response results in too much pressure on the governments of Pakistan and other fragile states, these states may collapse—with radical Islamists left to pick up the pieces. This is where American allies need to play a part. Above all, a new U.S. policy needs to be shaped by three linked realizations.

First, since the end of the Cold War, there has come into being the basis of a unified world system in which the world's other leading states are partners, not enemies, and in which all these states are under threat from similar forces. In other words, there really is the makings of an "international community"—or would be, if the United States could stop acting as if it alone constituted this community. The community is based on shared adherence to Western-led modernity. The only categorical opponents of this modernization project are indeed religious fanatics—who are not to be found in Moscow or Beijing. Second, with the exception of certain Middle Eastern states, the real threat to the world order comes not from states, but from below, from alienated populations. And third, since the United States cannot occupy and police the Muslim world in the struggle against Islamist terrorism, it is essential to have the cooperation of leading Muslim states. This is something that was already emphasized by the aftermath of the attacks on the Khobar Towers and the U.S.S. *Cole*.

THE NEED FOR NEW FRIENDS

The failure, until now, to move away from the Cold War has its roots not only in various forms of inherited bigotry but also in very strong interests within the U.S. security establishment. This establishment was a product of the Cold War, and it needs a Cold War–type enemy: huge, identifiable, and most important, armed with either high-tech conventional arms or with old-style nuclear missiles. Hence the endless insistence on the danger of a restoration of the Soviet Union.

Russia is no longer strong enough to fulfill that role, so China has been widely promoted as a replacement. But a pathological loathing of Russia persists in important parts of the U.S. establishment, and some bizarre arguments can still be heard concerning Russia.

The leaders of the only institute in Washington explicitly devoted to the study of the Caucasus and Central Asia had been arguing for an American reconciliation with the Taliban as part of a new strategy of driving Russian influence out of the region. In other words, these advocates wanted to revive American policies of the 1980s (with which some of them were closely associated) of support for the Afghan *mujahideen*—this despite the fact that the Soviet global threat had disappeared, Russia was not in occupation of Afghanistan, and this very policy was what helped to produce Osama bin Laden and the safe haven given to him by the Taliban. Such people have sought to deny the presence of international Muslim radicals in Chechnya—though the latter have a Web site that publicizes their victories and casualties, and despite the fact that bin Laden's aides have spoken publicly of sending volunteers and supplies to Chechnya.

Concerning NMD, both critics and allies of the United States, plus other states, have been arguing that the real threat to the American mainland comes not from ballistic missiles but from terrorism, that a ballistic-missile defense system would therefore be a form of Maginot line that our enemies would simply outflank. After all, if a missile had been fired at the United States on

September 11, the country responsible would have been obliterated by an American counterstrike hours later. Compare the difficulty of finding out who was responsible for the October anthrax attacks. In fact, in some cases, we may never be exactly sure which group or combination of groups was responsible and therefore exactly know how and where to retaliate.

More than five years after the bomb attack on the U.S. barracks at the Khobar Towers in Saudi Arabia in 1996, which killed 19 U.S. soldiers, American intelligence analysts are still at odds over whether the perpetrators were agents of bin Laden, of Saddam Hussein, of Iran (and, if so, of which Iranian-backed group), or even of some combination of those nemeses. One reason for this failure has been the attitude of the Saudi authorities and intelligence services, who for their own security reasons have refused to seriously investigate an Iranian role. An even less helpful stance was taken by the Yemeni authorities after the attack on the U.S.S. *Cole.*

One way of combating the kind of attacks we saw is, of course, better security in the United States, but this will not necessarily prevent a terrorist attack, as long as that terrorist is prepared to die. In the end, the key to fighting this war successfully has to be good intelligence. Given the difficulty that American agents have in penetrating the world of the Islamist extremists, the West desperately needs Arab and Muslim allies for such intelligence. The Saudis in particular will have to be persuaded to drop the decades-old strategy begun by Saudi Arabia's founder, King Abdelaziz ibn Saud, that turned a blind eye to Saudi-based radicalism beyond the kingdom's own borders, as long as the radicals did not cause trouble within Saudi Arabia itself.

The help of leading Muslim states will also be essential if there is to be an invasion and occupation of some part of the Muslim world. In their different ways, the 1998 U.S. bombardment of targets in Sudan and Afghanistan and the aftermath of the 1999 bombardment of Yugoslavia by forces from the North Atlantic Treaty Organization have shown the inadequacy of long-range bombardment when it comes to destroying enemies on the ground who are dispersed and hidden in a friendly civilian population.

Unfortunately, over the past ten years, America's Muslim allies have been severely undermined by Israel and its American backers, who have stuck with outdated policies that were necessary at a time of threats to Israel's existence. These former threats came not only from its Arab neighbors, but also indirectly from their superpower backer, the Soviet Union. The collapse of the Soviet Union not only crippled the remaining radical Arab states militarily, but also released a flood of Soviet Jewish emigrants to Israel. This immigration established Jewish demographic superiority (within Israel's pre–1967 borders) beyond challenge. Due to this link, but, more important, because of a common threat from Islamist extremism, Russia has since become in many ways a de facto ally of Israel, at least when it comes to intelligence sharing.

Saddam Hussein's invasion of Kuwait in 1990 united most of the Arab world behind the West's response. A key part of the price the United States had to pay for putting together this broad anti-Saddam coalition was to promise its Arab allies that it would push Israel toward a just peace with the Palestinians. The failure to achieve this objective has reduced America's Arab allies to what a pro-Western former Jordanian minister described as "shell regimes." This ex-official—a senior fellow at an American think tank at the time—said that the repeated humiliations of the Arab world by Israel had destroyed the domestic prestige of his own and other Arab elites, now seen as pro-American, and hollowed out the entire state system. "The only reason we are still standing is because no one is strong enough yet to push us over."

THE STATE OF THE MUSLIM WORLD

Simply to blame Muslim-based terrorism on Israel, however, would be unfair and inadequate for a whole set of reasons. The humiliation of Arab and Muslim world by Israel is so infuriating to them in part because it is only the last in a long history of defeats starting in the seventeenth century and extending far into the twentieth—overwhelmingly at the hands of the Christian Western world. It is of course true that the West has, at least in the twentieth century, repeatedly betrayed its own professed ideals in its behavior toward Muslim peoples. However, the key reason for these defeats has been the prolonged decline of the Muslim world relative to the West—defeats that were already producing radical Muslim responses (whether in Sufi or Wahhabi guise) in the last decades of the eighteenth century. The key reason for this decline has been the multiple failures of development and progress within the Muslim world.

It is the pathologies produced by these failures, as well as the appearance of Israel and the United States as objects of hatred, that have produced the phenomenon of modern Islamist extremism. Although they have found their most widespread and powerful expressions in the Muslim world, these pathologies are not restricted to that world. They are to be found wherever proud people, with strong but in part irrational traditions, feel defeated or radically unsettled by aspects of Western-dominated modernity.

Timothy McVeigh, the Oklahoma City bomber, can be seen in these terms, as can the Aum Shinrikyo sect in Japan. McVeigh comes from the white, Anglo-Saxon (or Scots-Irish), American lower-middle classes and farmers, who have always seen themselves as the backbone of the United States but now feel pushed to the cultural and economic margins. In the 1930s, similar classes in Japan turned to fascism in part as a response to the radical modernization and Westernization that had begun in the mid-nineteenth century. Having been crushingly defeated in the Second World War, these classes in Japan constructed a new state—in some ways modern, Western, and democratic, yet preserving many aspects of the former authoritarianism, crucially in attitudes toward work, duty, and family. In recent years, these segments of society have been undermined as a result of economic stagnation and moves toward a more Western model of economics and behavior—with destabilizing cultural and psychological consequences.

The danger to world order comes not from the ruling elites, who are increasingly integrated into the global market order (even in China, Russia, and India). It comes from the numerous social and ethnic groups that, for whatever reasons of culture, history, or geography, are unable to take part in the world banquet—or that have declined in status, even if they have benefited economically. After all, the great European political pathologies of the twentieth century did not have their roots in underdevelopment as such; they stemmed from the effects of uneven development and cultural change on deeply conservative societies.

Many of these excluded groups and individuals are simply pitiable, far too weak and miserable to threaten anyone. Others, however, have proud cultural traditions that make it very difficult for them to accept second-class status. Their strong fighting traditions give them a distinct edge in certain kinds of warfare, in organized crime and in the areas where the two intersect. Such groups give hostile states the chance to hit at the West without exposing their hands directly and thereby suffering retaliation.

Of course, such alienated groups form a relatively small minority of the world's population. The greater part of humanity has benefited to a greater or lesser extent from economic growth and "globalization" in recent decades. But those who have not—or think they have not—are still too numerous. They can certainly not be mastered by the high-tech fighter aircraft, heavy battle tanks, and enormous aircraft carriers on which the post–Cold War U.S. military remains determined to spend so much money.

This, then, is the dark side of the global village—the ability of that village's alienated minorities to lash out at their perceived oppressors over huge distances. Because the Muslim world was the oldest and grandest rival of the West and its greatest "victim," because "fundamentalist" Islam provides a singularly tough and yet flexible ideological framework for modern extremism, and because of the role of Israel and the United States as a focus of hatred, it is in the Muslim world that these pathologies have assumed their greatest and more dangerous forms.

It would be wrong to parrot the caricature of Samuel Huntington and posit one single Muslim cultural-political world united in difference from and hostility to the West. In the largest Muslim state by far—Indonesia—radical Islam as yet plays a rather limited role. But, sadly, one thing that does unite most Muslim countries is relative political and socioeconomic failure.

With the exception of some of the oil-endowed Persian Gulf states and—to a limited degree—Turkey and Malaysia, every single Muslim country has failed to enter the developed world. Almost all are menaced by rapid and, in some cases, virtually uncontrolled population growth, which floods inadequate labor markets with unemployable and embittered young men. Almost all are failing to educate or use their female populations, in some cases disgracefully so. Afghanistan has collapsed altogether, becoming a murderous theocracy and international menace. Others are threatened with this fate as well. The behavior of elites and state services across most of this region presents a deeply depressing picture. And very importantly, this is also true across the political spectrum, from authoritarian traditional monarchies and Western-backed semi-democracies through anti-Western radical nationalist and military regimes to ex-communist ones in the former Soviet Union.

It is not surprising in these circumstances that many people in the region have fallen back on revolutionary Islam as a last resort when everything else has failed, and on belief in a supposedly "Koranic" or *shari'a* (Islamic law) system. As a result of all these factors, the Muslim world finds itself in a profoundly peripheral position vis-à-vis the Western-dominated world. At the same time (unlike Africa or Latin America), it retains a deeply felt—and assiduously cultivated—collective memory of the Islamic sphere as a great cultural, economic, and political metropolis in its own right.

So in attacking America, Muslim terrorists would certainly be attacking not only Israel's key backer, but also the central symbol of their own failure. And anti-American Arab nationalism is—in the classic fashion of all nationalisms—an ideology that is capable of sucking up and drawing strength from a whole set of other, unconnected resentments, including bitter resentment of the corruption and oppression of the Arabs' own regimes. Israeli and American behavior has provided a dangerous focus for this.

NOWHERE TO TURN

The Chinese have some of the same historically based feelings that, in the past, contributed to the appalling pathologies of Maoism. But China also has one of the world's fastest-growing economies. Economic success has been the hallmark of the other Chinese states: Taiwan, Singapore, and Hong Kong. Indeed, the Chinese diaspora has been one of the most economically successful groups in world history. China is a genuinely powerful, relatively orderly state under a leadership that is nationalist and authoritarian but also rational and pragmatic. It has become a successful participant in the Western-defined modernization project. The position of the Muslim world is very different.

I gained certain insights into the roots of Muslim extremism during my work as a stringer for *The Times* (London) in Pakistan and Afghanistan in the late 1980s. I met not only some precursors of the Taliban among the Afghan *mujahideen* but also members of radical groups in Pakistan. I especially remember a long conversation with some young members of a "fundamentalist" group in Lahore. None were from the bottom of society. They came from that age-old breeding ground of fascistic and religious extremism, the struggling lower-middle classes and the upper peasantry.

They faced the threat of sinking into the immiserated, semi-employed proletariat—with the *hira mandi*, or prostitutes' quarter, as the possible destiny of their sisters and daughters. One of their very few ways of escape was through entry into the junior ranks of organized crime, especially heroin smuggling. Given the state of the Pakistani economy, legitimate economic opportunities were few. Their traditional communities and cultures were being undermined by urbanization and "atomization." The semi-Western, semi-modern new culture being thrust on them was of the most repulsive kind, especially concerning the treatment of women—a mixture of Western licentiousness with local brutality, crudity, and chauvinism.

In these depressing circumstances, adherence to a radical

Islamist network provides a sense of cultural security, a new community, and some degree of social support—modest, but still better than anything the state can provide. Poverty is recast as religious simplicity and austerity. Perhaps, even more important, belief provides a measure of pride: a reason to keep a stiff back amid continual humiliations and temptations. In the blaring, stinking, violent world of the modern "Third World" Muslim city, the architecture and aesthetic mood of the mosque is the only oasis, not only of beauty but of an ordered and coherent culture and guide to living. Of course this is true ten times over for a young male inhabitant of an Afghan, Chechen, or Palestinian refugee camp.

So it is hard not to have a measure of sympathy for some of the roots of Muslim radicalism. There was certainly considerable Western sympathy for the radical fighters in Chechnya, and especially in the figure of the great commander Shamil Basayev. I met him several times before and during the Chechen war of 1994–96—the only terrorist leader I have known personally—and at one stage I liked and admired him.

The key role in Basayev's progressive fanaticization was due to that war and the deaths of so many of his family at Russian hands. But a deeply malignant influence on Basayev was also exerted after 1995 by the international Muslim radical volunteers—the so-called Wahhabis (even though most are not Wahhabis in the strict theological sense) from the Middle East. They were led by an Arab commander with the nom de guerre of Khattab, and came to fight in Chechnya as they had previously fought in Afghanistan. Their influence over Basayev has been visible in his public language, which has more and more imitated their own. More than anything, it has been visible in the growing vicious contempt on the part of Basayev and his followers—so typical of a self-appointed revolutionary vanguard—for the rest of humanity, including the mass of the Chechen people.

This religiously ordained revolutionary mandate seems to have contributed to Basayev's revolt against the authority of President Aslan Maskhadov, which has helped to destroy Maskhadov's authority and any possibility of constructing a stable Chechen state.

Basayev—and indeed Khattab—are also examples of something else. Like their analogues in the Middle East and Afghanistan, these people have become deeply hateful. But they do not lack courage and ability. The endless Western media description of Muslim terrorists as "cowards" is absurd. As the last attacks make clear, these are formidable enemies. Their technological skills may be limited, but they do not need such skills if with a few simple weapons—including the simplest and oldest, knives—they can seize the West's own technological creations and use them with shattering effect against us. In the future there remains the threat of even more devastating attacks using unconventional weapons to achieve mass destruction.

CHANGING AMERICAN WAYS

To fight these enemies successfully will require radical changes in the international posture that the United States has taken during the past decade. During this period, U.S. world hegemony has often been exercised—sometimes benignly, sometimes arrogantly—in a generally lazy, half-hearted, absentminded way. One key reason for this attitude is that, as every opinion poll and election has shown, the great majority of Americans, while proud of their "world leadership," are also profoundly uninterested in the details of its implementation.

The reason for this lack of interest is that, until September 11, 2001, few Americans believed that anything the rest of the world could do could seriously harm them. The exception, alas, has been small but powerful ethnic lobbies and other fiercely committed groups, whose organization and determination have given them remarkable power compared to the much larger but apathetic and unorganized mass of the American population.

The other face of American unilateralism in the world has been a belief in America's invulnerability at home, with NMD supposed to complete the image of "fortress America." Now this fortress has been breached in a way that no unilateral U.S. response can hope to prevent. Here is a paradox: In the short term, fierce unilateral U.S. action is probably necessary to punish and deter the perpetrators of these attacks, but in the longer term, a continuation of American unilateralism would be a terrible threat to victory in this war.

Now the United States, like other hegemonic states before it, is paying the price of empire. And the time for absentmindedness is past. So, too, is the European tendency to rely on American help while moaning endlessly about American policies—without having the courage to stand up and demand change. The United Kingdom and the rest of Europe must participate fully in the war against terrorism. But if they are to do so alongside America and share America's risks, then they have not only the right but the duty to influence key American policies and make sure we have as many allies as possible from the rest of the world. The first, simpler aspect of this is to end Cold War policies against Russia and China. The second is to change U.S. policies toward the Israeli-Palestinian conflict. That will be much harder and take much longer. But it, too, is essential if we are to win this war.

THE RETURN OF HISTORY

WHAT SEPTEMBER 11 HATH WROUGHT

■

FAREED ZAKARIA

In retrospect, the 1990s look like a brief respite from the drama of world politics. It was a giddy age. By December 1991 the Soviet Union had collapsed, communism was discredited, and Saddam Hussein's invasion of Kuwait had been repulsed by an international coalition, with Russia and the United States joining together for the first time since World War II. It did not seem strange to echo the visionary rhetoric of Woodrow Wilson and speak, as President George H.W. Bush did, of a new world order.

The heart of this new order was global capitalism. The entire world seemed to recognize that in order to succeed, societies had to move in the direction of Western economics, and perhaps even toward Western politics. There was no alternative. Countries around the globe scrambled to retool. Many that had once proudly thought of themselves as ancient civilizations now struggled to become "emerging markets." Where the focus of the world had once been on superpower summits and United Nations assemblies, it was now fixed on a small town in Switzerland where the new power elite gathered annually. Davos became the symbol of a new age, one in which business was the common language. The driving force of history, it seemed, was no longer war or ideology or power politics; it was technology. Where sophisticated people once aspired to master the minutiae of nuclear strategy or counterinsurgency, they now talked knowingly of Moore's law and bandwidth.

Government became a matter of navigating these new currents. Finance ministers—once obscure economic managers—were now the key figures in their cabinets and often the most respected faces of their countries. Men like Argentina's Domingo Cavallo, India's

Manmohan Singh, and Poland's Leszek Balcerowicz became better known and regarded than their heads of state. In the United
States, *The New Yorker* marveled at the power and influence
wielded by Lawrence Summers, then the deputy secretary of the
Treasury, comparing him to Henry Kissinger at the height of his
fame. No comparison, however, could do justice to the apostolic
stature of Federal Reserve Board chairman Alan Greenspan, often
named in public opinion polls as the most widely respected living
American. To understand just how sharp a change this was, try
naming the chairman of the Federal Reserve in, say, 1975. Or
1965. Or 1955.

It was a new age, all right. It just turned out to be a brief one.
This is not to say that in the years to come economics will lose its
importance or that the technological revolution has fizzled out.
Both have helped drive modern history and will continue to do
so. But they will have to share center stage once again, interacting
and competing with more traditional forces. What we are likely
to see over the next decade is the return of politics, the return of
culture, the return of government, and perhaps even the return of
History.

THE RETURN OF POLITICS

September 11, 2001, will prove to be a watershed because, like
all pivotal dates in history, it will mark both the emergence of
new elements in the game and the belated recognition of existing
ones that were quietly gaining strength in the background. The
new elements are the ones that have received all the attention in
recent weeks. The attacks were the first carried out on the American mainland by a foreign adversary since the War of 1812. The
enemies are elusive and shadowy. The means they employ are unconventional and asymmetrical. The animating vision behind this
new terrorism is not self-determination but existential hatred. Yet
the world we are entering also highlights a shift that had already
begun, a disillusionment that had been brewing with the supposed triumph of economics and technology.

During the 1990s one constantly heard that the world had

been transformed. Globalization was sweeping old models aside as technology was bringing us together. (Did I mention that the Internet changes everything?) All this was happening whether one wanted it to or not. The sense of frustration in the face of immovable forces was best expressed by James Carville, Bill Clinton's erstwhile campaign manager, who saw many of his and Clinton's cherished policy proposals get tossed aside after the 1992 electoral victory for fear that they would offend Wall Street. "I used to think that if there were reincarnation, I wanted to come back as the pope or the president," he said, "but now I want to be the bond market; you can intimidate everyone."

Of course there was, and is, a great deal of truth in his observation. In the 1990s, after communism's fall, market economics became the world's dominant ideology. After decades of flirtation with statism, countries around the world dismantled economic controls, deregulated industries, and liberalized their economies. Equally important, the rise of capital markets over the previous two decades proved a new and powerful enforcer of economic discipline, rewarding some countries and punishing others. Governments began to think that they had little power over their own destinies. In the metaphor of foreign-affairs columnist Thomas Friedman, they were forced into a golden straitjacket, limiting their policy options in order to get rich.

But by the end of the 1990s, countries around the world had come to realize that the constraints of capitalism, although real, were not nearly as tight or as predictable as many had believed. Consider northern Europe, which was hardly moving ineluctably toward less and less government. Most of the governments in the region spend more than 60 percent of their country's gross domestic product (GDP)—almost twice what the U.S. government spends. And yet during the 1990s, many of these countries' growth rates equaled America's.

The lesson of the 1990s appears to be that within certain constraints, countries have room to maneuver. The limits are real and powerful: governments cannot go back to their old ways of owning companies and overregulating industries. But if an economy is basically capitalist, with the market rather than government allocating resources, you can still maintain a relatively generous welfare state. This is, in fact, the new Scandinavian model, in which countries such as Sweden took the lead in deregulating their financial and telecommunication industries while maintaining their social safety nets. Redistribution seems to have fewer distorting effects on the economy than does government ownership or large-scale regulation. The debate over the welfare state thus returns to where it belongs, in the realm of political philosophy as much as economics. Americans will always place a higher premium on individual liberty and economic freedom than do Europeans, who are willing to pay a price in inefficiency for a certain kind of social order. But these are political choices, not economic necessities. Capitalism is a large house in which there are many mansions.

Politics has returned not simply to the industrialized world. In the countries that were most strenuously pursuing neoliberal economic reforms, the East Asian financial crisis of 1997–99 and now the current American recession have slowed the zeal for transformation. This is not because their reforms failed. On the contrary, the rising living standards of East Asia over the last 30 years remain the one true economic miracle of the last quarter-century. But the roller coaster of contemporary capitalism has given even its greatest enthusiasts pause. None of the emerging markets was prepared for the sharp plunges in growth and asset values that have accompanied their slowdowns. Rapid liberalization and growth produced their own set of problems: urbanization, social upheaval, and political change. In this region, if the 1990s were devoted to economic liberalization, the next decade may well be devoted to dealing with some of its political consequences.

Ignoring the political dimensions of globalization has already had its costs. Consider the fate of Indonesia in the wake of the economic crisis of the late 1990s. The International Monetary Fund (IMF) and Washington helped topple President Suharto's regime with the hope that radical economic and political reform would follow. Instead, the entire country has been unhinged. Over the last two years, the Indonesian economy has contracted by almost 50 percent, wiping out 20 years of economic growth, throwing tens of millions of people below the poverty line, and embroiling the country in ethnic violence. If there is one image that reflects the diplomacy of the 1990s, it is the famous picture of IMF chief Michel Camdessus, arms folded, glowering over President Suharto while the old man signed on the dotted line, agreeing to the fund's terms for a bailout.

There will be no more such photos. Politics has returned to the fore, and now Mahathir bin Mohamad of Malaysia is considered a hero for standing up to the IMF. One Indonesian scholar commented sadly, "Many in my country wish that Suharto had done what Mahathir did—defied the IMF, moved at our own pace—and we would be better off today." The point is not that Mahathir's strategy was wise but that most people in the region seem to applaud it.

Or consider trade. Talks over the expansion of global trade are stalled, and not because of a few hundred latte-sipping protesters dancing outside World Bank meetings, though they are also part of the new politics of globalization. Developing countries believe that without major concessions from the West, these talks have become a one-way street on which they alone open their markets. But Western countries are not about to get rid of domestic subsidies that have powerful constituencies, such as European farmers, no matter how much they distort global markets. Again, politics has reared its head.

Finally there is the Middle East, where the seductions of globalization have not fared well. Bill Clinton, Shimon Peres, and others painted a picture of a new Middle East based on cooperation, economic interdependence, and growth. But the rulers of the region understand that in such a world their regimes and bases of power would not prosper. Countries such as Ireland and Israel benefit greatly from their access to the global economy, and so they take political risks. But much of the world, and crucially almost all of the Arab world, is governed by political elites that dare not liberalize because to do so would unsettle their own power. To them, globalization is not an opportunity but a threat.

These varied policies and attitudes come from diverse parts of the globe, but they do have one element in common. They are political responses to the dominance of global capitalism during the 1990s. Depending on one's views they may seem admirable or wrong-headed—I see them mostly as the latter—but they were gathering steam even before the fall of 2001 and now they are here to stay. And many of them have been, and will continue to be, couched in the language of anti-Americanism because the United States is, correctly, seen as the chief exemplar, representative, beneficiary, and protector of globalization.

THE RETURN OF GOVERNMENT

People have made far-reaching predictions about the social and cultural effects of the events of September 11. American exceptionalism is finished. American innocence is lost. Irony is dead. It is too soon to tell whether the culture will maintain this sense of shock or return to normalcy over the next six months. But one change that is likely to endure is the renewed power of government. The state is back, and for the oldest reason in the book: the provision of security.

By certain measures it never went away. Government spending as a percentage of GDP actually increased during the laissez-faire 1990s. But this was largely because aging populations required the disbursement of ever-greater health and retirement benefits. During the 1990s, governments around the world, from the United States to Brazil to Italy to India, were cutting their budgets in order to convince markets of their fiscal health. This trend is likely to slow down, at least for a while. When President Bush's spokesperson was asked whether the president's new spending proposals (for rebuilding lower Manhattan and bulking up the national security agencies) would bust the budget, the question was dismissed with a simple line: "National security comes first." In an October 2001 *Newsweek* poll, 52 percent of Americans said they would prefer a government that provides more in services, even if it cost more in taxes. In 1996, only 27 percent had answered similarly.

It's not just money, but power as well. Government is going to get itself involved in areas of life that, before September, people thought it should avoid. Consider the Internet. A few European governments had recently announced that they intended to try to regulate the Internet in some fashion. This was widely seen as lunacy, the desperate efforts of old-fashioned *dirigisme* that would not work. Yet it is now not unlikely that governments are going to set about trying to do just that and find some way to monitor the Internet—along with almost every other form of communication and information distribution.

And this will likely happen even if the Al Qaeda network is destroyed, even if other terrorist organizations are crushed, even if the states that sponsor terrorism are "ended." We have now seen that the chief vulnerability of Western societies is also its greatest strength: openness. We have also seen that this new terrorism can be so easy and so lethal because of the wondrous aspects of the new economy—cheap technology, communications, and distribution—which will only become more pronounced over time. This means that we will live with the knowledge that these dangers exist around us, and that events as bad or worse could happen again. No one will fault governments for doing what they can to protect us. The war on terrorism will strengthen government even more than the Cold War did, since this is a war that will be fought both at home and abroad.

The fundamental shift that is likely to take place is that counterterrorism will move from the realm of law enforcement to that of national security. The difference is significant. Law enforcement operates after the fact of a crime and gathers evidence and testimony within the tight constraints of the law. Eventually only a court can determine whether to punish a criminal. National security tries to anticipate events before they happen and uses all kinds of methods—overt and covert, peaceful and violent. It is its own police, judge, jury, and executioner. Its appeal is not to law but to *raison d'état*.

If civil liberties will take a back seat at home, human rights will do the same abroad. The return of the state implies the return of realpolitik. We saw this with brutal swiftness in the case of Pakistan, in the immediate aftermath of September 11. Until then the United States had viewed Pakistan with great suspicion. Not only was it a military dictatorship, but it was also supporting religious extremists in Afghanistan and Kashmir and had recently tested a nuclear bomb. But Washington needed Pakistan's help in battling the Taliban regime, and so within days a new and close relationship between the two countries was forged. Washington lifted its sanctions on the country and gave it promises of aid, arms, and enduring friendship.

The speed of this turnaround was startling, but a similar process is likely to take place around the globe. When security concerns are pressing they trump everything else. And as countries cooperate with Washington on a broad antiterror front, they will have more leeway at home to handle their own internal threats as they see fit. This is not a pleasant development, especially not for the minorities who live under authoritarian regimes. Already Russia's president, Vladimir Putin, has indicated that he sees his battle against the Chechens as part of the broad war against terrorism.

Realpolitik also implies respect for and attention to other governments. We have already seen President Bush develop a new fondness for building close relationships with his counterparts abroad. A marked shift has also taken place in America's attitudes toward its allies. This is partly because the nature of this war requires a great deal of cooperation from other countries, but it is also partly because there is an ideological and cultural dimension to this struggle and the United States wants to be seen as part of "the international community" and not a lone cowboy. Legitimacy has always been an important component of power; now it is vital. The new multilateralism of the Bush team came about with startling speed, but it is real and will persist because it is born not of choice but of necessity.

THE RETURN OF HISTORY?

It is not so unusual for politics and government to return to prominence. After all, in very few eras of world history has economics reigned supreme. The hopes for untroubled peace and prosperity are always disturbed by international competition or human nature or both. And the rise of threats and security problems was hardly unexpected. But the nature of this new threat—tied as it is to radical, political Islam—suggests a more complex struggle than against, say, the Barbary pirates or the Irish Republican Army. Indeed, we may be in for another long battle over History.

Ever since Francis Fukuyama wrote his elegant and insightful essay "The End of History?" in 1989, he has had to suffer through a series of critiques that made the error of assuming that when he said "History" he meant "history," thereby reducing his argument to an absurdity. But as Fukuyama used the term, History—with a capital "H"—is the Hegelian idea of a clash of ideologies over the organization of society. Each ideology claimed that History was going its way. The end of the Cold War settled that debate and ended the much longer tussle between liberal democracy and its various competitors. Countries everywhere, Fukuyama argued, would inevitably converge on liberal democratic capitalism as their model to organize society. The problems we would face in the future would be those produced by too-fast technological change and too-crass commercial life.

Fukuyama actually considered the threat that radical Islam might pose to this world order and dismissed it, pointing out, correctly, that it had no appeal to non-Muslims. In an ideological sense, therefore, it posed no threat to the West. But he did not recognize that the West posed a threat to radical Islam, one that its followers feel with a piercing intensity. Perhaps History can be restarted by one side unilaterally.

It is true that Islam has no appeal to non-Muslims and thus most of the West is immune from its ideological challenge. But that is surely not the only yardstick by which to measure a Historical struggle. After all, by 1970 very few people in the West believed in communism. And fascism held little appeal in the United Kingdom or the United States. Even the nineteenth century clashes between systems were not really about two equally universal ideas. After the mid-nineteenth century, monarchies were simply trying to preserve their own power structure, not launch a counterrevolution. But all these contests involved not merely land and power, but ideas.

Radical Islam contests not simply the power of the West and

the United States, but also the principles they hold dear. It rejects the Western liberal model in much the same way that communism did. And although radical Islam may not have many adherents in the West, more than a billion people around the world are potentially receptive to this message. In this sense they do have an argument with the West over the direction of History. The West might not want to take part in this debate, but that was also true about the struggles with fascism and communism. History finds you out.

Moreover, although the nature of the challenge from radical Islam is unique, it comes out of a broader phenomenon and thus might resonate in other parts of the globe. Radical Islam has risen on the backs of failed states that have not improved the lots of their people. It festers in societies where contact with the West has produced more chaos than growth and more uncertainty than wealth. It is, in a sense, the result of failed and incomplete modernization. This is a phenomenon we are likely to see more of over the next decades.

In debating Americanization over the past decade we have neglected to focus on the real and growing danger: the backlash against modernization itself. For Western intellectuals, modernization is seen as largely benign and, in any case, as inevitable. So the debate here has been an intramural one, among the varieties of modernization. (Too many McDonald's and not enough French films is one of the usual complaints.) But in large parts of the world modernization is a grueling, alien process that threatens to denude cultures and disrupt settled ways of life. Around the world, as societies develop, however slowly, people leave villages full of poverty and security and go forth into the chaotic, noisy modern world of the city. Once there the experience can be so disorienting that many try to "escape from freedom," in Erik Erikson's words, to find something safe and secure, some connection to the old world. Some have handled it better than others, but all have gone through the stresses and strains.

Over the last two decades the process of modernization has accelerated around the world as governments have been forced to open up their economies and their societies in ways that they had not done in half a century. And the revolution in information, communications, and distribution has meant that even if government didn't open up, the outside world entered anyway, through satellite television, videocassettes, clothes, games, and the Internet. The effects of this involuntary modernization have been more powerful and more unpredictable than we had imagined.

In his celebrated lecture titled "Our Universal Civilization," V. S. Naipaul, now a Nobel laureate, asked why "certain societies or groups are content to enjoy the fruits of progress, while affecting to despise the conditions that promote that progress." He dismisses this attitude—particularly prevalent, he says, in the Muslim world—as "philosophical hysteria." As always, Naipaul is acute in pointing to the foibles and hypocrisies of the developing world. But he assumes that people can get over their past easily, that protestations otherwise are merely affectations. In doing so he hits upon a great truth about the attractiveness and seductiveness of the West's universal civilization. But he misses the ferment of societies trying to come to grips with a modernity that they did not make.

Every dominant power in history has defined modernity. This is the West's moment, and for those outside, this version of modernity is not easy to take. Naipaul assumes, in a sense, that people can be like him—a non-Westerner who has found comfort and security in the West. And of course there are tens of millions who have done just that. East Asia has been able to combine modernity with its own cultures in remarkable ways. But there are also tens of millions who have not been able to make their peace with the West, many of them in the lands of its great historical rival, Islam. The cultural backlash against the West is wrongheaded, destructive, and futile. But it is no affectation, as we discovered on September 11.

Naipaul ends his lecture with the firm belief that the West's universal civilization will triumph in the end. And it is true that the power and attractiveness of concepts of individual rights and freedoms are stronger than any force in human history. They will prevail. But there may be one more struggle before the West can declare a final victory.

ACKNOWLEDGMENTS

To say something worthwhile about an important subject is always difficult. To say it in real time, chasing a moving target when the world has been turned upside down, is simply remarkable. The authors who appear in these pages managed to pull off a major intellectual accomplishment under incredible time pressure, and for that we are deeply grateful. Peter Osnos and Paul Golob from PublicAffairs were engaged at every stage of the project from conception onward. Others from PublicAffairs who played a crucial role were Robert Kimzey, Kate Darnton, David Patterson, Melanie Peirson Johnstone, Dan Geist, Jenny Dossin, and Evan Gaffney. On the *Foreign Affairs* side, Rosemary Hartman, Jonathan Tepperman, Traci Nagle, Helen Fessenden, Ann Coleman, Celia Whitaker, Siddarth Mohandas, and our publisher David Kellogg helped make sure that the right things were said, in the right ways, and that the magazine came through the experience with flying colors. Under the leadership of Les Gelb and Pete Peterson, the Council on Foreign Relations continues to live up to its traditions as an ideal place to think clearly about American foreign policy. And finally, Kathy Lacey and Sheri Berman inspired us and put up with us, giving us the guidance and support necessary to get the job done. Without them, it would never have happened.

JAMES F. HOGE, JR.
GIDEON ROSE

New York
October 2001

CONTRIBUTORS

FOUAD AJAMI is Majid Khadduri Professor of Middle Eastern Studies at the School of Advanced International Studies, The Johns Hopkins University. His most recent book is *The Dream Palace of the Arabs*.

KAREN ARMSTRONG is the author of *Islam: A Short History; Jerusalem: One City, Three Faiths; The Battle for God: A History of Fundamentalism;* and *A History of God: The 4,000-Year Quest of Judaism, Christianity, and Islam.*

MARTIN N. BAILY is Senior Fellow at the Institute for International Economics. He was Chairman of the Council of Economic Advisers from 1999 to 2001.

MILTON BEARDEN served as the Central Intelligence Agency's Station Chief in Pakistan from 1986 to 1989, where he was responsible for that agency's covert action program in support of the Afghan resistance to the Soviet-supported government.

SAMUEL R. BERGER served as National Security Adviser to President Bill Clinton from 1997 to 2001 and is Chairman of Stonebridge International, LLC.

RICHARD K. BETTS is Leo A. Shifrin Professor of War and Peace Studies and Director of the Institute of War and Peace Studies at Columbia University. He is the author of *Surprise Attack: Lessons for Defense Planning.*

RICHARD BUTLER is Diplomat in Residence at the Council on Foreign Relations. From 1997 to 1999 he was Executive Chairman of the United Nations Special Commission, the body charged with disarming Iraq. He is the author of *The Greatest Threat: Iraq, Weapons of Mass Destruction, and the Crisis of Global Security.*

WESLEY K. CLARK was Supreme Allied Commander, Europe, from 1997 to 2000 and is the author of *Waging Modern War: Bosnia, Kosovo, and the Future of Combat.*

MICHAEL SCOTT DORAN, who taught for three years at the University of Central Florida, is Assistant Professor of Near Eastern Studies at Princeton University and the author of *Pan-Arabism before Nasser: Egyptian Power Politics and the Palestine Question.*

GREGG EASTERBROOK is Senior Editor for *The New Republic* and Beliefnet.com, Contributing Editor for *The Atlantic Monthly* and *The Washington Monthly,* and Visiting Fellow at the Brookings Institution.

STEPHEN E. FLYNN is Senior Fellow in National Security Studies at the Council on Foreign Relations and commander in the U.S. Coast Guard.

LAURIE GARRETT is a Pulitzer Prize–winning science and medical writer for *Newsday* and is the author of *The Coming Plague: Newly Emerging Diseases in a World Out of Balance* and *Betrayal of Trust: The Collapse of Global Public Health.*

F. GREGORY GAUSE III is Associate Professor of Political Science at the University of Vermont and the author of *Oil Monarchies: Domestic and Security Challenges in the Arab Gulf States.*

JAMES F. HOGE, JR., has been Editor of *Foreign Affairs* since 1992. He was previously Publisher of the New York *Daily News* and Editor and Publisher of the *Chicago Sun-Times.*

BRIAN M. JENKINS is Senior Adviser to the President of the RAND Corporation. He is the author of *International Terrorism: A New Mode of Conflict* and the coauthor of *Aviation Terrorism and Security*.

WALTER LAQUEUR is Chairman of the Research Council of the Center for Strategic and International Studies and the author of *The New Terrorism: Fanaticism and the Arms of Mass Destruction*.

ANATOL LIEVEN is Senior Associate at the Carnegie Endowment for International Peace and the author of *Chechnya: Tombstone of Russian Power*.

MICHAEL MANDELBAUM is Christian A. Herter Professor of American Foreign Policy at the School of Advanced International Studies, The Johns Hopkins University, and Senior Fellow at the Council on Foreign Relations.

RAJAN MENON is Monroe J. Rathbone Professor of International Relations at Lehigh University and Director of Eurasia Policy Studies at the National Bureau of Asian Research.

JOSEPH S. NYE, JR., is Dean of the John F. Kennedy School of Government at Harvard University and has served as Assistant Secretary of Defense for International Security Affairs and as Chair of the National Intelligence Council. His most recent book is *The Paradox of American Power*.

WILLIAM J. PERRY served as Secretary of Defense from 1994 to 1997 and is Professor in the Department of Management Science and Engineering at Stanford University.

GIDEON ROSE is Managing Editor of *Foreign Affairs*. He has served as Associate Director for Near East and South Asian Affairs on the staff of the National Security Council and has taught American foreign policy at Princeton and Columbia universities.

MONA SUTPHEN, a former Foreign Service Officer, served on the staff of the National Security Council from 1998 to 2000 and is now Vice President of Stonebridge International, LLC.

WILLIAM F. WECHSLER was Special Adviser to the Secretary of the Treasury from 1999 to 2001. He previously served as Director for Transnational Threats on the staff of the National Security Council, where he chaired the interagency working group on Osama bin Laden's financial network.

ALAN WOLFE is Director of the Boisi Center for Religion and American Public Life at Boston College. His most recent book is *Moral Freedom*.

FAREED ZAKARIA is Editor of *Newsweek International* and the author of *From Wealth to Power: The Unusual Origins of America's World Role*.

FOREIGN AFFAIRS

Published by the Council on Foreign Relations since 1922, the 110,000-circulation bimonthly *Foreign Affairs* is required reading for government leaders, business executives, scholars, and journalists. Its editorial authority and prominent readership have earned *Foreign Affairs* a reputation as the "most influential periodical in print." Essays like George Kennan's famous "X" article outlining the policy of containment, Henry Kissinger's controversial essay on nuclear policy, Samuel Huntington's "Clash of Civilizations," Paul Krugman's prescient "The Myth of Asia's Miracle," and Fouad Ajami's seminal essay on America's role in the Arab world have made *Foreign Affairs* the premier forum for provocative analysis and new policy initiatives.

Visitors to *Foreign Affairs*' website, www.foreignaffairs.org, may read the text of feature articles, interviews with authors, special background briefings on current global developments, search the magazine's vast full-text archive of articles, and read the reviews of thousands of books on international affairs.

A Japanese version of *Foreign Affairs* has been published since 1990, and in December 2000 a Spanish edition, *Foreign Affairs en Español*, was launched in Latin America and Spain. Both are also available on line at www.foreignaffairsj.co.jp and www.foreignaffairs-esp.org respectively.

For more information about the magazine, including how to subscribe, please e-mail foraff@cfr.org.

PUBLICAFFAIRS is a new publishing house and a tribute to the standards, values, and flair of three persons who have served as mentors to countless reporters, writers, editors, and book people of all kinds, including me.

I. F. STONE, proprietor of *I. F. Stone's Weekly,* combined a commitment to the First Amendment with entrepreneurial zeal and reporting skill and became one of the great independent journalists in American history. At the age of eighty, Izzy published *The Trial of Socrates,* which was a national bestseller. He wrote the book after he taught himself ancient Greek.

BENJAMIN C. BRADLEE was for nearly thirty years the charismatic editorial leader of *The Washington Post.* It was Ben who gave the *Post* the range and courage to pursue such historic issues as Watergate. He supported his reporters with a tenacity that made them fearless, and it is no accident that so many became authors of influential, best-selling books.

ROBERT L. BERNSTEIN, the chief executive of Random House for more than a quarter century, guided one of the nation's premier publishing houses. Bob was personally responsible for many books of political dissent and argument that challenged tyranny around the globe. He is also the founder and was the longtime chair of Human Rights Watch, one of the most respected human rights organizations in the world.

·   ·   ·

For fifty years, the banner of Public Affairs Press was carried by its owner Morris B. Schnapper, who published Gandhi, Nasser, Toynbee, Truman, and about 1,500 other authors. In 1983 Schnapper was described by *The Washington Post* as "a redoubtable gadfly." His legacy will endure in the books to come.

Peter Osnos, *Publisher*